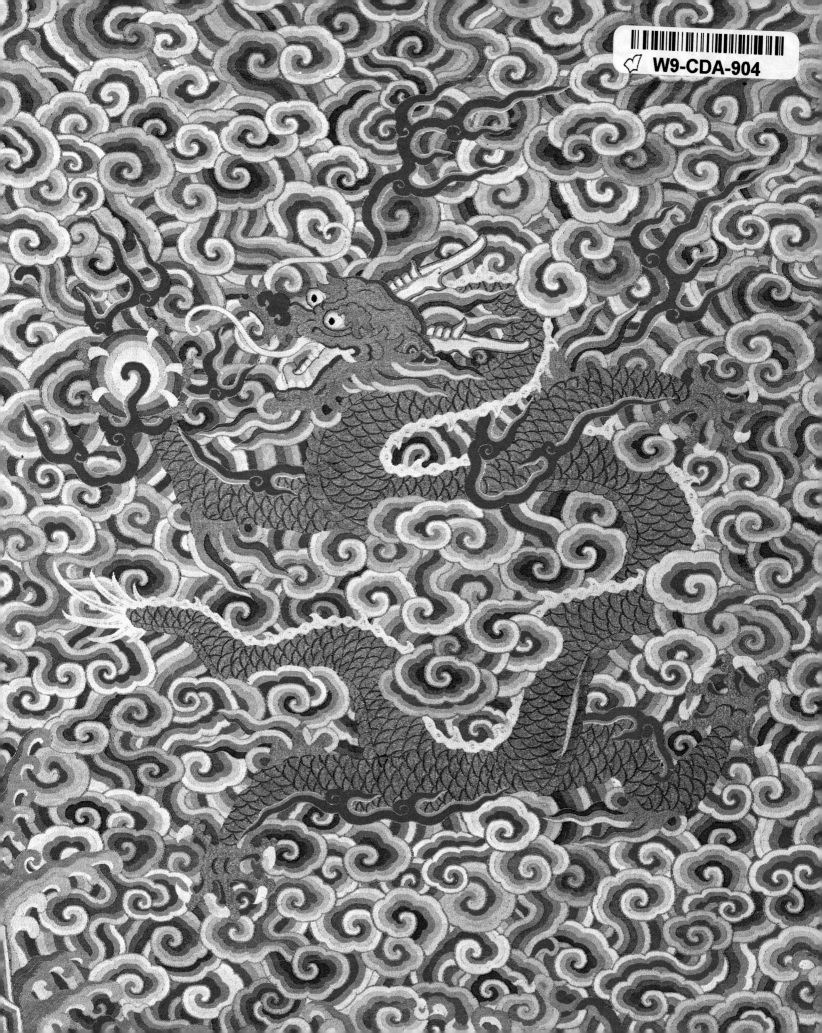

JOURNEY INTO CHINA

JOURNEY INTO
CHINA

National Geographic Society

JOURNEY INTO CHINA

Published by
The National Geographic Society

Staff for this book

Kenneth C. Danforth
Editor

Mary B. Dickinson
Assistant Editor

David M. Seager
Art Director

Anne Dirkes Kobor
Illustrations Editor

Robert Arndt
Ross S. Bennett
Edward Lanouette
Elizabeth L. Newhouse
David D. Pearce
Robert M. Poole
Margaret Sedeen
Editor-Writers

Diane S. Marton
Kyna E. Rubin
Elizabeth C. Wagner
L. Madison Washburn
Anne Elizabeth Withers
Editorial Research

Greta Arnold
Illustrations Research

Gilbert M. Grosvenor
*President and
Chairman of the Board*

Owen R. Anderson
Executive Vice President

Charlotte Golin
Layout Assistant

Paulette L. Claus
Georgina L. McCormack
Teresita C. Sison
Editorial Assistants

Richard S. Wain
Andrea Crosman
Leslie A. Adams
Production

Karen F. Edwards
Traffic Manager

John T. Dunn
Technical Director

Ronald E. Williamson
Engraving and Printing

Contributions by
Thomas B. Allen
Wayne Barrett
William P. Beaman
Thomas Bolt

Todd Carrel
John L. Holden
Susan B. Levine
Kyna E. Rubin
Field Interpreters

Robert L. Breeden
*Senior Vice President,
Publications and
Educational Media*

Maps painted by
Robert Hynes

John D. Garst, Jr.
Virginia L. Baza
Lisa Biganzoli
Gary M. Johnson
Geographic Art

Jolene M. Blozis
Anne K. McCain
Index

Chief Consultants
Jay Mathews
*Former Peking Correspondent
The Washington Post*

Linda Mathews
*Former Peking Correspondent
The Los Angeles Times*

Jonathan D. Spence
*Professor of History
Yale University*

Michael Sullivan
*Professor of Oriental Art
Stanford University*

The Asia Society's
China Council
Washington, D. C.

Prepared by
National Geographic
Book Service

Charles O. Hyman
Director

Photographs by
James P. Blair
Jim Brandenburg
Jodi Cobb
Dean Conger
Bruce Dale
Lowell Georgia
George F. Mobley
Thomas Nebbia
Galen Rowell
James L. Stanfield

Endpapers: detail of an 18th-
century Qing Dynasty dragon
robe, now in the Metropolitan
Museum of Art. Photograph by
Victor R. Boswell, Jr. Pages 2-3:
Guilin; Hiroji Kubota, Magnum.

First edition 420,000 copies
Second printing 50,000 copies
Third printing 50,000 copies
Fourth printing 40,000 copies
Fifth printing 115,000 copies
Sixth printing (1987)
  200,000 copies

Library of Congress CIP data
page 518.

CONTENTS

FOREWORD

When I was a child my mother warned me, as I dug a large hole in our backyard flower garden, that if I kept on digging I would end up in China. For a boy growing up in the post-Depression Midwest, this was a welcome adventure to contemplate. I conjured up visions of exotic people and places I felt I knew intimately from *Terry and the Pirates* comics, the frightening tales of Fu Manchu, and Charlie Chan Saturday afternoon movies. It was a land of contradictions, where beautiful, dark-haired women wore brocaded trousers and evil emperors silken gowns; where Confucian sages gave stern counsel in fortune-cookie prose.

For many of us, the Chinese stereotypes stem partly from Hollywood, but mainly from China's self-imposed isolation. Since ancient times, Westerners have yearned to plumb the mysteries of the Orient. Early Romans knew the Chinese only as the faraway makers of the silk they coveted. Marco Polo regaled 13th-century Europeans with tales of his adventures in Cathay and the great cities he saw there. It was while trying to find a new route to Asia that Columbus discovered the New World—which Europeans soon took as their own, leaving China, as always, a land beyond the wind.

The United States did not develop close relations with China until World War II, when the Nationalist government desperately sought allies in its death struggle with the Japanese invaders. As soon as that war ended, the Chinese resumed their own civil war with increased violence and hatred. From that time forward, relations between the United States and the victorious Chinese Communists became ever more strained and unpredictable. Most Americans were barred from the country for decades, and only one National Geographic staff journalist—Luis Marden—was allowed to work in China between 1948 and 1979. When the Communist regime first began to loosen restrictions on working visas, the National Geographic Society eagerly sought entry to a nation which is home to one-fourth of the world's people.

If China could be positioned over North America, the Heilong Jiang (Amur River) would be on the same latitude as Hudson Bay, Hainan Island on a level with Haiti. China's 3.7 million square miles include the cold, high Himalayas and the sweltering Turpan Depression, 505 feet below sea level. The landscape is so broken, the extremes of climate are so great, that only about 10 percent of the land is arable. The lofty Qin Ling range divides China into the parched north and the well-watered south. Other physical barriers further fragment the landscape. For a while separate states existed as in Europe, but

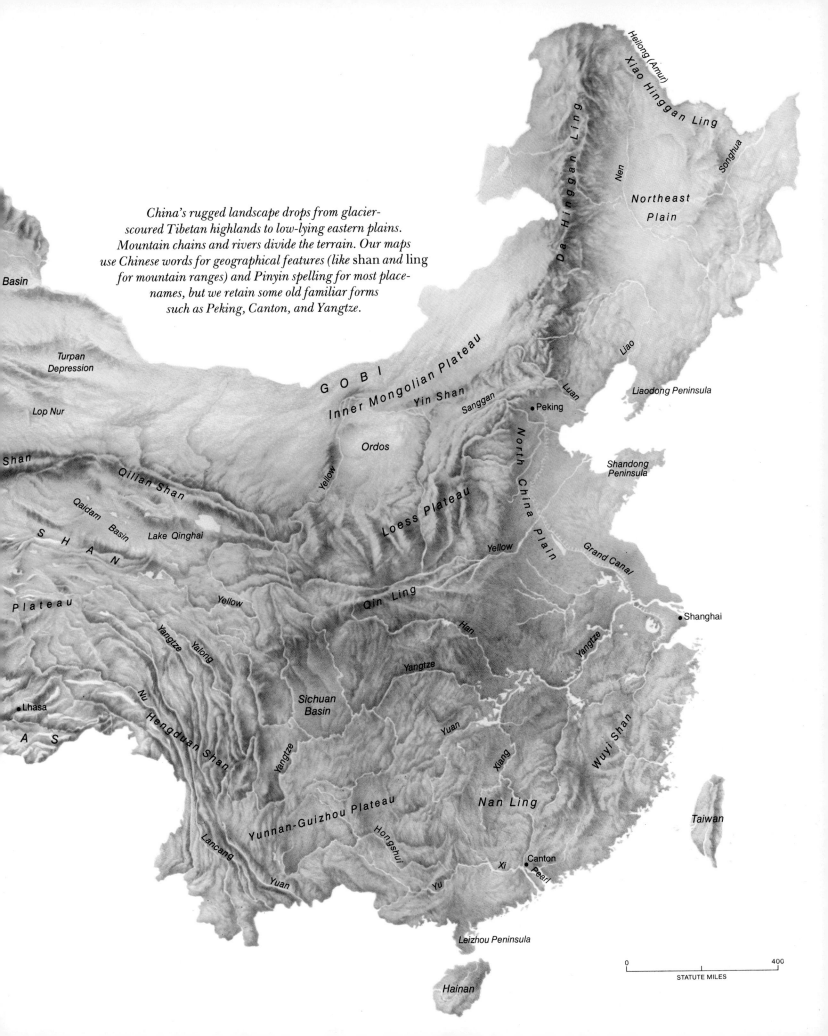

China's rugged landscape drops from glacier-scoured Tibetan highlands to low-lying eastern plains. Mountain chains and rivers divide the terrain. Our maps use Chinese words for geographical features (like shan *and* ling *for mountain ranges) and Pinyin spelling for most place-names, but we retain some old familiar forms such as Peking, Canton, and Yangtze.*

Heilong (Amur)

Xiao Hinggan Ling

Da Hinggan Ling

Songhua

Nen

Northeast Plain

Liao

Liaodong Peninsula

Basin

Turpan Depression

Lop Nur

GOBI

Inner Mongolian Plateau

Yin Shan

Sanggan

Luan

Peking

Shan

Qilian Shan

Ordos

Yellow

Shandong Peninsula

SHAN

Qaidam Basin

Lake Qinghai

Loess Plateau

North China Plain

Yellow

Grand Canal

Plateau

Yellow

Qin Ling

Han

Yangtze

Shanghai

Yangtze

Yalong

Lhasa

Yangtze

Sichuan Basin

Yangtze

Yuan

Xiang

Wuyi Shan

A S

Nu

Hengduan Shan

Yangtze

Nan Ling

Taiwan

Lancang

Yunnan-Guizhou Plateau

Hongshui

Yu

Xi

Canton

Pearl

Yuan

Leizhou Peninsula

Hainan

0   400

STATUTE MILES

they eventually were welded together under aggressive rulers. (See the enclosed wall map, "The Peoples of China," which shows China's ethnic diversity.) As the core population of Han Chinese gained new territories, they carried with them strong unifying characteristics, including a written language and a bureaucratic tradition that prevailed through dynasty after dynasty.

China's frontiers, some of them newly under control, form natural buffer zones against the unwanted influences of alien civilizations. To the west looms the Qinghai-Tibet Plateau, surrounded by the most formidable rampart of mountains on earth. Beyond the Great Wall lies the broad Inner Mongolian Plateau, separated from the Soviet Union by the desolate Gobi.

China today, though open to daily airline flights and eager to receive package tourists and foreign businessmen, is suspicious of journalists who try to dig below the surface. More than 20 of our writers and photographers explored China for this book; all found that the most difficult and least romantic barrier to free travel and inquiry was the pervasive bureaucracy. Much of our energy went not into the travail of reportage in an underdeveloped country, but into getting permission to do the work of journalists.

A year of negotiations gained us unprecedented access for such a large project, and we finally started on our journeys. We followed mighty rivers and ancient trails; traced the Grand Canal and the Great Wall; found our way into oasis courtyards and bamboo huts; and everywhere sought the truth. The acceptance of aid from government agencies (a necessity for working in China) was two-edged: It brought us formal cooperation and opened many doors, but also placed those agencies where they could deter our plans if they wished. Our readers should know that Chinese officials—sometimes an unwieldy number—went along on every journey. They did so, they insisted, to "ease our way, attend our comforts, and protect us." Our writers and photographers, while hampered and frequently blocked, persevered and often were able to slip away and find rewarding surprises.

On my own visits to China, my attention was often torn between the country's great physical and cultural attractions and the demeanor of its people, who seem to be pouring all of their energy into the building of a modern nation. For most Chinese, the economic and social accomplishments of the last few years are matters of consuming interest and unconcealed pride. They view virtually all aspects of art, work, and even recreation in terms of how these efforts might advance China further into the 20th century.

Journey Into China does not attempt to analyze ideology or politics. Our aim is to portray the geographical and human diversity of China as thoroughly and sensitively as possible. In the process, we have developed a real affection for the Chinese people and an increased sense of wonder at their 4,000 years of culture. Working on this book was an experience I would not trade, as my mother would have said, "for all the tea in China."

CHARLES O. HYMAN
Director, Book Service

XINJIANG UYGUR AUTONOMOL

TIBET AUTONOMOUS

8

*Immense in territory, varied in people,
China is organized into provinces, autonomous regions,
and municipalities. Han Chinese predominate in culture and
politics, but 55 minorities enrich the national mosaic. This
map, showing each area with its capital, can be used as
a companion reference with the chapter
maps of our individual journeys.*

HEILONGJIANG

• Harbin

JILIN

• Changchun

INNER MONGOLIA
AUTONOMOUS REGION

Shenyang
•

LIAONING

• Ürümqi

REGION

Hohhot •

PEKING
MUNICIPALITY
•
HEBEI

TIANJIN
MUNICIPALITY

HEBEI

GANSU

• Yinchuan

Taiyuan
•

Shijiazhuang
•

SHANXI

Jinan
•

SHANDONG

NINGXIA
HUI
AUT.
REG.

Xining •

QINGHAI

Lanzhou •

Zhengzhou
•

JIANGSU

• Xian

HENAN

ANHUI

Nanjing
•

SHANGHAI
MUNICIPALITY

SHAANXI

Hefei
•

REGION

HUBEI

Hangzhou
•

• Lhasa

• Chengdu

Wuhan •

ZHEJIANG

SICHUAN

• Nanchang

Changsha •

JIANGXI

HUNAN

Fuzhou
•

GUIZHOU

• Guiyang

FUJIAN

• Taipei

Kunming •

GUANGXI ZHUANG
AUTONOMOUS
REGION

GUANGDONG

TAIWAN

YUNNAN

Canton •

• Nanning

0   400

STATUTE MILES

Hainan Island

GUANGDONG

EBB AND FLOW OF CONQUEST

By Jonathan D. Spence

For thousands of years China developed at its own speed in its own way, so that, to most Westerners, this ancient civilization seems a world apart. And yet the dilemmas that shaped China sound familiar to Western ears. The longest continuously recorded history in the world gives us a sense of China's concerns: How to tame mighty rivers and ensure good harvests. How to ward off hostile border tribes. How to build—and control—the bureaucracy needed to manage vast populations. How to keep the emperor—master of the known world—on a moral course through the ebb and flow of conquest and palace intrigue.

China's national beginnings lie in the inland valleys of the Wei and Yellow Rivers. By the middle of the second millennium B.C., a group of settled farming communities was partly organized under rulers who directed labor projects and warfare. These rulers turned to priest-advisers for predictions on government matters and the outcome of hunts and battles. The priests applied red-hot rods to the bones of sheep or cattle and to tortoise shells until they cracked, then interpreted the cracks as auguries from the spirits.

Sometimes records were inscribed on these bones and shells in the

Life-size clay warrior, one of thousands buried near China's first emperor. By Lowell Georgia.

scratched figures of the earliest Chinese pictograms. In 1899 a scientist noticed inscriptions on "dragon bones" being ground up for medicine, and archaeologists traced them to Anyang in Henan Province. The dramatic discovery provided the first firm archaeological evidence for the Shang Dynasty, the earliest authenticated ruling house in China. Signs of large-scale human and animal sacrifice in the royal tombs demonstrate the power and cruelty of these rulers. At the same time, superb ritual bronze objects, cast in pottery molds and elaborately decorated, testify to the high level of Shang technology and their brilliant aesthetic sense.

The Shang were overthrown by the new regime of Zhou in the 12th century B.C. Then Zhou power weakened, and about 25 rival states spread out to the south and east, some building territorial walls. Fragmented chronicles show the slow erosion of central power and the growth of international relations between the states. As diplomacy failed, the fourth and third centuries B.C. earned their bleak name, the Era of Warring States.

Incessant warfare brought death and misery, but written history, philosophy, and sophisticated ethical argument were developing at the same time. Confucius, born in the sixth century B.C., had drawn an example for the present from the records of the past. His humanistic code of virtuous behavior in the service of the state was to have its impact throughout imperial history. As if in answer to his cautious moralizing, a rival "legalist" school taught the stern lesson that states should be run by harsh punishments and iron control of trade and agriculture. And a third philosophy, known as Daoism, sought to escape from the political turmoil of the times by abandoning personal will to a mystical harmony with nature.

Under the guidance of legalists, the small kingdom of Qin at the southern bend of the Yellow River won its independence from Zhou. Equipped with bronze and iron weapons, war chariots, cavalry, and masses of organized foot soldiers, Qin crushed rival states and in 221 B.C. achieved a unified Chinese empire. The victorious ruler took the title Qin Shi Huangdi (First Emperor of Qin) and declared that his dynasty would last "ten thousand generations." He designed a new tax structure and strict legal code, cruelly silenced intellectual critics, and, consolidating state walls, completed the Great Wall with the forced labor of hundreds of thousands. His reign was as unpopular as it was ruthless. Civil war erupted, and in 206 B.C. the Qin Dynasty fell to the house of Han. Little remained save the name Qin (Ch'in), by which the West came to call China, and the passionate conviction that China could be a unified nation ruled by a single man and governed by law.

The new and powerful Han Dynasty, founded by a rebel military leader, Gao Zu, sent expeditions and settlers out to Central Asia and down to the Pearl

River Delta, and ruled, with one interruption, until A.D. 220. Its name survives today as the one by which ethnic Chinese are known.

In the long succession of dynasties after Han—through civil war, fragmentation, and reunification that led to the Sui and then the prosperous Tang era—the population rose to over 60 million, and a truly Chinese civilization flourished. The ideographic writing system, now standardized, gave rise to exquisite calligraphy and poetry. Buddhism, introduced from India, blended with local traditions into a distinctive Chinese faith and inspired new forms of painting and sculpture. Glazed masterpieces of the Tang potter's art heralded dynamic achievements in ceramics. Silk production thrived, providing the base for paintings of utmost delicacy. The codified works of Confucianism became components of education and guidelines for moral conduct.

By the time of the Song Dynasty in the tenth century, an effective bureaucracy had emerged to help the emperors control the state. Scholar-officials were recruited through examinations based on memorizing and interpreting Confucian texts—now known as the "Classics." This new merit system signaled the demise of the old aristocratic order that had dominated most cultural and military life since the Han. Song China became a rich and cosmopolitan realm, with Asian traders arriving by land in the northwest and Arabs by sea in the southeast, with a flourishing iron industry fueled by the wood and coal of north China, with artistry in porcelain and landscape painting that has never been surpassed, and with an urban life of immense variety and ebullience.

Then, in the midst of Song richness, came collapse. The country had already been cut in half in 1127 when the armies of the Jürchen state of Jin overwhelmed the capital in Kaifeng and drove the Chinese armies out of the north. But the Song had established a new capital at Hangzhou, some 100 miles south of the mouth of the Yangtze River. In 1279 the tragedy was repeated, though this time without recourse. Kublai Khan and his highly-trained Mongol cavalry overran central and southern China, wiping out the Song and establishing a new dynasty, the Yuan. The conquest was terrible in its thoroughness and took a great cultural and economic toll. China never regained the technical brilliance of the Song, which had placed the country far ahead of any rivals in medieval Europe or the Middle East; and the Chinese never quite transcended the cultural shock of "barbarian conquest."

In the early years of Kublai Khan's reign, many scholars simply withdrew from an active life to the study of philosophy and the arts. And in return, Kublai Khan, having, as Marco Polo noted, "no confidence in the natives," concentrated political power in the hands of his Mongol countrymen and foreign advisers. After his death, internal dissension in the ruling class, coupled with disastrous floods and famine, carried the dynasty toward its demise. A native rebellion led by Zhu Yuanzhang, a peasant turned monk, flared against the Yuan in central China and brought the country once more under Chinese sway with the founding of the Ming Dynasty at Nanjing in 1368.

The Ming was an empire of power and splendor at many levels. Emperor Yong Le sent fleets to Africa and Arabia in the 15th century. He constructed

a new Ming capital at Peking, with the Forbidden City at its center, rebuilt the Great Wall, and improved the Grand Canal, begun about the fourth century B.C. Rice and tea, from the agricultural heartland of the south around Hangzhou, and porcelain, from the imperial kilns at Jingdezhen, flowed north to the capital. Commerce flourished, and exports included the famous blue-and-white porcelain of Ming, known in Europe as "chinaware."

But the Ming Dynasty retained some of the harshness and inflexibility that had permeated life under the Yuan. Punishment was ruthless; political leaders, even revered scholars, were beaten to death in public. The emperors wielded an extreme if erratic power, and they often deferred the day-to-day management of national matters to court eunuchs, who enriched their relatives and friends and paid little attention to national goals. Depression and cynicism grew in the 16th century, as fresh Mongol tribes roamed across the northern borders, pirates laid waste the eastern seaboard, and peasant unrest brought plundering and alarms in the countryside.

Much of this disarray passed unnoticed by the first Italian missionaries, who began to arrive in the 1580s. They saw an empire of unparalleled richness and splendor, with cities surpassing Venice or Florence. They saw, too, an urban society mirrored in its arts. In the 16th century, the popular short story and drama came into their own, playing on themes of social pretension among newly rich merchants, and romantic and erotic love between young men and women. To Europeans, weary of the violent struggles of Catholics and Protestants in the Wars of Religion, or of the mercenary armies that roved between northern Italy and the Netherlands, China seemed supremely civilized.

The collapse of the Ming Dynasty in the middle of the 17th century seemed almost a cliché out of history, a series of disasters somehow shaped by a classic "dynastic cycle" that drove power from its apogee to its nadir and led to violence and death. Great famines ravaged north China. One major bandit leader, Li Zicheng, sprang up in Shaanxi and another, Zhang Xianzhong—known as the Yellow Tiger—in Sichuan. Each swiftly took over his whole province and began to move outside in giant raids. Manchu tribesmen, uncontrollable in their mountainous forest areas between the Heilong Jiang (Amur River) and Liao River, struck at will in the northeast. Some of the Ming armies mutinied. Salaries went unpaid. The morale of the bureaucracy fell ever lower.

The end of the Ming came as a mixed result of all these causes. In 1644 the imperial armies allowed the rebel Li Zicheng to enter Peking almost unopposed. Rather than face the shame of capture, the last Ming emperor

15

Han Dynasty bronze horse. Opposite: Ancient royal grave by the Yellow River.

Highlights of Chinese History

Yuanmou Man	1.6 million years ago	Earliest prehuman traces. Growth in skills and social organization as early hominids develop into modern humans. Stone tools and use of fire.
Lantian Man, Peking Man	700,000-500,000 years ago	
Upper Cave Man	18,000 years ago	
Yangshao culture	5000 B.C.	Farming villages in Wei and Yellow River Valleys (such as Banpo, near Xian). Painted pottery.
Longshan culture	2500 B.C.	East China and heartland river valleys. Wheel-made black pottery. Early divination and ancestor cult.
Three Rulers and Five Emperors	?2852-?2205 B.C. (traditional dates)	Mythical hero-rulers, credited with inventing skills such as farming, building, medicine, silk culture.
Xia Dynasty	?2205-?1766 B.C.	Chinese claim as first dynasty. Founder said to be Yu, master of flood control and irrigation.
Shang Dynasty	?1766-?1122 B.C.	First verifiable dynasty. Cities at Anyang and Zhengzhou. Ancestor worship employs ritual bronze vessels and "oracle bones." First writing.
Zhou Dynasty	?1122-256 B.C.	Western Zhou later cited as model period. Capital near Xian. Feudal states gain power, build walls for defense. Zhou move to Luoyang. Confucius born 551 B.C. Flowering in classical literature, arts, and philosophy; Confucianism, Daoism. First canals begun.
Eastern Zhou	770-256	
Spring and Autumn	722-481	
Warring States	403-221	
Qin Dynasty	221-206 B.C.	First emperor unifies China, joins state walls to form Great Wall, constructs a palace and mausoleum near Xian, standardizes weights, measures, writing.
Han Dynasty	206 B.C.-A.D. 220	Prosperity and expansion. Splendor of capitals at Changan and Luoyang rivals that of Rome. Buddhism enters along Silk Road. Birth of Confucian civil service. Paper invented. Sima Qian first great historian.
Western Han	206 B.C.-A.D. 9	
Eastern Han	25-220	
Three Kingdoms Wei, Shu-Han, Wu	220-280	Han generals turn warlord and divide empire. Period romanticized as time of chivalry and heroism.
Western Jin	265-316	China briefly united. Capitals at Luoyang, Changan.
Southern and Northern Dynasties	317-589	Succession of dynasties (including 24 short-lived ones) north and south of the Yangtze. Important period for Buddhism. Cave temples begun at Dunhuang, Yungang, and Longmen.
Eastern Jin	317-420	
Northern Wei	386-534	
Sui Dynasty	589-618	Northern Chinese general conquers south and reunites China. Grand Canal built. Capital at Changan.
Tang Dynasty	618-907	Rebuilt Changan becomes a cosmopolitan capital. Scholarship and arts flourish. Gunpowder and block printing invented. Height of Silk Road trade.
Five Dynasties (north) **and Ten Kingdoms** (south)	907-960	Another period of warlordism and fragmentation.
Song Dynasty	960-1279	Age of high culture: painting, poetry, calligraphy. Strong bureaucracy, but military power declining. Invention of compass. Northern invasion by Jin. Song move capital from Kaifeng to Hangzhou.
Northern Song	960-1127	
Southern Song	1127-1279	

Yuan Dynasty (Mongol)	**1279-1368**	Kublai Khan conquers China. New capital established at Peking and Grand Canal extended to supply it. Marco Polo serves khan in China.
Ming Dynasty	**1368-1644**	Mongol defeat. Stable, prosperous era under strong emperors. Forbidden City and imperial tombs built. Arrival of Jesuits. Changan now called Xian.
Qing Dynasty (Manchu)	**1644-1911**	Han subjugated by sinicized Manchus. Neglected Forbidden City restored, Summer Palace rebuilt.
	1839-1842	Foreign trade pressure leads to Opium War; Chinese forced to open treaty ports.
	1850-1864	Taiping Rebellion in the south: anti-Qing revolt, inspired by mixture of Chinese and Christian ideas.
	1858-1860	Anglo-French invasions at Canton, Tianjin. Foreign troops destroy Summer Palace; it is later rebuilt.
	1894-95	Sino-Japanese War. Japan dominates Korea, Taiwan.
	1900	Anti-foreign Boxer Rebellion suppressed by foreign troops. Qing court flees. Westerners occupy Peking.
Republic of China	**1911-1949**	1911 Revolution. Attempted democratic government.
	1912	Sun Yat-sen briefly serves as first president. Kuomintang (KMT), or Nationalist Party, formed.
	1916	Warlord period begins.
	1921	Chinese Communist Party (CCP) founded.
	1926-27	Joint KMT-CCP expedition against warlords has some success but ends in hostile division.
	1934-35	Long March of Communists to northwest.
	1937-1945	Second Sino-Japanese War. Nationalist government under Chiang Kai-shek. American military aid during World War II. Japan surrenders.
	1946-49	Civil war between KMT and CCP.
People's Republic of China	**1949-present**	Nationalists flee to Taiwan. Mao Zedong proclaims People's Republic of China (PRC). Soviet aid.
	1950-53	Korean War. PRC institutes land reforms.
	1956-57	Hundred Flowers Movement.
	1958	Great Leap Forward. Communes formed.
	1960	Soviet technicians withdraw.
	1966	Ten-year Cultural Revolution begins.
	1972	President Richard M. Nixon visits Peking.
	1976	Premier Zhou Enlai and Chairman Mao Zedong die. Gang of Four arrested; sentenced in 1981.
	1977-78	Deng Xiaoping emerges as preeminent leader.
	1979	USA and PRC establish diplomatic relations.
	1980s	China woos foreign capital, trade, and tourism.

OVERLEAF. *Castle in the sand at Dunhuang: Tiered galleries enclose rock-cut Buddhist shrines.*
James L. Stanfield

hanged himself on Coal Hill behind the Forbidden City. The one remaining Ming general with a major army in north China, Wu Sangui, turned back from guarding the Manchurian frontier in order to confront the rebel regime in Peking. Seizing the opportunity, Manchu troops swept through the undefended Pass Between the Mountains and the Sea—Shanhaiguan—at the eastern terminus of the Great Wall. Trapped between two forces, Wu Sangui threw in his lot with the Manchus.

This may seem a strange and traitorous decision, but the Ming forces were by then in total disarray. Li Zicheng's bandit army, though Chinese, had behaved with incredible savagery in Peking, humiliating or killing officials and looting homes, and now showed little sign of being able to establish a stable regime. The Manchus, on the other hand, though an alien people with strange customs like shaving the front of their heads and plaiting their hair in one long pigtail down their backs, had imitated Chinese court and bureaucratic customs in Manchuria. They had accepted numerous Chinese into their own ranks, and offered the promise of a peace based on the Confucian principles they had so recently learned.

Within less than thirty years joint Manchu-Chinese forces, led by Manchu generals and by Wu Sangui and other defectors, had consolidated their hold over China. Dissatisfied with the rewards given to him by the new Manchu dynasty, known as the Qing, Wu himself rebelled in 1673, sparking a civil war that engulfed half the country and nearly made the Qing one of China's shortest dynasties. But slowly and steadily the Qing armies fought back, recaptured the south, and in 1683 seized Taiwan from the last Ming supporters, bringing the island firmly under Chinese political control for the first time.

For a century and a half, under three of its greatest emperors, Kang Xi, Yong Zheng, and Qian Long, the Qing Dynasty grew in wealth and territory. The population rose from 120 million to 300 million or more. Qing armies pushed into Tibet and dominated the court of the Dalai Lama in Lhasa. They advanced far across the Lop Nur basin to the great western deserts on the Russian border. In the northeast, they destroyed encroaching Russian settlements and drew a line between the two countries, using the course of the Heilong Jiang as the border. The Western trading powers—Britain, France, Holland, and later the United States—were forced to restrict their trade to the city of Canton. There they had to conduct their business in tea and silks strictly on Qing terms, acknowledging, as it were, the central role of the emperor of China in the conduct of world affairs.

This time it was not so much internal collapse that brought down a dynasty but the fact that a new and aggressive group of trading nations would not let China run things by her own rules. Britain especially, strong with the new power brought by the industrial revolution and flushed with imperialist visions after the defeat of Napoleon in 1815, sought to open a range of new trading ports and to end irksome restrictions. To balance the payments of her trade with China, the British began to sell large amounts of opium grown in their Indian domains in Bengal to eager Chinese traders, who paid in silver.

Opium sales proved all too successful, and the damaging effects of opium addiction on the Chinese psyche and the economic drain caused by the huge outflow of silver to the West finally led to military confrontation. In the Opium War of 1839-1842, British forces broke the Qing defenses in south and central China and imposed a humiliating treaty. Its provisions opened five ports to trade, promised direct contact between foreign powers and the Chinese bureaucracy, extracted a large cash indemnity, and protected foreign traders and missionaries in certain Chinese cities.

In the 1850s and 1860s China was wracked again by major rebellions and fresh foreign wars with England and France. A second round of treaties saw the opening of more ports, deeper penetration by foreign merchants and missionaries, and an even wider sale of opium. The possibilities of dynastic collapse were evident to all.

To shore up Chinese power, desperate Qing officials tried belatedly to adopt certain Western skills. But neither the small number of adaptable bureaucrats of the old regime, nor the scattering of newly trained managers and scientists, could make much impression on a government mainly interested in preserving its own power. The Empress Dowager Ci Xi, who dominated Chinese politics between the 1860s and her death in 1908, made sure that Manchus stayed in key government positions, wasted scarce money on lavish palace construction, and took an intransigent foreign policy position. The seizure of major spheres of influence within China by the British, Germans, French, and Russians, coupled with the taking of Taiwan by Japan in 1895, hastened the court's collapse. At a time when internal forces demanded government reforms, the imperial status quo was further eroded by Ci Xi's support of the anti-foreign Boxer rebels and her declaration of war against the foreign powers. The Boxers' 55-day siege of Western legations in Peking and Tianjin in 1900 brought massive foreign intervention and led to the frantic flight of the court from Peking and the imposition of yet another adverse treaty.

By 1908, the year the empress dowager died, China had started tentatively on the road toward a constitutional monarchy, and the Qing rulers had agreed to convene representative assemblies. Yet these institutions had little connection to executive power. Instead they focused the angry frustrations of China's nationalists, and provided a forum for the exchange of new ideas. Here were aired the bitterly anti-Manchu views of patriotic Chinese like Sun Yat-sen, who had been driven into exile in 1895 after an attempted rebellion. Sun had built up strong backing among activists in his own country, among Chinese students studying military tactics and economics in Japan, and among the Overseas Chinese communities in Southeast Asia and the West.

OVERLEAF. *A man, a plow, and the good earth—a timeless pastoral scene in Sichuan Province.*
Thomas Nebbia

In the years immediately after the empress dowager's death, frustration and anger grew in China, and could not be placated by the clumsy actions of the Manchu regents who ruled in the name of the boy emperor, Pu Yi. Riots over high food prices, provincial protest against the government's centralizing railway policy, fledgling politicians' disgust with the delaying tactics of the central government—all came to a climax with a series of army mutinies in October 1911. Barely four months later, bereft of almost all support, the regents of the young emperor had no choice but to announce his abdication. The Mandate of Heaven—the divine sanction—had been withdrawn from the last Chinese emperor. In January a Chinese republic was declared, with Sun Yat-sen as temporary president. Realizing his military weakness, Sun yielded the presidency to Yuan Shikai, once one of the empress dowager's most trusted generals, now seen as a progressive "strong man" who could lead China into the modern world.

There was a brief period of euphoria in 1912 and 1913 at the prospect of Chinese democracy. Elections were held across the country for a national parliament—limited to male electors, it is true, and only to those with property or educational qualifications, but nevertheless unprecedented in China's history. Yet when some of the victorious candidates began to criticize the acting president, Yuan Shikai, and to suggest the modification of his powers, Yuan saw this as a personal threat rather than an attempt to gain true representative government. He had the leading opposition spokesman assassinated, banned the major opposition political party and exiled its leaders. Just before his death from natural causes in 1916, he even tried to install himself as emperor, though he had to abandon the move in the face of frenzied public protest.

The rise of both the Kuomintang (Nationalist) Party and the Chinese Communist Party can be traced back to the years after Yuan's death, generally known as the period of "warlordism." With Yuan gone there was no general strong enough to control all the armies, and no forceful central government. Accordingly, China slowly broke up into dozens, then hundreds of small units controlled by groups of militarists and politicians or by individual military leaders. From this fragmentation, and the often ruthless exploitation of peasants in the countryside and workers in the mines and factories, sprang a social and intellectual rage. These bitter feelings gave nationalism a new cohesive force and released revolutionary energies in the pursuit of social justice.

Strengthened and reorganized after years of exile, Sun Yat-sen's Kuomintang Party reasserted itself in Canton, determined to make this the southern springboard for a drive to reunify China. There Sun was joined by leaders of the Chinese Communist Party, which had been founded in Shanghai in 1921. Despite their different ideologies, they could agree on the major priorities for a China they defined as "semi-feudal and semi-colonial." Sun Yat-sen died in 1925, and the Nationalist government struggled to pursue his goals.

In 1926 and 1927, a "United Front" of joint Communist-Nationalist armies wiped out many of the southern and central Chinese warlords and reached the Yangtze River cities of Wuhan and Nanjing. There, however,

Imperial reception room at the Summer Palace. Such luxuries drained the Qing treasury.
Dean Conger

major ideological differences surfaced. Bloody internal wrangling was followed by Kuomintang massacres of workers and peasants who had supported the Communist cause. By October 1927, Mao Zedong and other Communist leaders found themselves fugitives in the poverty-stricken border region of Jiangxi-Hunan, or else hiding underground in major cities.

Seven years later, effective police measures and a series of concentrated rural campaigns, orchestrated by the Kuomintang military leader Chiang Kai-shek, led to Communist flight from all eastern bases. Some 100,000 soldiers and supporters embarked in 1934 on the disastrous yet heroic Long March from eastern Jiangxi. Fighting continuously, they wound their way through 11 provinces, covering 6,000 miles in one year, much of the route through high mountains. About 20,000 survivors finally reached the arid loess hills and valleys surrounding Yanan in Shaanxi Province. Here they entrenched, perhaps remembering in their desperate straits that it was in this region that Qin power had grown over two thousand years ago, and that here the bandit armies of Li Zicheng had first assembled to challenge the Ming in the 1630s.

In the face of renewed Kuomintang attacks during 1936, the Communists probably owed their survival to the Japanese. Following treaty concessions at the end of the Sino-Japanese War of 1894-95, Japan had converted her economic expansion in Manchuria into a virtual protectorate by the 1920s. Emboldened by this success, she attacked Shanghai in 1932, set up a puppet government in Manchuria, and moved troops into the Peking region. Concerned with unifying his country by exterminating Communist rebels, Chiang Kai-shek was not ready to declare war on Japan. But public outcry at Japanese arrogance was so great that Chiang found it hard to marshal support for his attacks on the Communists: "Why should brother kill brother?" Chinese asked. In December 1936, Nationalist troops mutinied in Xian, and Chiang agreed to a new United Front with the Communists. When total warfare with Japan erupted in 1937, the Communists led their resistance from Yanan in Shaanxi while Chiang, pushed inland by Japanese forces, fought from his base far up the Yangtze in the Sichuan riverside city of Chongqing (Chungking).

Separated by ideology, yet united by patriotism, the Communist-Kuomintang alliance during World War II was inevitably a complex one. To American diplomats, and to military advisers under Gen. Joseph W. Stilwell who came to China in 1942 following Pearl Harbor, the alliance was quite inscrutable. American aid and advice went mostly to the Chongqing regime, which was the official Nationalist government of China and seemed to be bearing the brunt of the fighting against the Japanese. Chongqing appeared a heroic place in those days. Its factories had been reassembled from machinery hauled up rivers and over mountains all the way from Shanghai. Its universities were full of faculty and students who had carried their books across China. Gen. Claire Lee Chennault's Flying Tigers echoed the heroism of the old Lafayette Escadrille, and Mme Chiang Kai-shek presented a vivid and elegant symbol of the Chinese people's will to resist.

As the war dragged on, however, and American attention swung first to the African campaigns against Rommel, then to Eisenhower's thrust into Europe, and to the savage battles for the Pacific Islands, China began to seem a military and political backwater. The Chongqing regime looked less attractive the more one knew about it—corruption, laziness, inefficiency, bigotry, all seemed rampant. By contrast, the few foreign observers in Yanan described the Communists as ebullient, dedicated, honest, and apparently totally open about their dreams for a reunified society in a free postwar world.

When World War II ended in August 1945, civil war in China flared up almost immediately. The Kuomintang forces were stuck in southwest China. Even when troops were airlifted north by American planes, they could not prevent Communist armies led by Lin Biao from racing to Manchuria and seizing control of the northern regions. Nor could the Kuomintang stop the catastrophic inflation, restore China's war-wrecked industry, or bring order and decency to the life of poor peasants in the countryside. The government lacked mass support from its own people, was disdained by the intellectuals, and received only minor military assistance from the United States. Its armies slipped from disaster to disaster in the battles of the late 1940s, until Chiang Kai-shek retreated to Taiwan in 1949. On October 1, 1949, in Peking, Mao Zedong declared the inauguration of the People's Republic from the Gate of Heavenly Peace on the edge of the Forbidden City where pageants of emperors had passed in their palanquins.

Communist rule over China between their victory in 1949 and the early 1980s passed through several major phases. The first, lasting until the mid-1950s, concentrated largely on rebuilding the economy. Foreign ownership of China's industries was abolished through nationalization, and the age-old patterns of exploitation of landless peasant laborers were ended by a land reform program of confiscation and redistribution. To arrest the terrible erosion of China's hills, a huge program of reforestation was begun. With the aid of the Soviet Union, railways were extended and huge hydroelectric dams constructed on the Yellow River. Military forces were modernized and re-equipped after their serious mauling in the Korean War, and modern communications were developed. Some of these events caused immense disruption. Violence—often death—was meted out to hundreds of thousands of dispossessed landlords and former members of the Kuomintang. The intellectuals were at first reassured with revitalized universities, a vigorous world of publishing, filmmaking, history writing, and archaeology. But the Hundred Flowers Movement of 1956-57—in which they were encouraged to speak out and criticize abuses by the party bureaucracy, then penalized in an "anti-rightist" campaign for doing so—came as a serious jolt.

27

From the mid-1950s to the early 1970s, during the second phase, things took a very different course. Strengthened by the successes of these first years of rule, Mao Zedong moved to more radical policies which promised to yield a transformation of the human spirit beyond the transformations already achieved in the economy. Land deeds, once distributed to the poor peasants, were withdrawn, and all Chinese land was now collectivized in a new commune system of joint work and pooled wages. The Great Leap Forward, proclaimed in 1958, brought hundreds of thousands of laborers together for vast irrigation and construction projects, and forced peasants to work in backyard furnaces—a plan designed to move the gains of industrialization out of the cities and into the countryside. Supervision of intellectuals was intensified.

The Leap was criticized, and the massive suffering its disruptive policies caused led to a backlash against Mao in the early 1960s. But he regained his hold in the mid-1960s as Lin Biao, his Defense Minister, threw the weight of the army behind Mao and presented the "Little Red Book" of Mao's sayings as the collective wisdom of the ages—the blueprint for China's future.

By 1966, in an upsurge of radical fervor which Mao called the Great Proletarian Cultural Revolution, the inner structures of the Communist Party itself were assaulted. Student Red Guards, encouraged to root out all "revisionist" tendencies, paraded before Mao at the Gate of Heavenly Peace. The staffs of schools and universities were purged, examinations abolished, and the schools closed, some for years. Tens of thousands of intellectuals, youths, and party workers were sent off to hard labor in distant communes. Anyone linked to the West by education, sympathy, or upbringing was suspect. As the cult of Mao reached its peak, China turned against all foreign powers—the Soviet Union along with the United States, Japan, and most of Europe—preaching a new doctrine of unity with the deprived "third world."

By the seventies this process had run its course, and China entered another phase. Lin Biao was killed in 1971 after allegedly attacking Mao. Mao received President Richard M. Nixon in Peking in 1972, opening a new era of accord with the United States. After Mao's death in 1976 his closest radical supporters, now labeled the Gang of Four, were purged from office and put through humiliating trials, their guilt a foregone conclusion.

When Deng Xiaoping, vice-premier of China and Mao's de facto successor, visited Washington in 1979, the way was opened to broader cultural exchanges and new levels of economic development for the People's Republic. The Chinese were reminded of the backward nature of their industrial plant, of their low housing standards, and of the staggering problems in health care, birth control, and food production and distribution posed by a population that had edged up steadily to the one billion mark.

Though China and the West remained separated by huge gulfs of tradition, the early eighties were years in which, perhaps fleetingly, new kinds of journeys could be undertaken: journeys into a present dominated by Communist government yet seeking a future with Western overtones, journeys across a country still bearing the weight and majesty of a slowly fading past.

30

Portrait of Mao, Great Helmsman of the People's Republic, haunts Peking's Gate of Heavenly Peace.
Jodi Cobb

CITY OF THE KHANS, CAPITAL OF THE CADRES

By Jay and Linda Mathews
Photographs by Dean Conger

Remote and inhospitable, the North China Plain seems an unlikely site for a capital. Peking—called Beijing in Chinese—stands neither on the sea nor on a major river; instead, the nearby hills are its reason for being. Peking was founded over 3,000 years ago as a frontier settlement, a shield against barbarian tribes who swooped down from the passes to the north.

We first saw Peking in April, when the city was under assault by another old adversary—the weather. Peking's annual dust storms were at their peak, and the city was suffocating under tons of fine soil blown in from the Gobi and the arid northwest. The fine yellow powder stung our skin, clogged our throats, and penetrated the windows and doors of the Peking Hotel. A golden haze hung over the entire city; day after day, the curving, gold-tile roofs of the Forbidden City, just two blocks from our hotel balcony, vanished in the amber dust by midafternoon.

Through the grit, we watched poker-faced commuters pedaling home, bowed by Siberian winds and choking on the dust. It was not the best time for a clear and dispassionate view of a many-layered city. When our dust siege was

Curved rooflines poised above Beihai Lake reflect Peking's graceful past.

over, we gladly returned to Hong Kong, where we lived and worked as journalists from 1976 to 1979, covering China from afar.

Fortunately, half a dozen later visits to Peking gave us chances to get to know the city better, and we soon grew envious of our Japanese and European colleagues, who were permitted to live in the city we wrote about every day but seldom saw. More and more, we wanted to return for a longer stay. Our chance came in 1979, with the normalization of U. S.-China relations. Soon we were on our way to Peking again—with eight suitcases, our two sons, and a three-months' supply of Pampers—to be residents, not tourists.

We looked around the grimy foyer of the old Capital Airport and realized that most of our fellow passengers, though Chinese, were as strange to the capital as we were. We eavesdropped on the clickety-clack accents of Cantonese import-export officials, the soft slur of commune leaders from the hills of Shanxi, the nasal buzz of Shanghai navy officers.

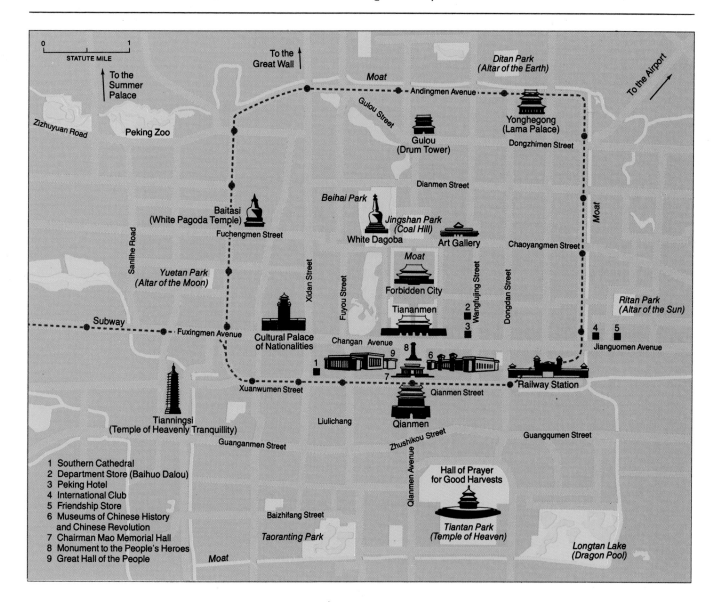

Since the 13th century, when it first became China's capital under the Mongols, Peking has been a city full of people from somewhere else. It still draws them from all over China. A few come as tourists, but most are dispatched to Peking for meetings or conferences, representing their factories or communes on business. Those who are lucky, well-connected, or talented enough to attract the attention of the "central authorities"—as the leadership in Peking is invariably called—sometimes wangle permanent assignments, a step up from their jobs in the provinces.

Power is the lure: What happens in Peking matters—to China and to the world. Decrees on everything from population control to the size of peasants' private plots of land emanate from the Communist Party authorities in Peking. The official language is standard Peking Chinese, the tongue Westerners call Mandarin and the Chinese call *putonghua,* or ordinary speech. The entire nation, despite its 3,000-mile breadth, runs on Peking time.

Jay and Linda Mathews spent four years exploring Peking, at first on frequent trips from their Hong Kong base, and later, for 17 months, as journalists resident in Peking. Housed in the venerable Peking Hotel—then the only available quarters for them and their children—they looked out on the historic gate Tiananmen, heart of the old empire, and on Tiananmen Square, the center of today's People's Republic. Their explorations through China's capital led them to many well-known sights in the city center (opposite) and in Peking's environs (right), as well as to other places that expressed China's theme of mingled stability and change: A Qianmen Avenue teahouse run by youthful capitalists, the Bright and Flowery Bathhouse, the candy counter of Peking's leading department store, and the ramshackle cottage of a courageous subway worker.

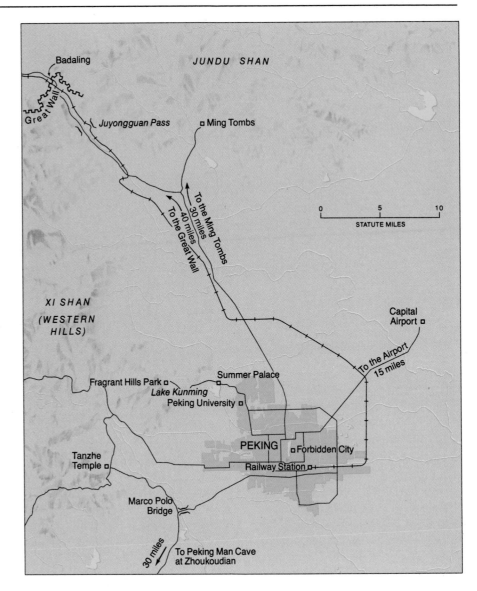

35

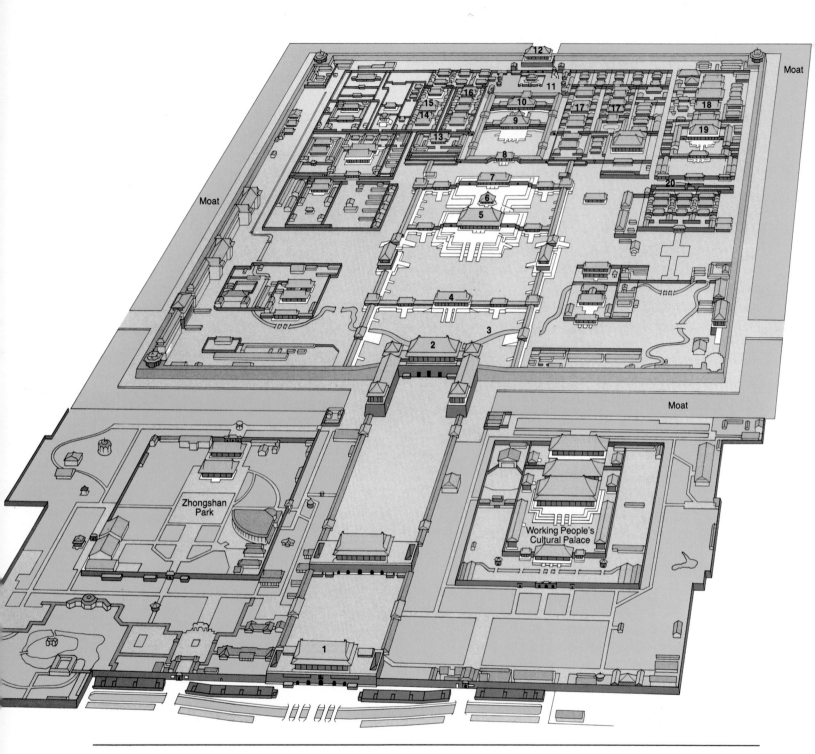

Symmetry and magnificence were Ming emperor Yong Le's goals when he began to build the Forbidden City in 1406. Its 250 acres were laid out under geomantic laws, aligned on a north-south axis. Colors, names, and shapes all had meaning. Today some of its buildings, numbered above, are open to the public.

1. Gate of Heavenly Peace (Tiananmen). 2. Meridian Gate. 3. Golden Water Stream. 4. Gate of Supreme Harmony. 5. Hall of Supreme Harmony. 6. Hall of Middle Harmony. 7. Hall of Preserving Harmony. 8. Gate of Heavenly Purity. 9. Palace of Heavenly Purity. 10. Hall of Earthly Peace.

11. Imperial Garden. 12. Gate of Divine Military Genius. 13. Hall of Mental Cultivation. 14. Hall of the Absolute. 15. Hall of Manifest Harmony. 16. Palace of Concentrated Beauty. 17. Pottery and Porcelain Exhibit. 18. Gold and Jade Exhibit. 19. Palace of Peaceful Old Age. 20. Nine Dragon Screen.

Living there, we came to appreciate Peking's tough and resilient people. Their ancestors labored to build and rebuild the city and over centuries impressed their own character on it, triumphing over a harsh climate and foreign invasions, and surviving indifferent and brutal leaders. Today's citizens are worthy successors, and their city's survival and growth make it a fitting symbol for all of China.

Today, despite Spartan living conditions and a government whose control reaches into the most intimate aspects of people's lives, many Chinese—even those in Peking, closest to the center of control—manage to enjoy happy lives with their families, to pursue their private passions, and to find pleasure in unlikely places.

Far from being the soulless blue ants of popular American imagination, the people of Peking are avid moviegoers (just try to buy a ticket to a new film), tireless tourists (there are crowds of sightseers at any scenic spot), and sports enthusiasts: At dawn, the parks of Peking are filled not only with old folks, moving through the ancient rhythms of *taijiquan*, but also with legions of young joggers in sweat suits.

Once, wandering down a narrow side street, we came on a crowd of teenagers and young adults; they shouted at one another, broke up into little groups, and caucused on the sidewalk. We were still fresh from Hong Kong, still accustomed to thinking of Peking in purely political terms. What was this, we asked one youngster—a street fight, a black market? He laughed shyly. "We're stamp collectors," he said. "We get together two or three days a week to look at each other's collections and do some trading."

As we settled into Peking's rhythms and learned where to look, we discovered that our new home was also a city of songbird fanciers, some of whom congregated with their caged pets every Sunday near Longtan Lake. Amateur horticulturists abounded; it was a poor household indeed that didn't boast a garden of flowering plants on the balcony. Many teenagers, we learned, would play basketball around the clock if they could; on late summer nights, as we drove to the main telegraph office to file our stories, we passed dimly-lit basketball courts and heard the swish of balls through nets.

But the center of life for the Chinese is unremitting labor: They have overcome Peking's natural handicaps and the ravages of successive invasions, and established the city as a world capital. Ambitious irrigation schemes, some begun more than 2,000 years ago, transformed the arid North China Plain into a productive agricultural region. The Grand Canal was extended in the seventh century to link the Peking region to the towns of the Yellow and Yangtze River Valleys. And since 1949 the Chinese have added thousands of miles to their rail network to tie the rest of China more closely to the capital.

The modernization of Peking itself is largely a Communist achievement. When Mao Zedong's armies finally entered the city in January of 1949, it was a war-weary backwater of more than two million people jammed into tiny courtyard houses and squatters' huts, an oversize village without significant industry or even the ability to feed its inhabitants. Today Peking is second only to Shanghai in population; it has nine million citizens, counting those in the nine adjoining counties that Peking annexed to feed itself. In industrial output per capita, Peking ranks second among China's cities and has built an iron and steel complex, petrochemical plants, and textile mills to supplement the artisans' shops and small businesses that were once the basis of its economy.

Though still developing, Peking now boasts high-rise buildings, a subway system, even a brand-new (if little-used) freeway—as well as the by-products of modernization that the city fathers would undoubtedly rather forego: traffic jams, housing shortages, air pollution, and juvenile gangs.

The little frontier settlement of ancient times, with its rural hinterland, now sprawls across 6,900 square miles, but the Ming Dynasty emperors would probably have no trouble finding their way around central Peking today. The city retains the grid plan they established early in the 15th century, and most of the historical landmarks in and around Peking—the Forbidden City, the Ming Tombs, and the Temple of Heaven—date from the reign of the third Ming emperor, Yong Le, a compulsive builder and monument-maker. (The actual buildings tourists visit today are mostly 18th- and 19th-century restorations and reconstructions.) Around Yong Le's capital, 200,000 laborers raised a 40-foot wall, four miles on a side, that stood until the 1950s.

Within those now-vanished walls is the heart of Peking. Its layout is a variation on an old Chinese puzzle: Instead of spheres within spheres, there are boxes within boxes. The walled-in capital of the Ming Dynasty, called the Inner City, covered an area of roughly 16 square miles; Qianmen, or Front Gate, the massive blue-tiled stone arch now ringed by a traffic circle, was originally its main portal. Within the Inner City was the Imperial City, a 1,500-acre enclave which was Peking's administrative and governmental center; Tiananmen, or the Gate of Heavenly Peace, with its crimson walls and roof of golden tiles, was the southern entrance to the Imperial City. And within the Imperial City was the holy of holies, the Forbidden City, where the emperor himself worked and lived; Wumen, or Meridian Gate, marked its threshold.

Peking lies low. Two-story houses were long prohibited, to keep ordinary Chinese from the sacrilege of looking down on the emperor if his sedan chair should pass in the street. The streets obediently run parallel or perpendicular to the main thoroughfare—Changan Jie, or Avenue of Eternal Peace—in a nearly perfect checkerboard. The architects who laid out the city put the altars of the sun, moon, earth, and heaven at the cardinal points of the compass, and the Forbidden City at the center of the dial. Today, Peking's obsession with the compass lives on in taxi drivers who ask passengers if they want to turn north or south (not left or right) at the corner, and in hostesses who say they keep the wine on the east (not the right) side of the shelf.

After the ancient walls around Peking were destroyed, wide boulevards and shopping streets replaced them in many parts of the city. But Tiananmen remains the physical center of Peking and the spiritual hub of all China. The gate is the nation's symbol, reproduced on stamps, airline tickets, and policemen's caps, and Chinese children grow up singing "I Love Peking's Tiananmen," just as American children sing "My Country, 'Tis of Thee." Tiananmen is the place where 24 Chinese emperors handed down their edicts. When the People's Republic of China was born, it was here that Mao Zedong hoisted the red flag. In the square before the gate, troops mustered in the great orchestrated parades that Mao so loved; every paving stone was numbered to keep the lines straight. The first mass protest against the excesses of the Cultural Revolution, in April 1976, took place in Tiananmen Square.

We often strolled through the square on balmy summer nights, when it was dotted with card players and families escaping their stifling houses. One night we joked with some of the card players who squatted on the pavement playing hand after hand of "Swimming Upstream." Linda gestured at the portrait of Mao that hung over the Gate of Heavenly Peace. "Do you suppose he would have approved of this game?" she asked one 70-year-old. "Does it matter?" he retorted. "He's dead and I'm not."

Like the old man, the citizens of Peking wear their city's history lightly. Yet nearly all the Chinese we knew, even those jaded residents of Peking, had photographs of themselves at Tiananmen Square, with the gate itself prominent in the background.

Like the emperors and warlords preceding them, the Communists have tried to leave their mark on the capital. Preservationists complain that the building frenzy of the Great Leap Forward left Tiananmen Square an architectural jumble. True, the Great Hall of the People and other new buildings on and near the square owe more to Soviet inspiration than to Chinese tradition. But they demonstrate the nation's awesome ability to mobilize labor for giant projects: In 1959, ten important new buildings were completed in just ten months to mark the tenth anniversary of the People's Republic.

Finding our way around Peking was relatively simple; surviving to tell the tale was something else. A Peking traffic jam is a lurching, heart-stopping amalgam of motorcycles, three-wheeled vans, trucks, taxis, articulated buses with accordion-pleated middles, and, it seems, all of the city's three million bicycles. The basic rule of the road, apparently, is that the streets belong to those bicycles, which operate as if the automobiles did not exist, darting into traffic heedless of stoplights. Pedestrians, only slightly less daring, jaywalk with abandon. The beleaguered police periodically attempt to restore order, but nothing works for very long: When

Pekingese are in a hurry, red lights, traffic cops, and lane markings mean nothing at all, as we learned on one of our first taxi rides after our arrival.

Han, our driver, never stopped if he could swerve, never slowed if he could pass. On a stretch of highway just north of the city, Han passed a bus that was passing an army convoy. Our taxi plowed and bucketed through the dust and loose gravel on the far left shoulder for half a mile before we returned to the road again. When we arrived unscathed at the Great Wall, still trembling with fright, Linda asked the driver: "Where in the world did you learn to drive like that?" Han knew some English, but the nuances of inflection passed him by: "Oh, thank you," he beamed. "I learned it in the army."

For foreign correspondents like us, formal interviews had to be cleared in advance by the Foreign Ministry. We did our share of these, but we found that chance encounters with ordinary people could be just as illuminating.

Linda's sweet tooth led her to Zhang Binggui, who worked behind the candy counter at Beijing Baihuo Dalou, Peking's leading department store. An instinctive showman, Zhang drew crowds with his rapid-fire monologue and his knack for scooping up, with one stroke, exactly a pound of gumdrops or caramels—never more nor less—and pitching them onto the scale. Once, when business at the counter slowed, Linda drew the 62-year-old Zhang into conversation about what he called "the bitter past," the years before the Communist victory of 1949.

"As a child, I was hungry all the time," said Zhang, who went to work at the age of eight, carrying banners for traditional funerals and weddings. "My father was like all working people. He could never get ahead."

Zhang and his family have prospered since the revolution, but he worries about the more than 600 million Chinese born since 1949, for they are too young to remember the bitter past. They have wearied of the self-sacrifice demanded by the party, and in Zhang's view they are too eager for the freedoms and material rewards of the West.

We knew the youths he had in mind. We had talked with a 28-year-old Peking machine-tool worker who was cynical about his job and discouraged by the drabness of Chinese society.

"The government just won't let me earn what I deserve," he complained one day. "Besides, there is a group of bureaucrats above me—party secretaries, managers, and *pai ma pi* (those who 'pat the horse's rump')." These supervisors, he complained, divide up the scheduled pay raises among their cronies and favorites.

"How can they expect me to have any enthusiasm for work?" he asked us. "What I get is too little for the skills I have. And there are so many people my age, so many of us competing for so little, that things will never get better for me. It wouldn't be as bad, would it, if I were in a capitalist society?"

Our encounters with ordinary Chinese, though almost always cordial, rarely developed into real friendships, and we didn't expect them to. We—and the Chinese—could remember the Cultural Revolution, when xenophobia reached a feverish peak, and many Chinese with foreign connections were banished to the countryside to slop hogs and rethink their ways.

So it came as a surprise when Kong Lingliang, a subway worker, invited us to dinner for the lunar New Year, the most important holiday on the Chinese calendar. We had talked with him before, and his bosses had urged him to break off our relationship. Did Kong know the risk he was taking? Were we putting him in jeopardy? We raised these questions, and he responded firmly, "Come." Like many Peking folks, he didn't like being pushed around.

Kong's home turned out to be unlike any we'd seen in Peking. We were accustomed by then to the city's stark new apartments and old courtyard bungalows which, however crowded and ill-heated, were at least sturdy. But Kong lived in a ramshackle construction of brick and salvaged lumber. It lay at the end of a muddy road northwest of Peking, surrounded by cornfields. Our car got stuck, so we set off on foot past the huts of Kong's neighbors and pushed open his front gate, a collection of scrap wood held together with wire.

Wonderful smells wafted through the front door—pork, scallions, eggs, garlic, and cabbage combined by the sure hands of Kong's wife. As he welcomed us, she continued to cook on their one-burner charcoal stove. A dusty gray cat sat underneath, watching his mistress transfer meat-and-vegetable combinations to old chipped plates. She had no counter, so she laid the plates on a bed in the next room until everything was ready.

For the Kong children, the cottage had two tiny bedrooms, each just large enough for a bed and a chest. The third room, which doubled as master bedroom and sitting room, was dominated by a *kang*, a brick bed platform heated from below by charcoal. We sat on two of the Kongs' four wooden chairs; Kong and another guest used the other two, while his children sat on the kang. His wife never sat at all. On a small table with a plastic tablecloth she had set bowls of peanuts and hard candy. We sipped tea in glasses, then began making our way through the many courses, working up to a heaping platter of *jiaozi*, the meat-filled dumplings so essential to a festive dinner in northern China. We ate them Peking-style, dipping them in tangy vinegar and a red-pepper paste. Later, sated with food, beer, and wine, we went outside and set off round after round of New Year's firecrackers to scare away bad-luck spirits. After nightcaps and hot cocoa, Kong sent us on our way.

On the way home we talked about our friend Kong. One of his sons had died mysteriously, beaten to death, his killers never caught and punished. And now Kong's daughter, 18, was out of school without a job. She was what the government euphemistically calls *daiye qingnian*, a youth waiting for work. Kong fretted that she might get into trouble if she had to wait two or three years for a job—not an irrational concern, for Peking's unemployed youths often loiter on street corners, keep the black market alive, and, in the view of the Public Security Bureau, perpetrate most of the city's crime.

The antidote the Peking authorities have prescribed for unemployment is a big dose of free enterprise. With the blessing of the Communist Party, jobless youths have been going into business for themselves in recent years, alone or in small collectives. Thanks to these enterprising youngsters, Peking's service industries, dismantled during the Cultural Revolution, have begun to revive. The youngsters operate street cafés and inns, repair furniture and bicycles, cut hair, resole shoes, and carry luggage at railway stations.

Many young entrepreneurs are clustered at the north end of bustling Qianmen Avenue. There neighborhood youths have transformed a former earthquake shelter into a teahouse that serves jiaozi, pastries, and steaming cups of tea to office-bound commuters. Linda stopped by one morning and learned that the young proprietors were hatching expansion plans. A dozen sidewalk stalls were to be added, selling everything from *binggun*—fruit-flavored ices on sticks—to photographs of Chinese movie stars. Several young women had begun to peddle hand-knitted sweaters and scarves to passersby. Amateur photographers affiliated with the teahouse were pursuing tourists across Tiananmen Square, offering to take their pictures for 80 fen (about 50 cents). All of them scrambled because, unlike the employees of government-run enterprises, they faced the hazards of capitalists everywhere: No one gets paid if there are no profits.

After work, another sort of enterprise looms large in the lives of young and old: The neighborhood bathhouse, perhaps the most blissful retreat in the city, the place to soak away the dust and annoyances of the day. The bathhouses are a necessity, for few Peking homes have bathtubs and only half have running water; most people get through the week with sponge baths. But our friends assured us that a visit to the Bright and Flowery Bathhouse, just up the street from our hotel, could restore our spirits as well as get us clean.

Jay finally decided to try the cure. He paid his 26 fen (about 15 cents) at the lobby window, then wound his way past a swinging door and down a tiled corridor to the men's locker room. Instead of benches, individual cots with paper-thin mattresses stood around the room—perfect for napping on after one's bath. A sign over the pay window offered a wealth of services—laundry, foot treatments, massages, haircuts—but Jay chose only a soak.

He had shed his clothes and, conscious of all the eyes on his hairy American body, started to dash into the bathing room. But a Chinese friend named Zhang put a hand on Jay's arm. "Slow down. Look around you," he said. No one else was rushing. The other bathers, still in their robes, lounged on their cots sipping tea and chatting quietly. Jay began to get the idea. He leaned back on the cot and closed his eyes, seeking the proper state of repose. He sampled his tea, listened to the murmur of conversation for a while, then padded off slowly toward the baths.

In the bath chamber, a skylight bathed the naked men and boys in soft sunshine. There were three enormous tubs to choose from—one lukewarm, one warm, and one hot enough to send steam rising from it in waves. Following the example of other bathers, Jay lathered up with a big, brown cake of soap, rinsed off in the shower, then slipped into the lukewarm vat—the one his host deemed suitable for a tender-skinned foreigner. As a matter of honor, however, Jay briefly dipped into the hottest tub, where he met 81-year-old Zhao Zhengfu. "I started coming to the baths when I was nine," Zhao said, nodding toward a five-year-old who had jumped into the hottest tub, impervious to the temperature. "Now that I'm retired, I come twice a week for four hours each time. I like to sweat. It's good for your health."

Jay, feeling his skin had acquired enough of a ruddy glow, padded back into the locker room. Wrapped in towels, he ordered more tea. Zhang reclined on an adjacent cot, sipped thoughtfully, and looked sad. Jay asked what was wrong. "People don't stay so long any more, most of them no more than an hour or two. Once you could come here and buy very good tea"—he sniffed his cup with faint disapproval—"and watermelon seeds, then sit for hours, talking with your friends. But now there are too many people, and the bathhouse can't let them stay very long."

When he finally had to leave, Jay emerged clean and refreshed, further fortified by the sight of young women leaving the ladies' bath next door, their hair streaming loosely down their backs, their skin glowing from the steam.

The day we left Peking, we had a few last reminders that the ancient city is forever changing, forever renewing itself. Our little motorcade whizzed over a freeway that had not existed four years before. We sped past new apartment complexes and past fields being cleared for a new 22-story hotel. We slowed down for the crowds at the free peasant markets which have sprung up, products of the government's new willingness to allow small-scale private enterprise.

At last we arrived at Peking's newly expanded airport, where the DC-10s and Boeing 747s from 14 foreign countries discharge their passengers into an air-conditioned terminal modeled on Paris's Orly Airport. With its interminable hallways and moving sidewalks, it was nothing like the modest building we had passed through on our first visit to Peking.

As the time for departure neared, we said good-bye to Chinese friends who had accompanied us. Hou Ying, the cheerful and capable interpreter for Linda's newspaper, would soon be off on her own adventure, which might take her entire family to a United Nations post in Geneva or New York. We mused about where we might all meet again.

"Oh, you will come back to Peking," Hou Ying said, hugging Linda and giving Jay one last firm handshake. "And when you come back, you will hardly recognize Peking. We are changing so fast."

Windrows of bicycles, some of Peking's three million, jam a parking lot (below). Loaded with luggage, bikes skirt a puddle in Tiananmen Square (right), where a baton-wielding policeman (opposite) directs traffic. "Pay Attention to Safety," warns the sign—a necessity in a city where busy intersections may carry 500 bicycles a minute.

OVERLEAF. *A warm spring night coaxes Peking residents into Tiananmen Square to talk and relax. May Day flags fly from the pillared Great Hall of the People.*

Opposite: Jim Brandenburg

P*heasant-plumed*
actress impersonates a warrior (above) in
Stopping the Horse, *a Peking Opera
production. She manipulates feathers to
convey anger or surprise, gestures to
symbolize deep thought, gaiety, or anticipation. Bearded Little White Dragon
(right) girds for battle with the Monkey
King in a traditional drama using acro-
batics and pantomime as well as song and
dance. Players must learn both lines and
stylized gestures, and never improvise.*

*Before donning silk brocade costumes,
performers make up (far right). Patterns
emphasize facial expressions, colors symbolize character: Red stands for loyalty,
black for boldness, white for treachery.*

OVERLEAF. *Five marble bridges cross
Golden Water Stream, curved to resem-
ble a Tatar bow, before the Forbidden
City's Gate of Supreme Harmony.*

48

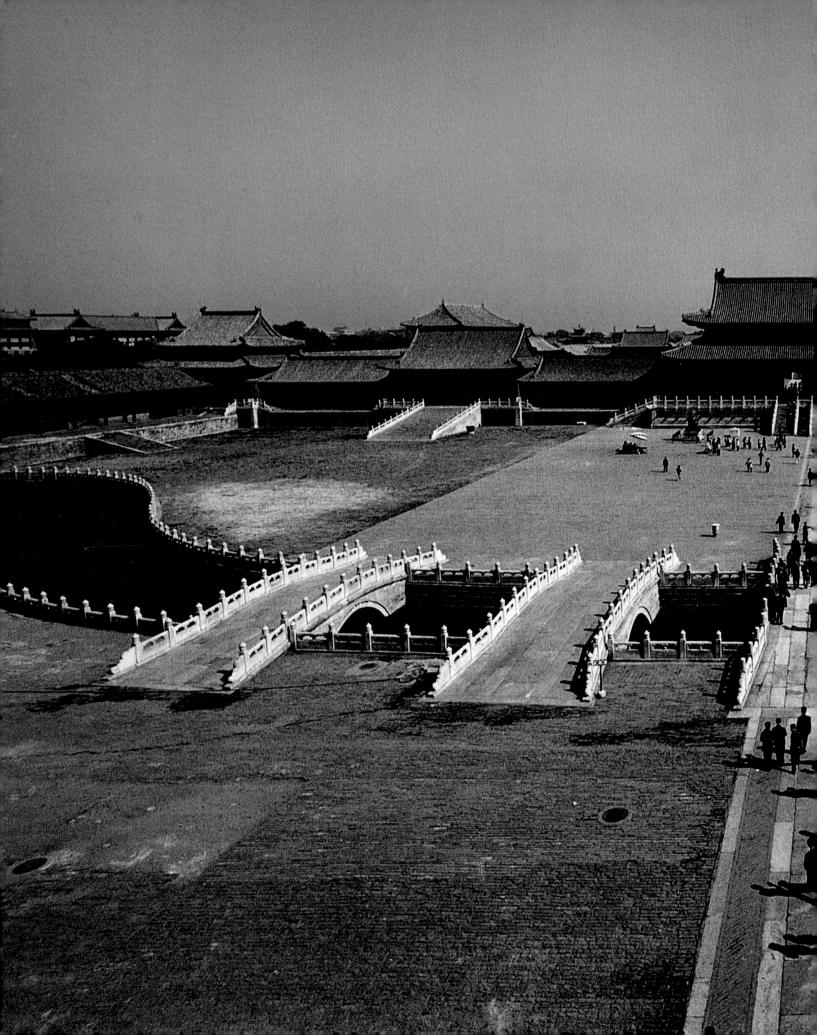

Seat of power during the Qing Dynasty, the imperial throne in the Hall of Mental Cultivation (far right) intrigues visitors to the Forbidden City, now a vast museum. Behind the throne, hidden by a screen, stands another royal seat; from it, Empress Dowager Ci Xi whispered commands in the names of two puppet rulers. Before her death she arranged the enthronement of a third.

A museum visitor rides a gilded bronze lion (above). A gold-and-pearl celestial globe like this copy (right) once modeled the constellations for a Qing emperor.

James L. Stanfield

Jim Brandenburg

Jade-green willows sway in the breeze, trailing their branches over the lotus-carpeted lake of Beihai Park (above). Set like a jewel in the center of Peking, adjacent to the Forbidden City, the park was an imperial retreat for Liao Dynasty rulers a thousand years ago, and remained the private domain of emperors until 1911. Its tile-roofed temples and pavilions recall the imperial dynasties that dug the lake, built Jade Isle, and created the gardens and rockeries. From the island's highest point towers the White Dagoba, a reconstruction of a hilltop shrine commemorating the visit of Tibet's Dalai Lama in 1651. Since the park was declared a "major cultural relic," workers have repaired its buildings, restored its gardens, planted more trees, and dredged and stocked the lake.

Fishing in the Forbidden City's 57-yard-wide moat, an angler concentrates on his line (right). During the winter, teams saw ice blocks from the frozen moat and store them for warm-weather use.

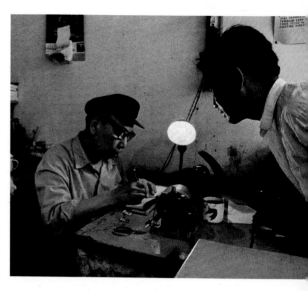

Force-feeding a Peking duck, a young commune worker (left) presses its open bill to a rubber nozzle, then pumps a rich grain-and-soybean paste down its gullet. She can process two dozen ducks a minute; five feedings a day for two weeks fatten the birds for busy city kitchens. Several Peking restaurants specialize in all-duck dinners, from duck soup to "pearly duck tongues."

Glazed with a malt-sugar liquor, their body cavities filled with boiling water, the ducks hang over an open fire and absorb the aromas of burning fruitwood. Cooks turn the birds with long poles (lower left) till they are done a glistening dark brown.

A charcoal oven tinkered from an old oil drum roasts yams at a farmers' free market (opposite). The vendor weighs out the hot potatoes by the catty—a traditional weight of slightly more than a pound.

A pen repairman (above) tests a point for a waiting customer. Now officially encouraged, self-employed artisans and merchants stimulate China's economy.

P eking's "long underground dragon," China's first subway, can carry more than half a million passengers a day—some napping—in its air-conditioned cars. The sleek trains have supplementary braking systems to stop them automatically in an emergency.

The first section, completed in 1969, runs 15 miles from the western suburb of Pingguoyuan to Peking's downtown railroad station. Destinations are marked on clock-faced signs above the often crowded platforms (far left). A second section, opened in 1982, tunnels ten miles around three sides of the Inner City, tracing the path of Peking's ancient city walls, now destroyed.

*S*hadow boxing in a Peking park, elders begin the day with the slow, ballet-like gymnastics of taijiquan (right), a centuries-old ritual for keeping fit. At Tanzhe Temple, a restored Buddhist monastery, a photographer poses a Chinese tourist in a cardboard cutout of a mounted warrior (above).

Marble "imperial road" ramps, carved with dragons, clouds, and cranes symbolizing good fortune and longevity, lead up to the Hall of Prayer for Good Harvests in Tiantan Park. Arriving here to intercede with heaven, the emperor was carried up the ramps in his palanquin, his bearers treading the steps on either side.

A galaxy of color and pattern swirls in the dome of the Hall of Prayer for Good Harvests, part of the ceremonial enclave of the Temple of Heaven. At the ceiling's center is a carved dragon, emblem of royalty. Crafted entirely of wood and built without nails, the building soars 125 feet high on four central cypress columns representing the seasons. Twelve pillars in a middle ring represent the months of the year; twelve others, set in the outer wall, stand for the "hours" of the Chinese day. Ingenious brackets reach inward from the column tops to support straight and ring-shaped beams. Color, carving, and gilt gleam from every edge and surface.

China's emperor journeyed to the Temple of Heaven complex for solemn ceremonies: To be reconsecrated as ruler, to pray for bountiful harvests, and—in the eleventh month—to take on himself his people's sins. From the Forbidden City the royal processions moved in silence through streets deserted by ordinary citizens, who were forbidden even to glimpse the spectacle, and hid at home behind closed doors. Any flaw in the carefully rehearsed ceremonies could call down heaven's wrath upon the empire. While incense smoldered and musicians played, priests read prayers from silken scrolls and slaughtered an ox on the roofless Altar of Heaven—symbolizing the emperor's willingness to sacrifice himself for the welfare of his people.

*S*unday Mass in *Peking's Southern Cathedral (far right) draws a capacity congregation. The cathedral owes its existence to 17th-century Jesuit missionaries, who converted many members of the imperial court. Today's Chinese Catholic hierarchy had to break with Rome, and now answers instead to the government-sponsored Catholic Patriotic Association, which most of the nation's Catholics do not support. China is officially atheist and bans proselytizing, but authorities permit services like Holy Communion (above).*

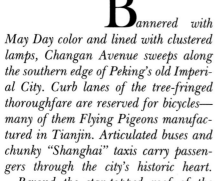

Bannered with May Day color and lined with clustered lamps, Changan Avenue sweeps along the southern edge of Peking's old Imperial City. Curb lanes of the tree-fringed thoroughfare are reserved for bicycles—many of them Flying Pigeons manufactured in Tianjin. Articulated buses and chunky "Shanghai" taxis carry passengers through the city's historic heart.

Beyond the star-topped roof of the Peking Hotel (right foreground) sprawls Tiananmen Square, at 98 acres the largest city square in the world. On its far side (background) looms the Great Hall of the People, where the National People's Congress assembles. Its cavernous auditorium accommodates an audience of 10,000 for political meetings or stage performances. Blocky buildings in center foreground are the Museums of Chinese History and Chinese Revolution.

An arena for rallies and demonstrations, the vast parade ground surged with 500,000 Chinese on October 1, 1949, when Mao Zedong proclaimed the People's Republic. Twice that number gathered there to mourn his death in 1976. Today a granite-pillared memorial in the square contains his crystal coffin.

Jim Brandenburg

April dust storms sweep down from the Gobi to assault Peking with powdery yellow grime. Pedestrians cover their faces with fine mesh bags (above). Street-cleaning teams, composed mostly of women, often work in surgical masks (left) as they wield their bamboo brooms. Troops plant grass (far left) in a campaign to lay the dust. Much of Peking's greenery was uprooted in the 1950s in a disastrous attempt to eliminate breeding places for insects, which had proliferated after the government ordered the eradication of the city's birds.

69

Topped with a straw hat for shade and a hardhat for protection, a construction foreman (opposite) rivets his eyes on activity overhead, ready to signal workers with whistle blasts. He is part of the all-Chinese labor team that built Peking's 78-million-dollar Great Wall Hotel, one of the first American-Chinese projects approved under China's recent joint-venture law. The 1,007-room, 22-story hotel has eased the growing pains of the capital's increasingly busy tourist industry.

Building badly needed housing, workmen pour the concrete floors and walls of an apartment building (above). In such new housing, a typical city family of five occupies an apartment with two small rooms about eight by eight feet, a kitchen, toilet, and entryway; tenants use their balconies to hang out clothes and keep plants. With lumber scarce, construction is usually of concrete and brick; builders are experimenting with synthetic materials and boxlike prefabricated units said to be earthquake-resistant. The loss of productive farmland to urban sprawl remains a problem.

OVERLEAF. Shimmering Lake Kunming reflects the bygone opulence of the Qing Dynasty, whose rulers rebuilt the Summer Palace and embellished the lake and its surrounding scenery. Windsurfers, members of a sports club, skim waters that royal barges once plied. Jade Fountain Hill, pedestal for a lone pagoda, and the pavilion-covered bridge anchoring West Dike are elements of a living scroll painting created by cultivated tastes—and built with backbreaking labor.

Stylized waves at its feet, the Summer Palace's bronze ox (left) gazes across Lake Kunming. The inscription that brands its flank glorifies the legendary Emperor Yu, who "harnessed the rivers" and made "flood dragons keep their distance." Beyond a pavilion where Qing emperors liked to drink wine and compose poetry, Seventeen Arch Bridge vaults across the lake's still surface.

High on Longevity Hill, surrounded by a gallery and four corner pavilions, stands the Pavilion of Precious Clouds (above). With elaborate decorations cast in bronze from carved wax originals, it was one of few structures in the Summer Palace to escape destruction by British and French forces in 1860.

A solid stone side-wheeler, the Boat of Purity and Ease (above) lies forever moored near the Bridge of Floating Hearts. A monument to Empress Dowager Ci Xi's excesses, the marble folly was part of her restoration of the war-torn Summer Palace. The funds were supposedly diverted from the Chinese naval budget.

Tired strollers in the Long Promenade (right) rest beneath beams decorated with a combination of pictures and patterns. A battle scene of third-century warriors (opposite) adorns one section of the covered walkway, which stretches almost half a mile along the lake below Longevity Hill.

Underground palace for a dead ruler, the tomb of Ming emperor Wan Li rivals a pharaoh's tomb in ostentation. Marble thrones in the sacrificial chamber (left) attract visitors. The blue-and-white urns are "everlasting lamps" that once contained flaming wicks afloat in sesame oil, burning to nourish the spirits of the departed. The archway beyond opens to the burial chamber of the emperor and his two wives. Self-indulgent in life and death, Wan Li, too fat to stand unaided, employed 600,000 workers to build his tomb complex, then celebrated its completion with a lavish party in the funeral chambers.

Visitors enter the tomb (top right) through doors once barred by massive marble slabs. Sealed from view beneath a huge cedar-shaded mound for more than four centuries, this is the only Ming tomb yet excavated. At the foot of the hill sprawl three walled courtyards; the innermost contains an altar and a pavilion housing a stele engraved with Emperor Wan Li's epitaph.

Cyclists wheel past the 24 stone animal sculptures guarding the Spirit Road (lower right), the grand approach to the valley of the Ming Tombs. Each species, real or mythical, is represented by one standing pair of creatures and one reclining pair—to allow, legend has it, for a midnight changing of the guard.

Vacationers splash in the surf and climb on the rocks at Beidaihe (below), a popular resort about six hours from Peking by train. Founded at the beginning of the 20th century during the reign of Empress Dowager Ci Xi, the town on the Bo Hai gulf became a retreat for foreigners and high-ranking Chinese. Though still priced beyond the means of most citizens, Beidaihe now includes sanatoriums and treatment centers for workers. Visitors, many in Western clothes, may stroll to the Kiessling Bakery—a German relic of foreign hegemony in this part of China—to eat ice cream and pastries.

Huang Hai, the Yellow Sea, breaks against Qingdao's rockbound coast (opposite), some 350 miles southeast of Peking. Stone walls climb to the pavilion-capped aquarium, China's oldest marine research center; beyond it rises a new hotel. Developed as a naval base by occupying Germans before World War I, the city of 1.5 million people is famous as a summer resort and deep-water harbor. Exports range from cotton goods and coal to peanuts and "Tsingtao" beer.

Opposite: George F. Mobley

80

ON THE TRAIL OF THE LONG STONE SERPENT

By Griffin Smith, Jr.
Photographs by James L. Stanfield

Stony and gray, the Great Wall of China rises from the ocean surf at Shanhaiguan. As if to shake off the clinging waters of the gulf called Bo Hai, it twists across a narrow plain, contorts itself momentarily at a massive gate, and then uncurls to ascend the peaks of the Yan Shan range. From 214 B.C., when existing state walls were joined in a continuous rampart at the command of the emperor, Qin Shi Huangdi, to its elaborate reconstruction by the Ming Dynasty 1,600 years later, to the present, the Wall has been regarded as one of mankind's grandest achievements.

I came to Shanhaiguan to follow the Wall as closely as I could for 2,000 miles across China. The town lies on a five-mile pinch of plain between mountains and sea, a pass that opens like an avenue into the heart of China. The pass was strategic long before the eighth century, when Tang poets visited "the camps of China echoing with bugle and drum." The most significant moment in the entire history of the Wall came on a spring morning in 1644 when Manchu horsemen swept through the undefended First Gate here at Shanhaiguan, sealing the downfall of the Ming Dynasty. The Wall, largely irrelevant to these northern conquerors, drifted into eclipse.

Rugged symbol of China's strength, the Great Wall defies the ages.

Shanhaiguan is now far from China's frontier, but it still has some strategic significance. Coastline defenses include a nearby air base, and military jets roar frequently overhead. In the midst of the city, the eastern gate tower of the Great Wall bears the inscription: "First Gate Under Heaven." The words reflect the belief that the world was divided into a central and superior Chinese civilization, and a peripheral, inferior barbarian outland.

The Wall stood for the proposition that unbridgeable cultural differences exist among peoples, differences so profound that they could be dealt with only by separation. Today, however, Chinese authorities say the Wall and the divisions it stood for are obsolete. "Epoch-making changes took place at last," recites an official text, "bringing into being a new, unified socialist China where different ethnic groups live in peace like brothers." Nevertheless, the Chinese name for China, Zhongguo, means "Middle Kingdom," an echo of that ancient division of the world into inner and outer.

Walking through the streets of Shanhaiguan, I gradually acquired an unofficial entourage of curious townspeople who stared blankly and without embarrassment. A young woman dressed in white was operating a thriving *guotie* stand on a street corner. Receiving the trays of stuffed pork dumplings from an elderly couple who assembled them in a storefront room, she sprinkled

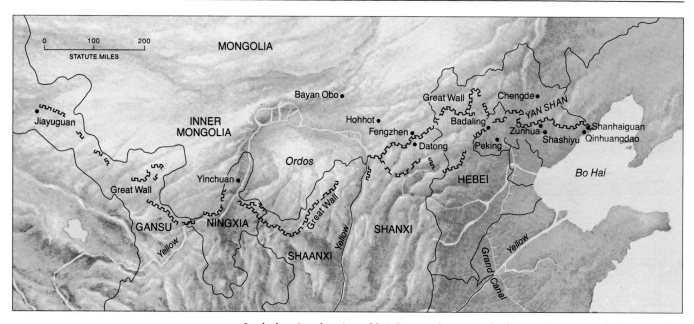

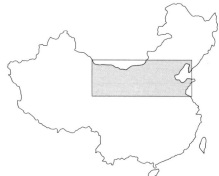

In the bracing dry air and bright sun of a typical north Chinese autumn, author Griffin Smith, Jr., followed the twisting course of China's legendary Great Wall nearly 2,000 miles from the coastal plain of Shanhaiguan to its desert terminus at Jiayuguan. Crisscrossing the brick, stone, and earthen remains of the "Ten Thousand Li Wall" that once guarded these inner Asian borderlands, he paused at such diverse locations as the imperial summer palace at Chengde; the tombs of the Qing emperors; the strategic high pass above Peking; the Yungang Caves; and the Ningxia region, homeland of hundreds of thousands of China's Muslims.

them with oil and water, covered them, and laid them tray by tray onto a smoke-blackened oil drum above a brisk coal fire. Tantalizing aromas began to fill the street. As the dumplings fried to a crisp brown crust she deftly scooped them up, a dozen at a time, and wrapped them in paper for a succession of customers. With a cordial smile she handed one such package, dripping juice, to me. They were delicious.

I made my first foray along the Wall outside Shanhaiguan at Jiao Shan hill. The mountains rose sharply. Here the Wall quit the narrow coastal plain and began the arduous climb inland. In town, I had seen Chinese honeymooners strolling the battlements of the First Gate arm in arm and posing for photographs beneath its soaring eaves. The clash of swords had seemed far away. But now, as I climbed toward a watchtower at Jiao Shan, I heard a menacing popping sound. Peering over the rim of the Wall I saw, far below, rows of soldiers manning gun emplacements. Targets shaped like toy planes whizzed back and forth along wires strung between the firing range and the watchtowers of the Great Wall. Now and then a bullet pinged a rock. I beat a hasty retreat. Soon the commanding officer, waving a red flag, trotted through a breach in the Wall. There was much discussion. Then he smiled. It was target practice, he said, but for American friends he would stop.

"Stopping" meant continuing the exercise without ammunition. The papier-mâché fighter planes again whined up and down the wires, a mimicry of MIGs screaming in low over the hills. I resumed my climb to the watchtower, occasionally glancing back unnerved at the 40 soldiers in battle fatigues snapping automatic rifles in my direction. Lengthening shadows stretched behind the Wall, and the fields below were bathed in a mellow light. At dusk the soldiers marched away toward a loudspeaker echoing with bugles and drums.

China awakens early, as I found when I set out before dawn the next day on the 14-hour drive to Chengde. At first light, women in white surgical masks began sweeping the dirt streets smooth with brooms made of stiff twigs. On the outskirts of Shanhaiguan, I passed an old man patiently scooping cow droppings from the road into a straw basket; these would be used for manure at planting time. People emerged from their walled houses, cup in hand, for the morning ritual of toothbrushing. Their breath frosted in the crisp October air.

The tempo of the morning quickened. Rural China is a place of endless labor, the bulk of it performed by the muscles of animals and human beings. One rarely sees the peasant harnessed to his own plow, as Western visitors reported as late as the 1920s; one does sometimes see a tractor, or a gasoline engine pumping water among the wooden locks and small arched bridges of irrigation canals. But China is still the bent back, the shouldered hoe. The man with the wheelbarrow, the old woman with the rake, and the young girl with the shovel are figures recurring kaleidoscopically, mile after mile.

The brown hills contrast with the brilliant green of vegetable gardens. In terraced canyons, every inch of arable land is committed to a purpose; millennia of trial and error have identified the ideal place for every use.

In autumn, farmers informally appropriate long sections of the narrow roads for drying corn or threshing obstinate foodstuffs like red beans and millet. They look up without annoyance as careening trucks, horns blaring, plow gustily across the object of their labor. Regular traffic can be a welcome aid, crushing the corn and separating edible beans from brushy chaff; but a hell-for-leather driver does leave behind a mess.

My route cut through a segment of the Great Wall at Yiyuan Pass where few visitors venture. Here the pavement ended. I crossed into wilder country.

For 20 miles I followed a lonely gravel road among steep hills, gaining elevation, until I could look back and see the Wall spread out upon the highest range of peaks behind me. It seemed to run along the roof of the earth, its watchtowers square and gaunt and almost too small to see, a row of bunkers on the topmost ridge. All across the northern frontier of China such sights had faced the wandering horsemen in times past. They could ride for weeks through the border country and never circumvent the Wall. Few were the heights from which they could even look down and glimpse what lay behind it. This utterly immovable object must have presented a numbing contrast to their own nomadic world, where nothing made by man's hands was ever too cumbersome to pack and move away.

Eventually evidence of agricultural China began to reappear along my route, field by field, village by village. The average Chinese, wrote historian John King Fairbank, "is seldom in all his life beyond earshot of other people." Soon I was back again in the familiar crowded landscape of gray-tiled rooftops and featureless walls. What did not change was the inhospitable rocky soil. Rock walls, rock cisterns, rock terraces, rock houses. So many rocks. So many had been used, so many more remained—an infinity of rocks.

It is known that the Great Wall began as the deliberate linkage, by Qin Shi Huangdi, of several separate walls built by different warring states for protection against one another in the period before China was forcibly unified as a nation. Only fragments of the Qin wall survive. The Han Dynasty re-established the Wall more or less along its present-day route. This line, dictated by climate and soil, stood for centuries as the northern limit of China proper. In time the Han wall was supplanted by the larger, more solid, and more advanced restorations of the Ming Dynasty, essentially the Wall we know today.

For the first Qin emperor, building the Great Wall was the climactic step in a totalitarian reign that transformed China. He had imposed a unified legal system administered by professional bureaucrats, and standardized writing, weights, measures, coinage, and even axle-widths. But the swift success of his soldiers' conquests left him with a huge pool of surplus manpower, dangerously armed and mobile. By sending them to work on the Wall he secured the boundaries of his dominions and stabilized his new society.

In the border region, trade and culture passed in both directions. When China was strong, its influence was propelled into the margin beyond the Wall; when it was weak, even the Wall might be breached. Barbarian tribes who could not be expelled by direct military force were tolerated if they could be subordinated to China's cultural influence through shrewd diplomacy. These "inner" nomads lived under Chinese protection, subsidized in indirect ways. In time they adopted Chinese values and enlisted for defense against the "outer" nomads beyond the border zone. The formulation is recognizable to this day along the frontier between Inner and Outer Mongolia.

Barbarian attackers, some motivated by the lust for booty and others by the desire to occupy well-watered Chinese lands, rise and fall like shooting gallery targets throughout the Wall's long history. Their names change—Yuezhi, Xiongnu, Xianbei, Qiang, Jürchen, Tatars. But no matter who they were, the Wall was an unmistakable defense line against them.

Early in my journey I had asked the director of the Cultural Relics Bureau at Shanhaiguan to tell me about the foreign invaders who had come through his pass.

"Foreign invaders?" He laughed out loud. "There were invaders through this route in ancient times. But they should not be considered foreign. That needs to be clear. These were conflicts between minority nationalities."

"But what about the Manchu in 1644?"

"We should not consider that a foreign invasion, but just northern nationalities."

"Then was Genghis Khan a minority nationality rather than a foreign invader?"

"Yes, of course."

I wondered if the Chinese who watched the Mongols first push through the Great Wall in 1211, or the Mongolian Oirats in 1449, had regarded them as minority nationalities.

The fact that the Great Wall was once China's boundary is suppressed in view of the ongoing border dispute with the Soviet Union. If pressed, officials launch lectures denouncing "the Soviet hegemonists who are trying to dismember China." One guide declared that a number of "minority nationalities" had built or modified sections of the Wall. "All these make clear to every sober mind that the Great Wall has never been the border line of China." This reasoning, though an understandable response to Soviet policy, eventually leads to such historical absurdities as "Genghis Khan's Chinese armies."

The Great Wall also helped keep the Chinese in, physically and psychologically. It defined the cultural frontier, the range of civilization. Chinese leaders did not want poor farmers along the border to drift off in search of a more prosperous life as herdsmen, diminishing the Chinese cultural presence at precisely the point strategic considerations needed it strengthened.

As a defense, did the Wall succeed? For its first 500 years—until the decay of the Han Dynasty—it largely frustrated the hit-and-run tactics of nomadic horsemen. Thereafter its success was intermittent. Genghis Khan's Mongols broke through in 1211. The Ming, at first firmly and then with increasing unsteadiness, tried to maintain it as a fierce and impenetrable barrier, until that fateful day at Shanhaiguan when the unopposed Manchus poured through the open gate. Their dynasty, the Qing, had a more conciliatory policy toward the northern nomads, epitomized in Chengde, my next stop.

The obscure provincial town of Chengde was transformed in 1703 when the monarch Kang Xi began to build an elaborate summer palace there. Its throne room, edict room, and imperial apartments still nestle among gnarled pines, preserving the dream world of mandarin China.

At its zenith, the summer palace at Chengde was also the destination of the British emissary Lord Macartney, who in 1793 sought an audience with Emperor Qian Long, Kang Xi's grandson, in order to promote trade. When Macartney's party passed through the Great Wall at Gubei Pass, its members were dazzled by what they saw. On the strength of a quick survey, one of the envoy's aides calculated the now-famous estimate that the Wall contained almost as much material as "all the dwelling-houses of England and Scotland," and the watchtowers alone "as much masonry and brickwork as all London." Though exaggerated, the appraisal of the Wall made better storytelling at home than the subsequent reception at the palace, where Qian Long brushed aside their diplomatic entreaties with a classic statement of Chinese insularity: "We possess all things. We set no value on objects strange and ingenious and have no use for your country's Manufactures."

Kang Xi and his Qing successors, northerners all, tried to conciliate the nomads by promoting Tibetan Lamaism, the religion of the Mongols. Seeking to weld the Mongols' loyalty to the imperial state, they erected eight impressive monastery complexes near Chengde. It may have been an eminently practical move: As Qian Long reportedly remarked, "Better a monastery than 10,000 troops." Since the tenets of Lamaism obliged at least one male in every family to become a celibate monk, the emperors' policy reduced the Mongols geometrically, siphoning off as much as one-half the male population into holy docility and undermining the Mongol economy. China's ancient foes were flattered and diminished at the same time.

Just outside modern Chengde, most of the monasteries remain. There is a feeling of decay in the cool air, among the peeling paint, the crumbling mortar, the rotting wood, the bricked-up windows. There are few monks now. Above the whispering of the wind through the poplars, I heard the steady tapping of two masons repairing a temple from the ravages of the Cultural Revolution and the wear of time, readying it not for reverent Mongol chieftains but for the tourists of the 1980s. The dusty gold-painted figures inside had tenanted a China wholly different from the one I saw outside. Theirs was a world of wind chimes, not loudspeakers, a world now laid aside by Communist decree. In one dark room, all the Buddhas have been assembled for safekeeping. Yet from their detention center they seem to preside over that old world still.

Today Chengde is a characteristically austere north Chinese industrial town, dominated by mining and textiles. At night the streets are dark, and bicycles bearing dark-clad Chinese flit like shadows through the gloom. The sole bright spot is the barbershop, emanating its white radiance for 200 yards.

One morning I strolled around the town. The long houses, half hidden behind walls, gave up few secrets. The best were on the highest ground; some, not many, had small flower gardens. The sidewalk markets sold vegetables with ruthless fidelity to the season. Pears, apples, peppers, scallions, coriander, and most abundantly of all, cabbage, lay on the ground in monumental piles. One vendor did a messy, slow business in gelid, caked chicken blood—a rubbery substance sliced and eaten with dip sauces.

Zunhua, 50 miles due south of Chengde, lies near the burial grounds of the Qing emperors, whose tombs are sheltered from the evil influence of the north wind by a range of hills that also harbors the Great Wall. Luowenyu Pass winds through these hills. Its strategic importance was confirmed in 1933, I was told, when outnumbered Chinese troops held off a Japanese invasion force for seven days. Today the war-damaged, unrestored Wall runs through a terraced pear orchard and across a canyon creek. I arrived there one morning as a flock of ducks stationed themselves downstream from a housewife washing lettuce, quarreling loudly over the discarded leaves. A bright sun glinted from the water to the Wall.

The Zunhua section dates from the Ming Dynasty. From Shanhaiguan westward past Peking, the Ming built with bricks and stone. In Shanxi Province workers also used packed dirt. And in the far west they used a technique known as *terre pisé*, in which dry soil is placed in rectangular forms and pounded solid. The forms are then raised and the process repeated until the desired height is reached. In the eastern portions the granite foundation stones were as large as 14 feet by 3 feet by 3 feet, the ashlars covering the core of rubble as large as 5 by 2 by 1½. Often, the Wall seems to have been positioned purposefully in the most inaccessible locations. Some parts consist of staircases; others are absolutely vertical. It looks as if someone, defying the natural terrain, simply said, "Put it there!" and the superhuman work was done.

The human cost of constructing the Wall was awesome. The orthodox history of Qin Shi Huangdi's wall says 300,000 troops built it, but others put the total at well over a million people, with as many as 400,000 dying along the way. Legend holds that thousands were entombed within its core. When a section near Datong was repaired in the year 555, two million laborers were conscripted for the job. In Ming times a Portuguese merchant reported serving a one-year sentence at a work camp with 300,000 fellow convicts.

The most poignant of the many tales of the Wall illustrates the cruelty of such toil. A young man—some say a brilliant scholar, others a prince—was ordered to the Wall because his views displeased Qin Shi Huangdi. Months passed, winter came. His devoted wife, the beautiful Meng Jiang, set out in the bitter cold to find him and bring him warm clothes. Eventually she reached the proper camp, only to learn that the frail youth had perished of privation and hard labor. His body lay somewhere within the Great Wall. Anguished, she wandered the battlements, thinking only to recover his bones and give them proper burial. Her mourning was so heartfelt that the Wall itself, at the intervention of the heavens, burst open, revealing a charnel house of bodies. From a cut on her hand, her blood flowed down to single out the remains of her beloved. Meng Jiang's story was a fixed part of Chinese literature by the third century A.D., reaffirming the power of love.

So painstakingly raised, the Wall has been coming down bit by bit. At Luowenyu Pass, whole sections had obviously been quarried and carted away to be used for something else. Zunhua's educational director, Huo Yixing, pointed out a neatly-lettered sign bearing the date 1975. "That says, 'Nobody Can Take a Rock or Brick From the Wall,'" explained Huo, a 60-year-old man in gray jacket and cap who carried a little rubber satchel full of documents. "During the Cultural Revolution the peasants living here carried away bricks to build their homes and pigsties. The local government did not stop them.

"But last year," Huo added, "there was a meeting in Zunhua. People were denounced and put on trial for damaging the Wall. Everyone has a duty to protect it." He removed a manila folder from his briefcase and spread the contents across the weeds: blueprints of the Wall, old photographs, and a hundred-page plan of cultural protection drafted in careful calligraphy. "This is the result of the meeting," he said. "Similar studies are taking place all along the Wall. We are trying our best now to save the Wall and let the younger generation see it."

That night in Zunhua the younger generation was more interested in seeing an ancient Charlie Chaplin film that had come to town. China is such an all-enveloping culture that the visitor who has been there any length of time feels as if he has been swallowed by Jonah's whale. So the very existence of a Charlie Chaplin movie seemed remarkable.

The theater was a cavernous building with no outward indication of its purpose. Inside, a packed crowd loudly chewed sunflower seeds—the Chinese equivalent of popcorn. Alternately, they hawked and spat, an activity seemingly without social stigma in China. They recognized Chaplin instantly, breaking into laughter at the mere sight of his figure on the screen. In silent cinema, across the gulf of language, Chaplin deflated the pomposities of the rich, the powerful, and the officious. The 1925 film may have been chosen for its ideological convenience—it gave away no secrets about an urban America that no longer uses horses—but the crowd's delighted uproar proved that the comedian's art was universal.

The Eastern Qing Tombs repose in royal splendor near Zunhua. Their curved approachway was formerly so sacred that only foot travel was allowed. I rode up in a jeep. Beneath the richly colored buildings of Emperor Qian Long's burial estate are somber underground vaults which artisans have decorated with intricate carvings that propound the Buddhist themes of sensual restraint. Their cold magnificence dates from the late 1700s, contemporaneous with the American and French Revolutions. A neighboring tomb for the Empress Dowager Ci Xi, who died in 1908, shows that within the long sweep of Chinese history such things have barely passed away. Her terminal extravaganza is a reminder of the excesses the Chinese people had to contend with during the memory of men still living. As if to drive home the point in microcosm, the empress's prayer hall has been converted into a small museum whose exhibits include dining bowls inscribed "Long Life to the Empress," and empty tins of Duke's Cameo Cigarettes.

Outside on the tomb grounds, along the ceremonial entrance path called the Sacred Way, I came upon a scene of utter tranquillity. The ancient pavement, piled with freshly harvested corn, was lined with the carved stone animals who had once been its mythical guardians; they stood loyally in matched pairs, wearing sly grins like escapees from some Noah's Ark of fantasy. The setting sun was pink, and one could hear the squeak of a wagon wheel, the rustle of cornstalks, the thwock of corn being threshed, the hum of crickets, and the far-off laughter of children. A man and his wife carrying two rakes cycled homeward, and in the field beside the road, members of the Eastern Tombs Commune were sowing winter wheat. The tableau spoke peacefulness, fruition, amplitude. The Sacred Way seemed puny in the encircling arc of the mountains, the vanished emperors' fanfares dumb against the eternal sounds of harvest. China was softly resurgent across the stones.

Badaling, northwest of Peking, is the crown of the entire Great Wall. Wave after wave, the Wall rises and falls across the mountains, disappearing behind one peak only to reappear at right angles running across another. Here the Wall seems to stretch on forever, its grandeur unmatched.

The hillsides were covered with maples blazing in full autumn foliage as I began a steep climb toward a watchtower which, like much of the Wall at Badaling, has been restored by the government to resemble as closely as possible the last Ming reconstruction. Along the way I saw patches of Chinese ideograms scratched onto the paving stones: Sun Duan from Guangdong Province had left his mark, and a little farther on, "Training Class of the Materials Bureau was here. In 10,000 years scientists will research these words."

Around me black crows, cawing, reeled across the valleys. Near the highest watchtower someone had paraphrased in black paint the lines from Mao's poem: "If a man fails to climb to the top of the Wall, he is not a real man." Few would dare turn back after that challenge.

From the vantage point of the tower I thought of the much repeated claim that the Wall is the only work of man that can be seen from space. The story has many variants—some say the Wall is visible from the moon, some say from Mars—and at Badaling the assertion seems almost credible. The legend began before the days of space travel, perhaps evolving from the myth that Qin Shi Huangdi rose up to the moon in a dream and, seeing how tiny his domain looked from afar, decided to build a wall around a larger area to encourage his kingdom to grow. Space travel has finally settled the question. The Landsat satellite's pictures, taken from 600 miles up, require magnification and scrutiny to see the Wall. But the old tale persists, and is solemnly reported.

After 5 p.m. the crowds are gone from Badaling; the crows and chipmunks reclaim the Wall, scavenging sunflower seeds and other tourist snacks. I left, feeling like a tenant who had overstayed his lease.

A predawn knocking on my door meant it was time to go to Datong.

China's railways are a last bastion of steam. The locomotives, their wheels lacquered fire-engine red, emit nostalgic whistles, hisses, and sharp short puffs. A cowling in front lends the engine a confident, head-held-high appearance. At small-town stations, porters disembark with buckets and brushes to scrub down the carriages (inexplicably avoiding the windows). At each crossing a uniformed guard holding furled red and green flags stands at attention while the train passes. Triumphal marches blare at every stop.

My sleeper was an oasis of graciousness, with wood paneling, green felt curtains, table lamp, and thermos bottles replenished twice a day with hot water for tea. Less welcome was the loudspeaker, which began broadcasting up-and-at-'em music before first light and could not be turned off.

Datong is famous for the Yungang Caves, whose masterpieces of early Chinese sculpture came into being during the fifth century A.D. when the Northern Wei Dynasty embraced Buddhism. The road to the site is black with dust from coal mines that are Datong's chief economic activity. Coal trucks and mule carts move toward the city—and ultimately toward the hearths, the power stations, and the trains of China—in ceaseless caravan. Local residents scurry beside them, gathering the lumps that jostle overboard at every pothole. Until Communism came, no foreign influence had a greater impact on the insular Chinese mind than Buddhism. Its vigorous growth is documented in the 51,000 sculptures at Yungang. The best are spellbinding. Angelic spirits called *apsarases* soar along the ceilings, radiating bliss. Serene Buddhas gaze down from their bays like satisfied boxholders at the opera. When travelers visited the caves in 1938, they reported that caretakers faithfully rang bells and burned incense at appointed hours. No longer.

The Great Wall at Fengzhen near Datong was of critical importance to the Ming Dynasty because it defended a major Mongol entry route from the northwest. Behind the Wall lay vast fortified garrisons from which soldiers were assigned rotating tours of duty at the front-line forts. During certain periods they were granted land around the garrisons and encouraged to marry, to raise a family, and to spend their lives as soldier-farmers at these outposts.

Today the Wall twists down from a plateau to the east bank of a river before resuming its course toward the Ordos desert region. Like melting pyramids, crumbling beacon towers dot every bluff; from them, sentries once signaled the appearance of hostile troops by firing guns and burning a mixture of sulphur, saltpeter, and wolf dung. The relayed alarm could reach the Forbidden City in Peking in a matter of hours. At these forts and others like them, soldiers have guarded borders for the better part of two thousand years.

Now the mile-square garrisons at Fengzhen shelter farming villages, occupied perhaps by descendants of those who first came here in obedience to a Ming command. Climbing over the walls of one, I startled a row of peasants cultivating cabbage fields inside. They stopped: eight curious upturned faces, eight diagonal shovels. I watched as the cattle came down to the shallow river to drink in the gathering twilight. On the far bank, smoke curled from the chimneys of the huts and the Great Wall threaded past, its watchtowers bristling, the valedictory of ruined dynasties. "The stream is cold and the wind like a sword," wrote Tang poet Wang Changling:

Old battles, waged by these long walls,
Once were proud on all men's tongues.
But antiquity now is a yellow dust,
Confusing in the grasses its ruins and white bones.

From Fengzhen I passed beyond the Wall to Hohhot, the capital of Inner Mongolia. When Chinese farmers emigrated to the fertile plain around this Mongol trading center in late Ming times, they gave the city a new name, Guihua, meaning "Return to Civilization." The choice suggests not only the uncertain acceptance the settlers brought to their surroundings, but also the profoundly different way of life that still exists in the grasslands.

Crossing the mountains beyond Hohhot in early autumn, I found the rolling steppe already patched with ice and snow. Homes here invariably face south, like cattle with their rumps to the bitter Siberian wind; not a chimney, window, or door interrupts the blank face they present to other points of the compass. Even the pigs have their own south-facing covered sheds.

The Mongols are a handsome and reserved race, with wide mouths, high cheekbones, and open, impassive faces. "They live on meat and milk and game," wrote Marco Polo, "and . . . are of all men in the world the best able to endure exertion and hardship." Their hospitality displayed the lavishness characteristic of nomadic peoples; I was toasted with three kinds of drink, serenaded at the table, and served more mutton than I could hope to consume. Could these be the descendants of "the inhuman Tartars, erupting as it were from the secret confines of Hell," against whom Pope Alexander IV in 1260 urged the leaders of all Christendom to rally?

One evening I was welcomed by a herdsman and his family whose traditional nomad's tent, the hide-covered yurt, had been pitched in the grasslands far from the nearest village. As the temperature sank below freezing, we shared a supper of steamed meat dumplings, sour cabbage, and boiled mutton which the herdsman whacked from the bones with a short knife. A cow-chip stove gave warmth, and candles cast shifting patterns on the ribbed walls, suffusing the inside of the yurt with a subdued and gentle mood. The family cat peered enviously down through a vent in the roof until the food was taken away and the women returned to sweep aside the crumbs. Afterward there was music sung to a homemade stringed *huqin,* melancholy tales of brave deeds. A kettle simmered on the stove and the listeners softly slurped their milk tea. The children, at first bright-eyed and intent, drifted into sleep. Outside in the cold air the Milky Way shone across the moonless sky.

Next morning I returned to Hohhot and took the train to Yinchuan. There the Great Wall completes its crossing of the Ordos and meets the Yellow River. On the east bank the Wall has been reduced to an eroded ridge of dirt about twice the height of a man. Nevertheless, there are few places where it is more useful today. An irrigation canal has been dug along the top, and water drawn from the river onto this high ground flows into the level fields of the surrounding area.

Yinchuan is the capital of Ningxia Hui Autonomous Region, a center of Chinese Islam. One third of its inhabitants are Muslim, whom other Chinese call Hui and consider a separate ethnic group. At the mosque, the imam and the mullah received me with tea.

"The government allows freedom of religion, as you will see," said the imam. "But during the Cultural Revolution the Gang of Four tried to stop the Hui religion. Now, after their downfall, the people are glad."

In the mosque, several dozen white-capped old men knelt on cotton pads over a plank floor, facing a *mihrab* flanked with green panels inscribed in Arabic: "*Allahu Akbar*—God is most great." The prayers were as universal as the Muslim's love of Mecca, where the imam and the mullah had long ago made the *hajj,* or pilgrimage.

Schoolboys crowded at the windows, whispering and laughing. The mullah urged them vainly to go away.

Afterward I asked him why none of the worshipers were young. "The young people are busy in their work," he said. "If you like, you can do these prayers at home. This is the freedom, to do as you like."

As he spoke, the students ran through the courtyard taunting the old men. After harsh words the imam picked up a stick and tried to shoo them out, but they dodged him, jeering defiantly, and continued their sport. It was the only time in China I saw such a display of disrespect toward elders.

Long before dawn, with the night sky still filled with stars, the inescapable loudspeakers made their presence known. They are the awakeners, the instructors, and the caffeine of daily life. At Yinchuan the mass alarm clock was antiphonal; from one direction came the chatter of China's morning news, from the other, something resembling Prussian military band music. These insistent sounds routinely cause the foreign guest to wrap a pillow around his ears and mutter against the sheer totalitarian intrusion of it all. I wondered whether the Chinese, so deeply civilized, shared such feelings. But an official from Peking was astonished when I raised the possibility with him. "Not everyone," he explained with the measured patience due small children and foreign guests, "can afford his own radio."

The final surviving section of the Great Wall, about 500 miles from Yinchuan to Jiayuguan in the western desert, protected the Silk Road both from bandits and from drifting sand. It is paralleled for much of the way by the Xinjiang railway line. The Yinchuan-Jiayuguan journey takes 28 hours. I calculated that for every second I traveled, at least six tons of material had long ago been laboriously moved in place to make the Wall, of which only the barest outlines remain today.

The last gate in the Wall is at Jiayuguan Pass. It stands isolated on a rise, a remnant of its former Ming grandeur. The once brilliant reds, greens, and yellows are surrendering to the brown baked earth. As I walked the battlements of the gate, I saw that the Wall veered off in a straight line to the left, past grazing camels. That which leapt boldly from the sea at Shanhaiguan ended abruptly at the high cliff of a river bank five miles from this, the ultimate gate of China. The landscape beyond, but for an occasional oasis, is a skeletal countryside of abandoned walled towns, dunes, and dust-colored mirage-cities shimmering in the air. For the Chinese this western frontier has symbolized danger, decline, and oblivion; on the dedication stone outside the gate at Jiayuguan are these words:

> *Looking westward we see the long, long road. . . .*
> *Who is not afraid of the vast desert?*

For most of the Great Wall's history, travelers from across this desert entered the empire at Jiayuguan. During the Ming Dynasty the three-story barracks pavilion must have been electrifying to those who first caught sight of it after months in the sinister outlands. *I am China,* it says; *who are you?*

T rucks and mule-drawn wagons vie for road space at a rail crossing outside Qinhuangdao, near the eastern end of China's Great Wall.

Farther north at Shanhaiguan, a woman cuts mian with a knife in a noodle factory after hanging strands from the rafters to dry. A staple in China's wheat-growing regions, noodles come in a variety of sizes, but the long thin ones, symbols of longevity, find a featured place in birthday party dishes.

A sleeping street peddler displays his brooms before a shuttered Shanhaiguan storefront. Reed disks serve as trays, wok lids, and tabletops in Chinese homes.

OVERLEAF. Like a fossilized guardian dragon, the Great Wall slithers over peak and gorge at Badaling. Built here of stone and brick, it averages 25 feet in height and 15 feet across the paved roadway, which breaks into hundreds of knee-high steps to surmount the rugged terrain. Sentries signaled from beacon towers with fire by night or smoke by day.

97

F amily feast draws near in a Shashiyu household with the preparation of jiaozi, or meat-filled dumplings, a traditional north China dish served on special occasions, and customarily on New Year's Eve. The daughter shapes the dough, made from wheat flour, into a roll that she will cut into inch-long pieces. Squashing each piece with her palm, she will roll it into a wrapper three inches in diameter. Mother fills each wrapper with a mixture of pork, cabbage, onion, garlic, and salt, folding and then sealing it with thumb and fingertip. The finished dumplings are boiled (above) in the kitchen guo (called "wok" in southern China) and dipped in spicy sauces during the meal.

References to jiaozi appear as early as the third century A.D.; dried specimens more than 1,000 years old were excavated in 1968 from a Tang Dynasty (618-907) tomb in western China.

OVERLEAF. Sunlight washes the 40 buildings of the Putuo Zongcheng Monastery near Chengde's imperial summer palace. Largest of the surrounding monasteries, it was modeled after the Potala Palace in Lhasa, Tibet, and built between 1767 and 1771.

Qing emperor Kang Xi began building the summer resort and the palace compound, whose brick wall is seen in the foreground, in 1703. The cooler climate of the encircling hills persuaded him to retreat here from the heat of Peking summers. Now a public park, the compound and nearby temples hold treasures of art and history amid landscaped gardens, ancient pines, and lotus ponds.

T he "Thousand-armed, Thousand-eyed" Buddha at Chengde's Puning Monastery evokes a religion that in its many forms has influenced everyday Chinese life for nearly 1,900 years. Actually, the 72-foot-high wooden statue in this Mahayana Buddhist chamber has only 42 limbs, and only 45 eyes on its face and palms.

Siddhartha Gautama, a high-caste youth of northern India, began to preach in the sixth century B.C. after contemplation led him to become Buddha, the Enlightened One. The "Noble Truths" of his teachings, which reached China by A.D. 100, offered an Eightfold Path of rightness, a way—or dharma—that led to serenity, compassion, and salvation.

The Sacred Way at the Eastern Qing Tombs near Zunhua is still guarded by a stone official (above). Once this road to the crypts could only be used on foot; today farmers pedal along it to their fields.

Balanced in a skiff beside a floating dredge pump, a worker cleans a large fish-farm pond near the Chengde summer palace. The circle of sticks in the foreground supports the submerged net of a smaller fish pen in this cove of a misty lake. Telephone and power lines stretch across the water above and behind the worker. In the distance, Mallet Peak—a natural formation— towers like a crude club. Sightseers climb to a terrace at its base for a breathtaking view of Chengde to the south.

Along Chengde's main street an elderly man offers for sale a Mongolian calandra lark, a loud and melodious whistler and an affordable pet for the average family. Once condemned as "bourgeois," keeping pets is restricted now only by the expense of feeding them. Children find free pets in crickets and other insects, perhaps like the cetoniine scarab beetle (left) chewing on this daisy.

107

Members of a commune production team near Yinchuan pitch in to harvest their crop of wheat. Some wear masks against chaff and dust as they feed sheaves into a threshing machine.

Nearby, at another commune in northern Ningxia, a team leader's wife models homespun headwear that identifies the area as Hui, Muslim Chinese. In the commune's administrative office, a master of memory chooses from a plate of 2,400 characters (above) to cut a stencil on a Chinese typewriter. She can type 10 to 20 characters a minute by manipulating a lever that moves the type-filled plate from front to back and side to side. When she has centered the desired character directly under the typing head, she depresses a key. An arm reaches down, extracts the slug of metal from its slot, carries it up to strike the platen, and returns it to the plate. She has 3,600 additional characters in reserve.

Weather-worn beacon towers of the Ming Dynasty march along the winding Inner Mongolian frontier northwest of Datong. In the foreground a village recalls the garrison forts that furnished manpower for the Great Wall. Today women share the burden of militia duty, like these two members of a commune militia unit at dry-run target practice (above) near Fengzhen. Factories, mines, schools, and government departments also have militia groups. Duty calls everyone at age 16; women serve until 35, men until 40.

111

Buddhist art both colossal and exquisite stands frozen in time and stone before a visitor to the Yungang Caves west of Datong (left). Carved during the Northern Wei Dynasty in the fifth century, galleries of some 51,000 figures in 53 caves reflect the music, dress, and architecture of ancient northern China. The 40-foot Buddha in later years acquired a coat of painted plaster, but weather and whirling dust scoured it away, revealing the holes that helped hold it in place.

In one of the finest wall panels, musicians with flute and mandolin-like pipa attend a bodhisattva—a Buddha-to-be—mounted on an elephant. A servant shades him with a parasol. In another panel (above) a form of the Hindu deity Vishnu, with multiple heads and arms, rides a phoenix. His presence underlines Buddhism's Indian origins.

One of the Great Wall's oldest sections, built of rammed earth in the fourth century B.C., once rose along the rumpled track opposite, near Hohhot. It winds toward the remains of Usutujo Temple, a reminder of the Mongolians' Lamaist religion.

Women cobblers work leather from local hides in a Hohhot factory. Traditionally a stockbreeding area of sheep and horses, Inner Mongolia produces many of China's hides.

In a village northwest of the city, a roadside vendor samples his own stock of roasted sunflower seeds, one of China's favorite snacks.

OVERLEAF. *Far Eastern cowboy reaches out his* urga—*a 15-foot birch pole with a leather noose—to rope a wild Mongolian horse. Small, tough, and treasured, horses serve the herdsman as transport, a source of milk, and subject of songs.*

115

Dawn stirs a peasant household to life at Bayan Obo commune in Inner Mongolia. A woman prepares breakfast in a pan atop the stove, while children feed milk and millet to a tot who later goes off to play with her broom (left). The platform bed, spread with a mattress of felt pads, also serves as a table. In the corner, thermos bottles stand beside a dish of lamb bones that will first strengthen a soup, then end up as food for the dogs waiting outside.

A pig and two chickens forage for food in a nearby village of Han Chinese farmers, part of an immigrant flood that has left the Mongolians a 20 percent minority in their own land. As they too settle down to farming, more and more once nomadic Mongolians are building similar permanent dwellings, in addition to their traditional nomadic tents. Politically, Han and Mongol representatives share local rule on the county level.

120

Snug and sturdy symbols of nomadic life, Mongolian yurts huddle on the windswept grasslands near Hohhot. Herdsmen build the collapsible dwellings by covering a willow framework, or khana, with hides, felt, and canvas lashed down with ropes. Inside, rugs help transform the hut into a cozy home. At the top of the framework a three-foot opening called a toono lets light in and smoke out. Flaps can be drawn over the toono and the single wooden door to seal the yurt against temperatures that may plunge to minus 30°F.

Popular evening entertainment centers around a minstrel with tea and talk. Here he sings and plays a modified hu-qin, a stringed instrument stroked with a horsehair bow.

121

olten iron, the lifeblood of China's industry, cascades from a blast furnace at the Jiayuguan Iron and Steel Mill, near the western end of the Great Wall. Other furnaces will process the iron into steel, which will be cast into ingots, then rolled into rails, sheets, and other shapes.

Casthouse workers wear heat- and flame-resistant pants, coats, and hoods. The goggles in this man's pocket (above) will be worn to protect his eyes from the molten metal's blinding glare.

This mill and others, fed by nearby iron deposits, have turned the once sleepy village of Jiayuguan into a booming industrial city of 100,000. The area's factories also churn out cement, chemicals, machinery, and electrical appliances.

Bactrian camels conjure up an ancient scene of Silk Road caravans as they plod through a crumbling cut in the Great Wall's western terminus at Jiayuguan Pass. Ming Dynasty rulers built this rammed-earth portion of the Wall and the magnificent brick fortress with its graceful watchtowers (above) in the late 14th century. Through the bastion's "gate to hell," banished criminals and disgraced officials stumbled out to face the merciless western wilderness: Central Asia.

125

THE LASH OF THE DRAGON

By Mike Edwards
Photographs by Lowell Georgia

At first it was only ankle deep, that wide sheet of ocherous water that crept into the village of Wangjiadi— Wang Home—about noon on a June day in 1938. By midafternoon it had risen to the higher ground of the village center, eating into the soft brick of the 20 meager houses clustered there.

Yang Kunshan, a man with a farmer's rough hands and cheeks burned to brick, remembers that, by evening, the water was over his head. He was about 30 years old then. "I knew water," he said, meaning, "I could swim." Just before dark, he roped his wife and two-year-old daughter to a raft of roof beams and, kicking from behind, departed the village he would never see again.

Yang had watched the soldiers of Chiang Kai-shek's Nationalist Army digging into the Yellow River dike less than a mile from Wangjiadi. Soldiers had gone to villages to warn that the dike would be breached to block the Japanese Army pressing Chiang's retreating forces. But few villagers fled. Most, like Yang, waited for the flood. It submerged an area almost as large as West Virginia. Drowning and starvation claimed 900,000 lives. Many survived as Yang and his family did, eating bark and leaves.

Celestial guardians keep evil spirits at bay in the grottoes of Longmen.

The Yellow River rises north of Tibet in the high, frigid fastness of Qinghai Province. It loops extravagantly across the desert wastes of the Ordos and through the Loess Plateau before starting across the North China Plain to the gulf of Bo Hai, a journey of 3,000 miles. No other river, not even the mighty Yangtze, is so emotionally joined to the Chinese people. "It is the mother of China," an engineer declared almost reverently. Six thousand years ago the streams of its lower basin were fished by people who shaped hooks from bone. As dynasties emerged, the river nurtured the great ones that underpin China's heritage: Shang, Zhou, Qin, Han, Tang, and Northern Song. The names of splendid dynastic capitals—Kaifeng, Luoyang, and the most opulent of all, Changan—volley across the centuries. As kingdoms grew wide and populous (the Han counted 58 million subjects in A.D. 1), the river became empire's servant, freighted with grain barges, stitched into a canal network that testified to the skill of ancient engineers.

My two-month journey in the Yellow River's lower basin was a ramble in a vast museum—a dowdyish old hall in need of patching and paint. Neglected for centuries, China's historic heartland accumulated a veneer of squalor and grime. Yet the heartland speaks powerfully of its former glory. It speaks in an old shrine here, a venerable pagoda there, in the shards of azure pottery I kick

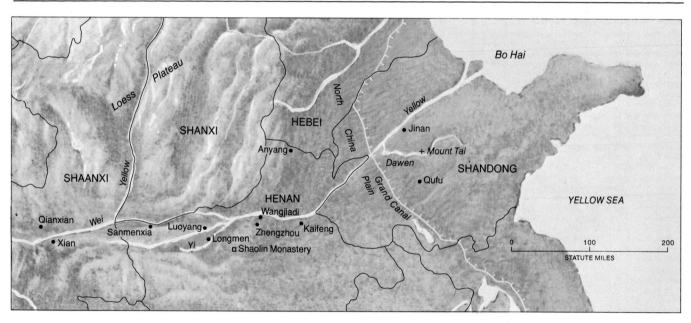

"Poor hills, furious waters," say the people of east-central China when describing their homeland—a swath of plains and gullied hills traversed by the Yellow River. Traveling a thousand miles by rail and highway, Mike Edwards journeyed two months along the lower reaches of China's "River of Sorrows." From Peking, he crossed the North China Plain, itself a creation of river silt, to bustling Jinan, capital of Shandong Province. He visited Qufu, birthplace of Confucius, and climbed Mount Tai, holiest of China's holy mountains. Rejoining the river at Kaifeng, he traveled westward to Luoyang, to Sanmenxia, and on to fabled Xian, site of one of China's most remarkable archaeological digs.

up from the rubble of a vanished metropolis, and in the elegant bronzes and statuary that archaeologists retrieve from long-buried temples and tombs.

The river shares in the credit for this splendor. But it also was, and is, a menace, prone to lash out at the countryside. Half solid after summer rains, it is the muddiest of the world's major rivers. Its name, Huang He, which can mean "yellow river" or "brown river," acknowledges the hue of its burden. It deposits millions of tons of silt in its own bed. The result is an *elevated* river, in places 11 yards higher than the countryside. It has flooded 1,500 times, at least two of them after its dikes were broken to thwart enemy armies. Twenty-six times it has changed course, six of those times swinging across the North China Plain like a sundered bridge cable to enter the sea at points 300 miles apart. Only resolute dikesmanship contains it now.

From those dikes, I watched small sailboats loaded down with coal and gravel where great grain fleets once worked. Ferries bring rural folk to town with their cabbages and chickens. Except for some traffic in its estuary, this is the sum of the river's commerce today. Shifting mud bars make navigation too tricky in low water; and when the water is high, the current becomes too swift.

So it was not the throb of a ship's engine that ushered me into the Chinese heartland but the clatter of steel on steel: I was taking a train south from Peking to Jinan, the capital of Shandong (Shantung) Province. Jinan is the last major city the Yellow River passes before it empties into the sea—creating seven or eight square miles of new land each year. Poets of old extolled Jinan's many springs and pools, but what caught my eye first was the railroad station—turreted and scalloped by the Germans who built it at the turn of the century. It would not have been out of place in Bavaria. And Jinan counts one other distinction: It is one of the few cities along the river that has not been built upon the ruins of an early dynastic capital.

In a tiny shop on City of Springs Street, two women ladled beer from barrels, filling mugs that customers drained on the sidewalk and bottles that would be taken home suspended from bicycle handlebars. Could this be another German holdover? No, the stand-up sidewalk beer garden and take-out store is a Chinese institution, not an import.

There is a little extra money for beer in Jinan. Factories in this city of nearly two million people make fine paper, produce steel and fertilizer, and assemble Yellow River trucks. The apples and pears that grow on ridges round about are high-profit crops for communes. So are the peanuts, cotton, and tobacco harvested on Shandong's plains.

In the company of engineers who wrestle with the problems of the river, I rode downstream a few miles from Jinan in a minibus, rolling along the plateau-like top of the dike, which is about 100 yards wide here. Beyond the dike, knee-high wheat stretched as far as I could see. In a few weeks, the same land would grow corn. Water admitted to the fields through a network of canals and irrigation ditches nourishes both crops.

On this spring day the river looked anything but menacing. It lazed along, wide, shallow, and braided with bars of silt. But in late summer the Yellow River may fill its three-mile-wide floodway near Jinan and rise to within a foot or two of the dike tops. The silt load can become so heavy that oxygen-starved carp leap into the air. Deposited silt has raised the riverbed in Shandong by two yards in the last 20 years. What solution is there for this troublesome torrent, other than building the dikes ever higher along the last 400 miles of the river's journey? An engineer with two decades of experience on the river fielded the question with a brief smile; he had debated it many times. His own pet plan: widening the floodway to usher the summer torrents harmlessly to the sea. Another engineer answered: "Conservation measures to hold the soil on the upper reaches while we strengthen the dikes on the lower."

In fact, erosion control efforts are under way, but the Yellow River still brings down 1.6 billion tons of silt in an average year, about what it carried in 1949. Some engineers are studying the feasibility of building a series of dams that would hold back silt; they would fill up after several decades. Meanwhile, the dikes grow higher and wider.

I briefly departed the Yellow River basin to climb to the top of Tai Shan—Mount Tai. It is 35 miles south of the river. Yet Mount Tai, 5,000 feet high, is firmly bound to the river's history. Emperors of old climbed this, China's most sacred mountain, to ask heaven to tame the unruly river long known as "China's sorrow." In turn, Daoists, Buddhists, and Confucians adopted Mount Tai, decorating its niches with temples and carving laudatory inscriptions on the granite boulders of its flanks.

It was especially the grandmothers who astonished me as I toiled up the Broad Way to Heaven, the 7,000 or so steps to the summit. Sausage-like in padded jackets and pants, many of them hobbled on feet no larger than a child's—the result of footbinding, the cruel stunting of feet into desirable "lotus" shapes. Yet these grandmothers moved right along. One, staring at my lug-soled boots, seemed to regard my ascent as difficult as I did hers.

They climbed to worship and to ask for favors. Some prayed for health. One confided that she would ask heaven for a grandson. "But we also have family planning now," she added dutifully.

The destination of most pilgrims was a quadrangle with pavilions sheltering several gilded Buddha-like statues. I watched a woman bow three times before one, then before another and another. For good measure, she bowed before two rotund plaster guards at the entrance. Many worshipers left a few small gifts: coins, an apple, a cookie.

To watch the sun rise from Mount Tai is counted a special treat. Although the temperature dipped below freezing, many visitors spent the night huddled by boulders. I hired a room in the small, plain, mountaintop hostel. Its rooms were unheated, but the management provided piles of blankets and heavy padded coats. At 5 a.m. a bell clanged in the hall. I donned my coat and hurried outside. Several dozen others already stood at the rim, oblivious to the chill. Applause crackled as the great red ball appeared above the horizon. "Long live the sun!" someone cried. "Ten thousand years to the sun!"

Going down was no fun. My calves ached for three days afterward. The old pilgrims descending alongside me cheerily scrambled off to collect souvenirs—a branch of pine or a spray of forsythia.

Among the emperors recorded as worshiping on Mount Tai was Zhen Zong, who reigned almost a thousand years ago. The mountain did not confer the longevity he desired, although he had a fair run at it. He lived 54 years and ruled for 25. He surely traveled the 200 miles between Mount Tai and his Northern Song capital, Kaifeng, on good roads. I covered the distance by train, lounging in a deluxe "soft sleeper" compartment as operatic arias floated through the car. Then came a tune the Chinese call "Ding, Ding, Ding." We know it as "Jingle Bells."

I stepped off in a disheveled city, low and gray, studded with boxy apartment buildings. In Song times, Kaifeng's streets were filled with traders from Japan, Indonesia, the Philippines, and the Muslim realms of Persia and Arabia. The click-click of countless abacuses proclaimed its position as one of Asia's greatest marketplaces. Historians guess that its population reached a million. Although only half that number live in Kaifeng today, the streets of a downtown bazaar were so crowded I could hardly move. Gray canvas shielded sidewalk vendors of new and used clothes, thimbles, shoe polish, and nails. Cobblers stitched on little hand-cranked machines. Only the crowds and a few small signs advertising Muslim cooking recalled the cosmopolitan atmosphere of Kaifeng a millennium ago.

The Yellow River is partly to blame for this melancholy decline. It went on a rampage in 1461. In 1642 embattled armies broke the nearby dikes, and 300,000 people perished. Floodwaters submerged Kaifeng again in 1887.

"When my father laid the foundations for this house, he discovered the roof of a former house underneath," said Zhao Pingyu, an oval-faced man of about 60 whose easy laugh revealed missing teeth. "That gives you an idea how much silt was brought by the river." Atop that silt, Zhao's father built the humble brick house I visited on a narrow lane known as South Alley of the Teaching of the Scriptures. The Foreign Heaven Chapel once stood just behind this lane. On its wall these words blazed in gold: "Hear, O Israel, the Lord our God, the Lord is One." Actually, at least three houses of worship stood on that site over the centuries, and Zhao believes that his Jewish forebears worshiped in all three of them.

The first Jews in Kaifeng—probably traders—founded a community that may have grown to a thousand or more. They built the first synagogue in 1163. Floods leveled it in 1461 and its successor in 1642. It vanished for the last time about 1855, when it was torn down by salvagers who sold its beams and roof tiles to local Muslims. After that, the Jewish community almost ceased to exist. Some Jews became Muslims. Zhao's grandfather became a Buddhist. I asked if Zhao followed any religion. "No," he said with a smile.

I walked through the former Jewish quarter: small houses crowded together, graced here and there by a fig tree. Mats made of layers of cloth glued together were plastered on a wall; a family would cut shoe soles from them. A hospital stands where the synagogue once stood.

On the edge of Kaifeng a section of old city wall juts through a dune of silt piled up by winds. It reminded me that, from an earlier wall, the Song in 1126 hurled gunpowder bombs and bamboo grenades down upon a besieging army. The grenades were loaded with chunks of iron and pottery. This "fire medicine" had been used in warfare in China for two hundred years. By the late 13th century it had reached Europe.

I ventured deeper into the North China Plain, heading for Zhengzhou, site of recent archaeological excavations. This time I traveled by minibus on a ribbon of asphalt that lay across the miles of wheat fields. Outside of Kaifeng, the traffic thinned and its character changed. Trucks snorted, tractors rumbled along, and wagons rolled behind mules, donkeys, and horses—sometimes one of each, a kind of Chinese troika. But rare was the village that boasted a passenger car. Young poplars were the tallest objects on the gentle landscape, except for the ubiquitous smokestacks of brick kilns.

Along Zhengzhou's wide boulevards paulownia trees sent forth lavender blossoms, returning the gaudy salute of red and blue long johns flapping on apartment balconies. A small, grimy city when the Communists took over in 1949, the capital of Henan Province has grown wide and tolerably handsome with a population of nearly a million. Signs in the huge No. 3 Textile Mill suggest that it may not grow much larger. Americans who visited the Zhengzhou mills in the mid-1970s saw signs that blazed political messages in boxcar characters. Now I found signs promoting "one child-ization," fetchingly embellished with lilies and peach blossoms. One sign proclaimed that, among the several hundred women employed in the weaving room, births had declined from 184 in 1963 to only 26 in the past year.

In the 1950s, when workers began digging foundations for factories and apartment buildings in Zhengzhou, they uncovered the foundations of ancient palaces and temples, along with pottery kilns, bones, and bronzes. In the compound of a surgical instruments factory, I was shown part of an earthen wall, pounded layer by layer into a hard mass. An Jinhuai, a historian who has devoted most of three decades to unraveling Zhengzhou's past, believes this wall encompassed the city of Ao.

Sketchy records say that Ao was the second of five (or perhaps seven) capitals of the Shang Dynasty, which ruled 500 to 600 years, until about the 11th century B.C. In recent decades historians have accumulated enough information about the Shang to call it the earliest dynasty of which a creditable history can be written. But not enough data has been collected to convince all scholars that the discoveries beneath Zhengzhou are the ruins of Ao. Some speculate that the site may be the first Shang capital, Bo, or even date back to the semi-mythical kingdom of Xia. If the Shang did indeed construct that wall, they ushered China to the threshold of history with mass and muscle. The wall was more than 4 miles around the perimeter; it was at least 10 yards high and 11 yards wide at the top. By An Jinhuai's reckoning, building it would have consumed the labor of 18,000 men for 10 years.

The Shang left a much clearer—and more impressive—record in the flat ground on the outskirts of the present city of Anyang, 100 miles northeast of Zhengzhou. A raw, dust-laden wind blew as I caught the train for that city. Women alighting at the Zhengzhou station pulled blankets over the heads of their babies. Through the train window I watched peasants bending in yellow clouds to plant sprouts of tobacco and cabbage. If they quit work for dust storms, the people of the North China Plain would be idle much of the year; dust storms are constants of life here.

When the wind subsides, people wipe a layer of silt from sills and tables. But some part of the plain has a fresh veneer of loess that may have traveled hundreds of miles from the Ordos, the Gobi, or the Loess Plateau. Crush a clod of this wind-supplied soil in your hand and you have talcum-like grains so fine they vanish into the whorls of your thumb. "It's good soil if it gets water," a farmer said. "It is *bazi*—it pulls up the seed."

As I approached Anyang, a steel mill came into view, puffing smoke that sent shadows scudding over a flat landscape green and yellow with plots of wheat and rape. I stepped off in a modest city with a workaday face that belies the remnants of turbulent history sleeping just beneath its suburbs. Here perhaps stood Yin, the last of the Shang capitals, where rulers once rumbled through the streets in chariots on their way to inspect nearby fields where war captives, leashed like dogs, worked under the gaze of overseers with whips.

"There is so much excavation to do that we won't finish for a hundred years," said Yang Xizhang, vice-director of the Anyang Archaeological Station. Eleven royal tombs already have been discovered. Grave robbers long ago bore off the valuables from most of them, but some treasure remains, as archaeologists discovered when they excavated the tomb of Fu Hao in 1976. She is believed to have been one of 64 wives of King Wu Ding. Her tomb contained 440 bronzes, 560 hairpins and other objects made of bone; 7,000 cowrie shells (used as money); and jade figures and ornaments that, in Yang's

133

words, "we carried out by the armload." When all was removed, the site was filled in. There was not enough money for buildings to protect the excavation.

The rich ground of Yin has yielded many grisly troves—in one instance, 164 skeletons of sacrificial victims who accompanied a king in death; in another, the remains of a hundred people killed to mark the construction of a building—perhaps a temple. The heads of other victims were interred separately from their bodies. Horses, cattle, sheep, and dogs also were sacrificed.

Other bones unearthed at Yin—hundreds of pounds of them—have greatly enlarged modern knowledge of this bloodthirsty dynasty. In the research station, Yang let me hold an ox bone upon which an inscription had been engraved. "This figure that looks a little like a box suggests a mouth," he said. "It means 'speak.' Another figure means 'hand' or 'catch.' Another is 'bird.'" Thus a question emerged: "Will I catch a bird on a hunting trip?"

Shang rulers made almost no move without addressing their ancestral deities. First the diviner asked a question: "Will the king have a hunting accident?" or, "Is it good to sacrifice one sheep for father?" or, "Should the king send this general against an enemy?" To get the answer, a priest touched a heated bronze rod or a glowing stick to the bone, waited for cracks to appear, and interpreted their pattern. Then, for the record, he inscribed the original question and sometimes the answer on the bone. Over the centuries these records piled up; written in archaic Chinese on what archaeologists call "oracle bones," they provide a fascinating account of China at the dawn of history.

Anyang is off the well-beaten tourist path. Around the corner from the city's hotel, three teenage girls sat on the sidewalk with baskets of peanuts. When I knelt to buy a double handful, their eyes grew wide. I must have been their first foreign customer, and I must have seemed monstrous. I got my peanuts, but then the girls seized their baskets and scurried away. When I strode toward them the next day, they fled before I could buy.

The weather turned hot as I caught a train for Luoyang, some 170 miles to the southwest. It was "hard sleeper" this time—a thin mattress and none of the starchy white antimacassars that embellish "soft sleeper" compartments. Trying to cool off, my companions—factory workers and bureaucrats—shed shoes and shirts and rolled up their trousers.

Emperors of both the Han and Tang Dynasties held court in Luoyang. In their time, the city enjoyed an importance second only to Changan, the great capital of these dynasties farther west. Like both Changan and Kaifeng, the city prospered in trade, luring dealers in spices and silks from far-off realms. Luoyang's flavor today is small-town (although, with nearly a million residents, the city is not really so small, save by Chinese standards). Pigs root in a vacant lot. Chickens scratch beside apartment buildings; at dusk, some fly to low balconies to roost. On a side street, sidewalk merchants vend hairpins, key chains, and rat poison. Nearby, a restaurant sign bears a picture of a friendly looking dog. For some Chinese, dog meat is still a delicacy.

One look around the foyer of the big Friendship Hotel in Luoyang and I knew I had reached a major stop on China's tourist circuit. It was piled with baggage tagged in half a dozen languages. In the dining room the maître d'hôtel, a sprightly little man of more than 70, moved solicitously from table to table, conversing in French and English. He had learned his trade before World War II in Shanghai's elegant French Club.

Japanese tourists especially are attracted to Luoyang's Longmen Caves, one of China's greatest Buddhist shrines. I found there a gentle, charitable side of ancient China, quite the opposite of Shang brutality. About 14 centuries ago, monks carved 120 or so prescriptions at the entrance to one of those caves: For malaria, breathe the vapors of mixed goose dung and liquor. To control "wild words and devil's talk," insert needles under the nail of the big toe. These remedies, the accepted medicine of the time, were posted out of concern for the afflicted.

By the time China entered one of the greatest periods of its antiquity, the three centuries of Tang rule that began in 618, Buddhism had long since arrived from India with its message of kindness and piety. At Longmen, rulers paid lavish homage to the imported religion, commissioning 97,300 figures—Buddhas, bodhisattvas, monks, heavenly maidens with sensuously trailing veils, acrobats, and musicians—in 2,100 caves and niches. Under earlier Northern Wei rulers some 800,000 workers spent 23 years making a shrine of a single cave. At its entrance I gazed upon two formidable stone figures: guards with bared teeth, armed with clubs. But within, the colossal seated Buddha radiated welcome with an expression suggesting that someone had just told a good but not great joke. Longmen's monumental celebration of life and felicity kindled good spirits among strolling families, school groups, and young lovers. They rowed on the lazy Yi River, clicked cameras at one another, and sat in the shade of willows, downing pop, beer, and boiled eggs.

I turned west once again, heading for the limits of the North China Plain. The steam locomotive pulling the train showered the cars with cinders. Soon we began to climb. From my window I could see sharply rising, thirsty loess hills. The ravines between them looked as if they'd been slashed with a knife.

I got off in a quiet town, Sanmenxia, and later drove north into the countryside. The road from town dips and climbs among ridges sliced into narrow terraces and planted in wheat. Villages are small and isolated. In one of these, Tangwa, wood and brick facades screened a couple of dozen cave dwellings burrowed into the hillsides. Poplars shaded a central area—a village square of sorts. Chickens wandered about and children played in front of three caves—the village school.

Homes tunneled into loess hills have a special advantage: They are expandable. A city dweller can't very well add a room to his small apartment, but a cave dweller can add another chamber (assuming he has no adjoining neighbors). Five-room homes are not unusual, providing far more space than the average family shares in Peking or Luoyang.

When I asked to see the inside of a cave, a young woman opened the door to a single long room. She and her husband, married the previous year, had begun housekeeping in this cave, which adjoins her mother-in-law's. The newlyweds had decorated the walls with colorful posters depicting scenes from Chinese operas. On cold nights, they could light a fire under their brick bed, which was covered with a thin mattress and quilts. Meals were cooked outside on a stove made of mud.

"The main advantage of a cave home is that it's cool in summer and warm in winter," a villager said. The major disadvantage, I suggested, might be the danger of a cave-in. "You would have warning," he assured me. "You would see cracks developing in the ceiling." The interiors of some cave homes are bricked to add strength, and also to stop earth from falling on bed and tables.

Plunging into a gorge beyond Tangwa, the road brought into view Sanmenxia Dam, about 300 feet high and half a mile wide. The water in the reservoir was not yellow; it was emerald. Slowing as it reaches this long lake, the Yellow River drops its silt. Soviet engineers who designed the dam in the 1950s apparently did not reckon with that silt. "They didn't have any experience with a river like this," a Chinese engineer said. In the 1960s, soon after the dam was finished, it became obvious that the reservoir would fill with loess within a few decades.

China had to tackle this problem alone; the Soviet advisers had departed after the rupture in relations in 1960. The Chinese engineers at length decided to reopen abandoned sluices bored through rock near the base of the dam, making tunnels through which silt accumulating on the reservoir floor could be flushed during times of heavy flow.

In ancient times the river sped past rocky outcrops where the dam now rises, and many a boatman perished while trying to thread a passage. Attempts by Han and Tang Dynasty engineers to widen the channels or to reroute the river through the gorge proved futile. The river always won. Ultimately, a road provided the safest way around the gorge. With several acquaintances from Sanmenxia, I traveled a stretch of that road, now a deep groove in the earth. We went to see the "Frog Pagoda"—the local nickname for a squat relic of Tang times, otherwise known as the Temple of the Precious Wheel.

My companions walked around the edifice clapping their hands and banging rocks together. "It is better over here!" someone shouted.

"No, come on this side!"

If the right sound were made at the right place, I was assured, the pagoda would respond with an echo like frogs croaking. Sure enough, after a few experiments, the pagoda sounded off like a swamp on a summer night.

My step had an extra spring the next day as I swung aboard one more train. How could a traveler not feel a quickening pulse as he started for Xian, the great Changan of old? Such excitement as I felt seemed not to have infected the young lady whose voice floated from the train's loudspeaker. Railroad workers were trying to improve service, she said, and would passengers please cooperate by not throwing trash or spitting on the floor? At last, we pulled into Xian's red brick station and I set out to explore the area that had been the capital of ten dynasties.

A massive wall—three stories high and wide enough on top for an army to march eight abreast—makes a rectangle inside present-day Xian. It is an interloper, only six centuries old. The walls which enclosed the million inhabitants of Changan in the opulent Tang era vanished long ago. No matter. Atop the newer wall as the sun sinks into haze on a May afternoon, I look toward a high tower crowning a gate and imagine an emperor's retinue passing through, a blaze of pomp and color entering the city as citizens bow low.

Today's wall is both park and pasture. A bell's tinkle, floating on the wind, announces the approach of a dozen sheep and goats mowing the grass on top of the wall. Old men ascend to chat and smoke, and lovers to hold hands while looking into the sunset. Boys with toy guns play at war upon the wall, as boys must have done in Changan with sword and bow.

Changan rose on a Yellow River tributary, the Wei, which flows into the Yellow River near the upper limit of the Sanmenxia reservoir. Beginning in the 12th century B.C., one dynasty after another raised capitals near the Wei, emblazoning the countryside with palaces and tombs.

Smokestacks rising all around Xian suggest power of a modern kind. Xian produces steel, chemicals, and textiles. With 1,600,000 citizens, the city extends far beyond its old limits—a low-slung, dusty metropolis spilling into wheat fields and cabbage rows.

One afternoon I strolled on West Avenue, one of four boulevards which meet in the center of Xian. (The three others are as functionally named: North, South, and East Avenues.) From a cubbyhole shop peered a decidedly un-Chinese countenance. It was as plain as the nose on the man's face that his forebears had reached Changan from afar. That hawk's bill of a nose would have been at home on a tribesman of Afghanistan.

His ancestors came from Arabia as missionaries, the shopkeeper said. "There were no Muslims here and China invited them." Perhaps they came by way of the Silk Road, that great artery of culture and commerce to which Changan owed much of its cosmopolitan atmosphere.

Farther along, a sign in a small restaurant window advertised Muslim fare. A young man with a cleaver paused in mid-chop to tell me that the restaurant had been open just one month. "But already," he declared, "we are famous for our food throughout China!" Surely his boast echoed the entrepreneurial style with which, during Tang times, 2,000 foreign firms vied for business in Changan.

I turned into the Lane of Great Learning and Practice and, presently, stood in the courtyard of a mosque. Elsewhere in Xian there is a refurbished mosque to which tourists are taken; the one I found was shabby. But several skull-capped men welcomed me with no hint of embarrassment. They especially wanted me to see two tall stone stelae, engraved in Persian and Arabic, which proclaim that the mosque dates to the eighth century.

Red Guards went on a rampage here during the Cultural Revolution. Imams were killed, one man said, and some died in prison. How many? He appeared uncomfortable with the subject. "Several," he answered.

Others told me that attendance at Friday prayer is increasing. And, one man added, life is much better for Muslims—there are 30,000 in Xian—than it was before 1949. "We were not equals of other Chinese people then," he said. "The kind of life I lived, I didn't know when I'd have a full meal. Now we have jobs. Many of us own small businesses."

I crossed the Wei River by taxi and moved along a highway crowded with trucks and wagons. The driver turned into a quiet lane. Lumpy mounds—the tombs of Han royalty—rose abruptly from level fields. Then we drove north half an hour, climbing into low hills that hold the tombs of Tang rulers.

A hill called Liang Shan is the final resting place of the Tang Emperor Gao Zong, who died in 683, and the ruthless Empress Wu. A palace concubine, she managed to depose Gao Zong's legitimate empress and take her place. When the emperor suffered a stroke, Empress Wu took over the government. Murdering, exiling, and ordering suicide for royal heirs and court officials, she kept power for most of the next 45 years.

The approach to the tombs is flanked by massive sculptures: lions, winged horses, rows of generals and officials. Sixty statues in a group represent foreign envoys who attended Gao Zong's funeral. It is a macabre sight; all are headless. Peasants beheaded the whole lot a couple of hundred years ago because they thought the statues embodied spirits that devoured crops. Although she usurped Gao Zong's power, Empress Wu honored him with a stele extolling his achievements. No one inscribed a stone praising Empress Wu; the reign of ancient China's only woman sovereign is commemorated by a slab devoid of laudatory inscriptions.

In recent years, archaeologists and historians have been keeping intense company with a ruler much more tyrannical than Empress Wu. But the First Emperor of Qin—Qin Shi Huangdi—who achieved imperial power in 221 B.C., is more difficult to categorize. Ruthless, vicious, arrogant, he nevertheless had qualities that enabled him to unify China.

His dust rests near Mount Li, in a man-made hill rising beside a road that strikes east from Xian. The wayside wheat fields were tawny as I passed in late May. Peasants scythed the grain, spreading some on the highway for a haphazard threshing under the wheels of trucks and buses.

Archaeologists began to explore Qin Shi Huangdi's burial complex, which covers many acres, in the 1970s. But it will take decades to piece together a complete picture of this grandiose personal cemetery, which includes the unexcavated tomb of the emperor himself, temple ruins, the graves of slain royal kin, mass graves of laborers executed to preserve the tomb's secrets, bronze chariots decorated with gold, the bones of animals buried to simulate stable and zoo, and who knows what else?

But a single discovery now open to the public affords one of the most awesome sights in China—the main body of the emperor's life-size terra-cotta army. Arrayed as if for battle, this army may have been intended to symbolize the emperor's conquest of vast regions—the first great Chinese empire.

Only a few hundred of the 6,000 soldiers in the largest burial pit have been restored and stand erect. Excavations behind them reveal jumbled arms, legs, and torsos—a chaotic scene, the result of plunder, fire, and the collapse of overhead timbers and earth. But look carefully at the faces of the erect figures when the sun is upon them. Focus on the eyes. When the light is right, there is only one way to describe the way these soldiers appear: *alive*.

Sometimes it takes two months to restore a single figure, said a young woman in a workshop near the pit. Repaired figures and half-figures stood in the workshop amid heads, feet, and limbs. Gluing the parts together may take only four or five days, she said. But sorting out and matching fragments may take weeks. One statue she put together was in 200 pieces.

Behind its victorious armies, the Qin state spread to the sea, and with unity came many positive contributions: good highways, standardized coinage and weights and measures, irrigation projects, an effective administrative system, and consolidation of the Great Wall. But Qin Shi Huangdi also punished cruelly, slew scholars, burned historical texts, dragooned great labor forces (700,000 to work on his mausoleum, it is said), and spent outrageously for palaces. On one occasion, he even took revenge on a mountain that had offended him—ordering workers to strip away its vegetation and paint it red, the color worn by condemned criminals. It was inevitable his dynasty would fall under the weight of such excess. And it did, less than four years after his death.

Today a pomegranate orchard crowns the small hill covering his tomb. The trees were gaudy with blossoms when I climbed to the summit. Two old men squatted there—one wizened, the other gap-toothed, both dispatched from a nearby commune to guard the mountain. In their black jackets and trousers, they looked like crows perched on a limb. "People try to pick the flowers," the wizened man said. Hefting a hoe as if it were a weapon, he added: "That's why we are here."

How did they view Qin Shi Huangdi? As a good man or evil? The wizened man thought a moment. "He's been in the ground a couple of thousand years," he said. "I didn't know him."

Spring flowers touch a field of winter wheat near Jinan, garlanding with apple blossoms a view of distant hills. Deep loess soil on the plains nearby becomes fertile when watered, producing bountiful crops that make the region a breadbasket for Shandong Province. Stone fences once cut fields like this one into myriad plots too small to cultivate efficiently. Removal of many of the fences in recent years—and introduction of modern farming practices—have boosted crop yields by nearly a third.

But change comes slowly to older generations (above). For this aged farmer, the timelessness of his calling echoes in an old peasant refrain:

I plow my ground and eat,
I dig my well and drink.
For king or emperor,
What use have I?

141

"**F**resh beer" proclaims the retouched sign in front of a refreshment stall in Jinan. "Warm and flat," remarked the author after sampling the brew—dipped from a barrel. China's thirst for beer has become unquenchable since the 1949 revolution. Once primarily a beverage for foreigners—and the rich—it is now sold in restaurants and hundreds of tiny stands. In many cities the local brewers' daily output is exhausted in a matter of hours. Most patrons drink their fill on the sidewalks or refill their own containers for home consumption. Well-known brands include Tsingtao, Shanghai, and Jade Fountain.

Playbills at a movie house nearby catch the eye of a passing cyclist. Tickets cost only 25 cents, but getting one may entail hours of shoving, bickering, and waiting—especially if the show is popular.

Loading a funerary floral arrangement aboard a bus requires patience and cooperation—as well as hardy paper flowers. Real flowers, an expensive luxury, are seen only on special occasions.

142

Thrusting between granite shoulders of Mount Tai, the Broad Way to Heaven gropes for the South Gate of Heaven, one of several temples crowning the summit of China's holiest mountain. Pilgrims—scholars, poets, peasants, and emperors—have prayed here since the dawn of history. Confucius, it is said, ascended the 5,000-foot mountain to contemplate the kingdom of Lu, as the region then was known.

Older pilgrims pile stone offerings in trees (above) hoping their prayers for grandchildren will be answered. Others bear away forsythia sprigs—a token in remembrance of the grueling climb.

OVERLEAF. Dawn floods the sky, illuminating the Dawen River and summoning spectators to a time-hallowed vantage point on the crest of Mount Tai.

Stone menagerie haunts the Forest of Confucius in Qufu, final resting place of the sage—and 76 generations of his descendants, members of the illustrious Kong family. The memorial park, once a simple plot, today covers more than 700 walled acres planted with pines and cypresses. Some 60 halls, pavilions, and temples—along with hundreds of tablets, tombstones, and sculptures (including the contemplative figure shown above)—pay homage to the philosopher who lived and taught in China 25 centuries ago.

149

R aindrops pummel the rooftops of Kaifeng, site of six ancient Chinese capitals. Long a center of culture and learning, the city's history reaches back some 3,000 years, far beyond the days when it served as the imperial capital of the Northern Song. Today, as in times past, trade and commerce flourish in dozens of shops, markets, and sidewalk stands (opposite).

Putting on a roof in traditional fashion (right), a worker embeds tiles in a matrix of clay mixed with straw.

150

Burnished by the noonday sun, the Yellow River flows across the North China Plain. Throughout recorded history the unruly stream has breached its dikes some 1,500 times, wreaking incalculable havoc. Now held in check by dams, reservoirs, and projects such as this pumping station at Mangshan, the river irrigates fields and slakes thirst in Zhengzhou, 15 miles away. Splashing fountain (above) adds a parklike touch amid terraced hills planted with shrubs to retard erosion.

152

Sculpturing a woven work of art with electric clippers (opposite), a worker at a carpet factory in Anyang outlines a spray of peonies—symbols of love and spring. A butterfly, emblem of summer and happiness, drifts among the tendrils.

The weaver (left) beats knots of wool yarn to produce a durable, densely woven carpet. The factory's finest products, destined mostly for sale abroad, may count as many as 120 knots per square inch.

onk strikes a martial pose at Henan's ancient Shaolin Monastery, home of Chan, or Zen, Buddhism. To balance the mental exercise of motionless meditation, Zen's founder invented exercises that evolved into a defensive martial art called Shaolin boxing. Legend says that 13 Shaolin monks used it to rescue a Tang emperor from rebel troops; 40 others routed a band of Japanese pirates. Today, Shaolin boxing claims more than a million adherents, but the monastery houses fewer than a dozen monks, all over 50 years old.

Forest of reliquary monuments (above) catches a setting sun outside the monastery walls. Each pagoda-like structure—called a stupa—houses the remains of a Shaolin elder known for his learning, virtue, or proficiency at the martial art of kung fu.

OVERLEAF. Buddha Vairocana, symbol of creation, presides over a court of disciples, demi-gods, celestial guardians—and sightseers—in the caves of Longmen near Luoyang. Begun in the seventh century, the cave measures 100 feet across and is the largest of thousands of grottoes and niches cut into the limestone cliffs above the Yi River. Square holes between the figures once held supporting timbers for a facade that sheltered the cave temple and its art.

Crawler tractors stand final inspection before shipment from a plant in Luoyang. The factory—first of its kind in China—can turn out a tractor every nine minutes. The 75-horsepower model (above) sells for about $14,000—a quarter of the price of comparable American-made machines. Industrial growth has swelled Luoyang's population to 20 times its 1948 level and dotted the area with more than 400 factories. In former times, when six dynasties established their capitals here, the city was known for jewelry and fine wine.

161

*S*ail hanging slack, a Yellow River gravel boat eases around a headland in the Sanmenxia Reservoir. The boatman waits, hook in hand (left), to anchor and unload. River silt settles out in the lake, leaving the water clear— but impedes power generation at the San-menxia Dam. The dam, completed in 1960, has helped restrain the river: Since then there have been close calls but no major floods.

Crowded ferry (above) crosses the Yellow River at Jinan, carrying commuters to their jobs in the city's factories. A new bridge nearby will speed the flow of goods and traffic across the river.

OVERLEAF. Terraces of wheat scale the hills near Sanmenxia. Precious rainfall, scanty in this area, produces a deeper color where terrace lips retain moisture.

163

Cave houses tunneled into the soil of the Loess Plateau make warm, dry dwellings in a country where living space is scarce and sometimes hard to afford. With hand tools, a family can carve out spacious quarters in a few months of spare-time work. Brick-lined or plastered ceilings, as in the classroom above, help prevent cave-ins.

Weaving (opposite) brings a better life for a cave-dwelling family near Qianxian. A village woman weaves homespun cotton for clothes and blankets at a time-worn loom. Ten lengths of the plaid will brighten a departing daughter's wedding; the rest provides extra cash.

*E*vening glow gilds Xian's Bell Tower, symbol of a city with a cosmopolitan past. The tower was first built in Tang times, when Xian—then known as Changan—served as China's capital and ranked as one of Asia's greatest trading cities.

Drawing on the past, a student at the Xianyang Museum (below) sketches sculpture from a Han general's tomb. The rounded rock shapes—China's first known monumental stone carvings—represent the Han Dynasty's innovative experiments with a new art form.

Stone memorial (left), recording the ancestors and achievements of a proud eighth-century Xian family, attracts visitors in the Shaanxi Provincial Museum's collection of stelae. Ancient texts displaying Confucian classics and a tablet recording the coming of Christianity 1,200 years ago form parts of the collection.

Overleaf: Chinese photograph

169

Chinese photograph. Left: Victor R. Boswell, Jr.

Brushing aside the centuries (above, right), archaeologists uncover a terra-cotta army entombed to guard the grave of China's first emperor, Qin Shi Huangdi. The 7,500 life-size clay soldiers were buried 22 centuries ago—in battle formation and with real war chariots and weapons of wood and bronze. A rebellious real-life army toppled the clay soldiers after the emperor's death. Today, one by one and often piece by piece, the ghostly imperial guard—one of archaeology's most spectacular finds— is being restored and returned to its post in the largest of three burial pits, where charioteers, horses, archers, spearmen, and officers muster in the dusty sunlight.

Both a museum and a working archaeological dig, the three-acre site (foldout, left) is part of a tomb complex that reveals abundant information about China's technology and its social and military organization at the time the country was first unified. Now under a protective roof, the emperor's troops fill the 11 corridors of the main burial pit, with robed bowmen in the van followed by four-horse chariots and ranks of armored infantry.

Each head individually modeled—perhaps to represent the various peoples Qin Shi Huangdi welded into one nation— the clay soldiers are painstakingly detailed, down to the last rivet of an archer's armor (above, left), and show the remains of painted uniforms.

173

Chinese photograph (also overleaf). Right: Victor R. Boswell, Jr.

Bronze horses harnessed in gold and silver lie in a pit near Qin Shi Huangdi's tomb. The bronze chariot carried an awning painted with a cloud design; the bronze driver's robes and hairstyle mark him as a high-ranking official. Half life-size, the rich equipage may be a replica of the ones the emperor used in life, standing ready to serve him after death.

An alert cavalry mount (right), fitted with a bridle of stone beads and a bronze snaffle bit, is one of 500 full-size clay horses buried with the terra-cotta army.

Fired in one piece, except for tail and forelock, the 500-pound statue bears testimony both to the potter's skill and the sculptor's detailing. Similar precision and personality mark the army's spearmen (overleaf), clad in terra-cotta replicas of plate armor.

174

Stone attendants stand watch before a royal tomb in a Shaanxi Province wheat field. The mound honors the mother of China's only recognized female ruler—the Empress Wu, who ruthlessly seized power in the seventh century.

Flag-bearing warriors (upper) form a royal guard in the tomb of 17-year-old Princess Yong Tai, perhaps murdered on orders from her scheming grandmother. Small ceramic grave figures (above) form a symbolic retinue of servants in a chamber of the princess's tomb.

CARAVANS OF PROFIT, CARGOES OF IDEAS

By Donald R. Katz

Istood on a balcony at the edge of the vast Taklimakan Desert, under the towering white walls of the Pamirs, some of the highest mountains in the world. Below me lay the bejeweled oasis of Kashgar, a place that was welcoming travelers from far-off lands for 14 centuries before Marco Polo rested here on his way to Cathay.

The path Polo traveled had at various times linked China to the realms of the Roman Empire. For hundreds of years after Rome fell, this and neighboring routes endured as the sole means of overland communication between East and West, as artifacts and new ideas were transported back and forth along the network of roads between the courts of India, Persia, and China.

Years after Polo's travels, the commercial trails came to be known collectively as the Silk Road—the name most widely used today.

I was about to spend two months working my way slowly toward central China. I planned to begin at China's farthest northwest rim, taking the northerly branch of the old Silk Road and calling at several of the oases that were once camel-stops for the travelers who conveyed cargoes and revelations from one edge of the known world to the other.

The frontier spirit of China's west animates a Kirgiz horseman. By Galen Rowell.

But first there was Kashgar, a frontier city rarely visited by Westerners during the 20th century. Only a few Han Chinese have seen the legendary outpost whose citizens neither look nor speak Chinese.

"Kashgar!" a group in Peking had said when I told them I planned to travel the Silk Road from Kashgar to Xian. They shook their heads with pity at the thought of a foreigner being subjected to such a "backward" region. "Kashgar," said one, "is very bad. Very bad conditions, very dangerous, and very, very strange." He had never been to Kashgar, some 2,100 miles to his west, and neither had anyone else I met in Peking.

A week later, I stood on that balcony in Kashgar and realized that I had been allowed to enter a place that hasn't changed much since the caravans and their cargoes stopped coming through four centuries ago. The scene below me was something from an old book, which preserves the sounds and colors of another time.

Women passed by in brilliantly patterned dresses with pants or thick bright stockings underneath. They wore their hair in glistening black braids, some so long they brushed their knees. Long gypsy earrings fell below red, green, or blue scarves interwoven with slivers of golden thread. Children swarmed through the streets and packed themselves in windows to form a lat-

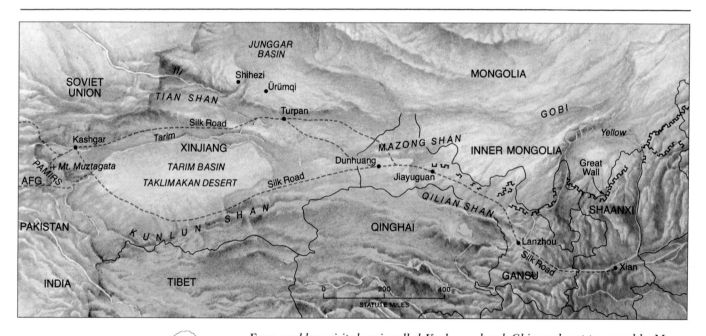

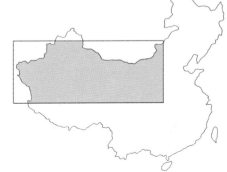

From a seldom-visited oasis called Kashgar at the farthest rim of China's wild west, Donald R. Katz began his trek along the ancient caravan trail called the Silk Road. The Silk Road is a popular label for the shifting network of desert routes whose exact locations have blurred with the passage of time. His journey took him from the awesome Pamir mountain range to lush oases that dot the same harsh Chinese desert traversed by Marco Polo 700 years ago. Along the way, Katz also visited pioneer settlements, members of China's national minorities, and a great repository of Buddhist art. He arrived after two months of travel at Xian, eastern terminus of the Silk Road.

ticework of black eyes and bright smiles. Little girls paraded in dresses more colorful than those their mothers wore. The girls in Kashgar connect their eyebrows with a black line—just like Fatima, the daughter of Mohammed.

The midsummer's morning was soon infused by wails, dust, and the falsetto cries of muezzins summoning men to prayer in some of the 4,000 mosques in the area. Merchants barked to be heard over the trundling of hundreds of carts and the braying of thousands of mules. Two-wheeled carts laden with fruit, sheep, or children filled the streets. Some were pulled by ponies, some by snorting camels, and others by tall, bearded men wearing long robes with silver-hilted daggers swinging from their belts.

More than 80 percent of the 220,000 people in greater Kashgar are Uygurs (pronounced wee-gers), a round-eyed and light-skinned people who are officially recognized as a national minority. Each day I wandered through the vibrant city of the Uygurs—all the time flanked by two friendly but nervous party officials of Han ancestry—it seemed that every citizen was bounding through the dusty streets.

In every alley, in crevices in the thick brown walls, and in the shade of trees or camels, the people came together to make, sell, buy, and use things at the edge of the streets. Tinsmiths pounded glowing metal next to men selling songbirds. Long-bearded barbers shaved the heads of men and boys alongside carts that held peanuts, cold noodles, bits of grilled lamb on long skewers, sour cherries, apricots, and fat, sweet mulberries. Hat makers sewed the colorful skullcaps called *doppa*, which all male Uygurs wear.

"Polo, Polo," said a jeweler, pulling on his beard. "Marco Polo?" He looked at a shoe repairman, then at a sausage maker who was sitting nearby. They both shrugged.

"Did he come before Liberation?" someone asked.

"Was he a Uygur?" asked a young man making nails.

"I know Polo," said another man in a sleepy voice. He hoisted himself onto one elbow in a cart overflowing with silk scarves. "Polo came for silk. All the foreigners came for silk," the man declared. "How much would you like to buy?" He held up a scarf. "Four thousand years we've been making this stuff. Everyone in the world loves silk."

Between a hat shop and a tiny mosque, a knife maker looked up when he heard the word "foreigner" ripple through the bazaar. He stared for a moment, then pointed at me with a smile. "Comrade," he said in Russian, "how good to see you here."

When someone in the crowd told him I was an American, the knife maker shrugged. "Everyone used to come here," he said, gesturing toward the mountains, which rose above the clouds to the west. "Everyone came. Emperors and princes, the great warriors and explorers, and the spies. The British came, even the Russians came. Everyone in the world came here to Kashgar."

The Pamirs are roughly 75 miles from the edge of town, but the awesome peaks appear less than five miles away. For most of China's history, foreigners who entered the empire from the west came through those 20,000-foot mountains, through what is now China's tightly-sealed back door to the Soviet Union. Those travelers who were brave and lucky enough to survive the journey came down from the cold and silent mountains and arrived in a lush depot that offered them hotels, entertainment, translators, money changers, warehouses, and even shrines where the weary could thank the gods of whatever land they'd come from for their safe passage.

This was the halfway point on the world's longest highway, a route that most Chinese schoolchildren will tell you was opened in 139 B.C. by the great Zhang Qian, who traveled to the edge of his world on a mission for Wu Di, a Han emperor. There was certainly traffic along the road before Zhang Qian's journey, but most of it came later. Hitchhiking along the road were powerful new fears and fervencies, new religions and dreams. Buddhism came in from India. Zoroastrianism, Manichaeism, and Nestorian Christianity came from Persia. And later Islam came storming in from Arabia. The caravans also carried jade, coral, linens, lapis lazuli, glass, gold, iron, garlic, cinnamon, tea, cotton, performing dwarfs, nubile women, and horses so fierce they were said to sweat only blood. The path was variously called the Fur Road, the Jade Road, or the Emperor's Road. It wasn't until long after the road had shut down that a 19th century German academic finally named it for its most important commodity: He called it the Silk Road.

Travelers tried to ignore the vivid tales of monsters and the stories about hot winds that cooked entire caravans in seconds. They would risk everything for the love of profit and silk, the material the ancient Chinese found they could bring forth from the bodily emissions of a fat, whey-colored slug. The fabric they wove was used to bribe and seduce, for silk was possessed of the sort of terrible beauty most societies attribute to gold. When the lust for silk was at its height, it was said that Romans would trade a pound of pure gold for a pound of silk. By the mid-first century A.D., writers in Rome were complaining about the sumptuous garments that "rendered women naked" in the streets. But the Chinese guarded the secrets of sericulture so closely that the Romans never learned it. Virgil thought the thread was derived from combing the fuzz off leaves.

Entire civilizations of traders, middlemen, and caravan specialists, such as the Parthians and the Sogdians of Samarkand, rose and fell along the road, their desert gardens bequeathed to others, their colorful cultures handed out to passersby like so many door prizes.

During my first week among the Uygurs, I asked about weddings. Before long, my hosts were conducting me down a quiet alley lined with delicate trees that they called augusia. At the end, a door swung open on an alluvion of sound and color. In a courtyard, the wedding guests stomped and pranced around, whooping and clapping, hugging and kissing. They swirled in dances made up of winks and coquettish hip thrusts, black braids twirling like windmill blades. Roosters crowed from the corners of the yard as a band furiously beat Uygur tambourines and strummed violins (played on one knee). Other musicians played long-necked guitars with such celerity that their right hands seemed to disappear in a blur.

The beaming father of the groom looked across his yard and pointed to his 22-year-old son, Dolkun, the eldest of five children. "He's been speaking love with the girl for a year already," the father yelled above the noise. "Uygurs usually get married after only a month. Dolkun's a little slow."

The Uygur courting ritual reaches its crescendo in several weeks of nightly parties like the one I saw at Dolkun's. The almost compulsive sense of enjoyment presented an astounding contrast to the speed and sobriety with which people back in Peking can dispense with a banquet.

As the wedding festival raced into dusk, Dolkun's father leaned toward me. "This is all good fun," he said, "but later it will be more fun when the women go home. Uygurs are great drinkers," he announced with pride. "Since Liberation we drink in public, but before that the *ahon* (Islamic clergy) forbade it. So we drank 'grape water' we made at home."

Everything about the joyous effusion at Dolkun's house—the look, tastes, smells, and rhythms—was made of a cultural amalgam born of the constant layering of one civilization over another in Kashgar. The silk gifts came from the looms of eastern China; the music sounded like the halting meters of northern Greece. Mountains of spicy Indian pilafs sat on bright rugs next to dishes of *korcu,* a lamb and potato mixture popular on the steppes to the north. The dances looked like a combination of movements from Egypt and Russia. The language was from an ancient Turkic empire, and the clothes bore the intricate and colorful Tang Dynasty patterns that went out of style ten centuries ago in the Middle Kingdom.

Despite its cosmopolitan history, the region around Kashgar has been relatively isolated from the West for 400 years, something I learned during a walk one Sunday through a village in Shufu County a few miles southwest of Kashgar. People stopped dead in their tracks or covered their eyes as I got out of the car. Women huddled together and pulled veils over their faces. Some children giggled; others cried. And a disconcerting number of old men appeared to clutch their hearts and stagger backward.

A man selling cold water from a block of ice that was melting in the sun stared at me for a moment. "I've never seen anything like you," he said. "I don't know what you are."

Standing to one side of the crowd were two herdsmen wearing thick sheepskin coats and pointed beige caps trisected by black felt lines. The hats were *kalpaks,* traditional for the Kirgiz people, another ethnic minority resident in the mountains around Kashgar. One of the herdsmen gripped my hand with painful force and didn't let go, while his companion just stood there with his mouth open, too emotionally overwrought to react otherwise. Someone in the crowd told the herdsmen I was traveling the Silk Road.

"The Silk Road! How wonderful!" the herdsman said. "The Silk Road—what's that?"

Kashgar sits at the edge of Xinjiang, a region of almost 13 million people living in an area more than twice the size of Texas. Xinjiang is in the heart of Central Asia, an amorphous geographical entity as historically severed by numerous political boundaries and diverse ethnicities as any place on the map. In the two millennia since the Chinese first deployed troops to secure portions of the region, the oases of the northwest frontier have been under their control for only 450 years or so. The boundaries of China, the Soviet Union, Afghanistan, Pakistan, and India all dissect the old concept of Central Asia, and almost all of the borders remain in dispute.

From Kashgar, I traveled a section of the Silk Road that cuts northeast across a landscape so buckled and torn that the hills appeared turned on their sides, their black and white bases thrusting into the air like ski jumps. Small slabs of green showed at intervals in the distance. Soon the earth fell away again and flattened into a burnished high desert marked only by occasional sagebrush. Those travelers who somehow crossed the forbidding Pamirs were on their own after Kashgar; before them stretched the desert of Taklimakan, which literally means, "Go in and you won't come out." Beneath its sands, legend says, hundreds of ancient towns lie buried. Few signposts pointed the way to China's heartland. "The continuous line of bones and bodies acted as a gruesome guide whenever we were uncertain of the route," wrote one visitor.

To the north, the desert is walled in by another barrier, the Tian Shan, or Celestial Mountains, whose streams still water the oases they created.

The mountains rise higher and the foliage becomes more lush farther north where a branch off the Silk Road cuts through the Ili Valley, a region where the Chinese-Soviet border blocks the ancient path. The border has also divided the rugged Central Asian people called the Kazaks.

Near Ürümqi, Xinjiang's capital, I visited a Kazak encampment, where I took to the hills on horseback with an old rider who offered to demonstrate the skills that have always made his people so famous and so feared.

The Kazak dug his heavy boots into the belly of his spindly-legged, broad-chested mount, and we began to gallop side by side through the rain. We loped past bluebells and waterfalls up the steep side of a forested ridge. We rode straight up without traversing back and forth, and I had to lean up over the horse's bobbing head to keep from falling backwards off the hard, pommelless saddle. On the flats I got in front of the old man and turned in the saddle to watch him. His long handlebar mustache flew back from his cheeks, just behind the long, fluttering mane of his horse. The old horseman sat so inert and straight-backed in the saddle that it was hard to see where he held on to the running animal at all, as if the motion beneath him was something he understood through some force of blood. His ancestors were challenged by generations of "pacifiers," yet he seemed to have been pacified only a bit. As I watched him glide easily through the rain behind me, I wondered what the

Kazaks were like *before* they were pacified.

Many of the tales of fierce horsemen descending on travelers along the Silk Road or falling from the hills onto yet another army of occupation are stories about the Kazaks. At one time, they and their herds roamed freely from the shores of the Caspian Sea, across the steppes, and well into northern Xinjiang. There are just under a million Chinese Kazaks now, almost all of whom have relatives in the Soviet Union because that's just where they happened to be when the borders were drawn up and down the hills of Central Asia. Kazaks, like other nomads from Xinjiang, often served as vassals and fighting men to a variety of emperors and conquerors. The once-nomadic Uygurs eventually settled down to farming, but the Kazaks have remained dedicated nomads, against long odds. Those living near new settlements the Han have established in Xinjiang come down from the high country after a seasonal absence now and find that more meadowland has been plowed into fields.

The Kazaks still breed their horses, strong, serviceable, high-altitude animals impervious to harsh temperatures, but hardly the magnificent, spirited stallions that animated the imaginations of horse traders and horse thieves along the Silk Road for centuries. "The eagle has his wings," a Xinjiang proverb instructs, "the man his horse."

Heading back to the old man's yurt, or tent, we galloped past a flock of sheep, and a spicy smell climbed the hill through the evergreens and the rain. When we broke into the clear, I saw that a lamb that had been playing with the children earlier in the day had been artfully reduced to 50 or 60 skewers of shish kebab and a broth from which a woman was blowing fat. At our approach, she picked a dripping rack of meat from the fire, waved it in the air, and smiled.

Back in camp a Kazak leader took me into his tent, where his wife was nursing their new daughter, Pretty Flower. He poured some warm goat's milk, and we sat on a bright rug in the middle of his yurt. Even Kazaks who have acquiesced to a more sedentary life continue to live in the felt tents which have served as homes for Kazaks for centuries. Later in the day, commune leaders sat in a circle in another yurt and rolled harsh cigarettes in dirty newsprint. The dream of an independent Islamic-Kazak state still exists in China, said one Kazak who seemed well aware of renascent Islamic nationalism in the Middle East. But an older leader insisted that his people will "remain part of the great Chinese family. Besides," he said, holding his thumb in the air, "if we destroy our relations with them, we're in trouble." Then he pushed his thumb into the dust and ground it back and forth.

Until quite recently, political boundaries have meant little in this region. The nearby border between China and the Soviet Union has been pushed around so many times that the current division between the two nations belies a cultural zone filled with Central Asian horsemen and perhaps the largest concentration of troops in the world.

Our Japanese van traveled 100 miles northwest of Ürümqi. The pitted highway meandered over a landscape so dry and brittle that it cracked and crumbled under foot. A patina of dust coated the inside of the hot van, which had been refitted with small hard benches that could have been borrowed from a doll's house. After a few hours we came to a stretch of desert that 30 years ago was the middle of nowhere. Now it is the Chinese settlement of Shihezi, the "desert pearl." In 1953 a thousand Chinese soldiers were sent to this lonely spot and told to dig up the desert and make a city.

"Oh, it was a wild, yellow land," said Ji Fenyan, one of Shihezi's founders and thus a man known as one of the "old soldiers" to others in the settlement. "There were wolves everywhere and we lived down in holes in the ground. Eight of us would wear harnesses and we'd pull sharpened cannons through the ground to dig canals. We drew straight lines in the earth with machine guns and melted down rifles to make plows." Ji's gray hair was cut in a clean flattop, and his leathery skin had the rosy coloring of people who have grown old in the hot sun.

Now 560,000 people live in and around the thriving city that Ji and his comrades made. Eighteen separate farms cover 375,000 planted acres. Shihezi produces wheat, corn, millet, sugar beets, cotton, and watermelons—one of which weighed more than 100 pounds.

The town has its own movie theater, an eastern Chinese musical troupe, a dance company from Hunan, and a Mandarin language radio and television station, which broadcasts only within the confines of Shihezi. Ninety-seven percent of the residents are Han Chinese, who live in a relatively wealthy world of self-containment. Young people in Shanghai and Peking call such plantations "Han farms"—places that grow Han Chinese to populate the ethnic wilderness of the west.

In Shihezi I was told that "every group in Chinese society is represented here." Yet no resident I talked to knew a single member of the 12 national minorities that comprise some 55 percent of Xinjiang's population. Minority people in nearby villages complained that they are not allowed to enter the lush confines of the "desert pearl" the Han built.

From Shihezi we returned to Ürümqi and then on along the Silk Road by van, running headlong into a wall of desert heat to the southeast. After four hours, the oasis of Turpan appeared, rippling like a dream in the distance.

By late morning, the temperature was 111°F. From the ground, the reflected heat measured 163 degrees—hot enough to start melting my rubber-soled shoes after only a short walk. Every donkey cart on the white streets of Turpan was adorned with a canopy to deflect the pounding sun, and the entire oasis was crosshatched by trellises, thick with vines, reminiscent of the Mediterranean towns to which Turpan was once connected. My eyes were so contracted by the intensity of Turpan's light that people sitting in the deep black shade of the grape arbors appeared only in silhouette, dangling their feet in the muddy irrigation ditches that run past each home or garden. Uygur children streamed from the shade and ran to the edge of the streets to clap at passing cars—a welcome the schools recently taught the kids as the first tourists returned to Turpan. Then the children ran back into the shade, where old men sat sipping ice-cold bowls of tea, eating apricots, and lazily waving fans at vast hordes of flies.

T urpan, the hottest place in China, would have no shade at all if it weren't for the 950 underground canals, or *karez*, which bring water from hills three miles away. The karez were developed in Central Asia, and came along the Silk Road into China with peaches, pomegranates, and long-staple cotton. The grapes, which also came down the road from Bactria (roughly where Afghanistan is today), produce sweet raisins and 20 kinds of wine, one of which is a clear, caustic substance that could also be used for removing paint.

Despite the karez system, Turpan's farmlands were threatened by encroaching sands in the 1960s. The *karaburan*, or black hurricanes that used to knock entire caravans on their sides, would fly in from the desert at 120 miles an hour and bury people in their homes for days. I was taken to the edge of town and shown a large wall the peasants had built 20 years ago because they thought it would stop the desert as earlier walls had impeded barbarians.

"We didn't know what to do," said a local official. "We didn't get any help from the government. We buried woven branches. We built walls. Then Russian advisors came in 1964 and said 'plant trees,' but that didn't work because we planted them in too large an area, as they did it in Russia."

It wasn't until the early 1970s that Turpan farmers, after years of experimenting, came up with the idea of planting the trees closer together, using them as fences or shelterbelts. Knitted rows of sturdy trees now enclose each field. Outside the shelterbelts, local scientists are testing deep-rooted desert plants in an effort to reclaim some of the cropland the desert took away. The experimental fields lie only a few hundred yards beyond the wall of trees and the thick roof of grapevines that shroud the oasis. The panicles of the plants look as delicate and brittle as old coral as they stand alone in the powerful sun, like outcasts.

Beyond the carefully nurtured plants, the Silk Road snakes deeper into the coruscating heat. I covered this stretch of territory by train, following the rails that parallel the ancient highway. The old route staggers through a reach of gobi that the wind has sifted down to a spongy dark floor studded with sharp pebbles. "As the horse steps on broken bits of stone, its hoofs bleed," a Silk Road traveler complained long ago.

For hundreds of miles—all the way from Turpan to Dunhuang—a series of ancient gates and towers rises up on this rude ground, and hundreds of sandy domes mark the undisturbed tombs of Han Dynasty citizens who came to guard the western edge of their world. The few tombs that have been opened revealed elegant chambers at the bottom of long stairways that lead 40 feet under the sand. The walls were covered in brick paintings that showed ancient plowing and silkworm feeding—and on one brick, the mating of the huge "heavenly stallions" of Central Asia with smaller Chinese mares.

This part of China is an archaeological sandbox. Every oasis peasant I talked to had found Tang, Persian, and Roman coins and bits of antique pottery in the fields. Some even pulled fanciful Tang hors d'oeuvres—petrified bits of food—from the earth. Others told of plowing up human bodies and preserved camels. Every local museum along the road had swatches of ancient silk that were finer of weave and bore more sophisticated patterns than anything produced today. Bamboo and wood shards that antedate the invention of paper have also been unearthed, bearing travel visas, drug prescriptions, and supply orders inscribed in languages devised thousands of miles from where these fragments were found.

Here, where the wind and sand advance and retreat in a fickle rhythm of their own, the visitor may stumble upon an ancient drinking vessel or a time-worn watchtower that rises over the landscape with all the lonely power of old things in a flat place. Outside of Dunhuang I climbed a 2,000-year-old watchtower, which stood a few miles off the caravan trail. Along these walls, sentinels once guarded the Chinese frontier and the Silk Road, whose northern and southern arms rejoin near Dunhuang after defining the edges of the Taklimakan Desert. On top of the watchtower I found bundles of reeds still at the ready. ("Light one bundle," the ancient instructions said, "if 1,000 barbarians are coming. Light four bundles for 5,000 invaders and five bundles for 10,000.") After a few moments of crouching next to the reeds, my temples felt seared by the desert heat; and my brain felt as if it had turned to fur.

On the jarring jeep ride back to Dunhuang, I thought about how fitting it was that Buddhism came into this earthly inferno so long ago, offering snow-faced gods and a world of eternal peace. There was even a chance to come out of the sun and observe gorgeous earthly depictions of the new religion's promise in the cool of a dark cave.

I entered one of the most beautiful of these chambers in Dunhuang, where twin bodhisattvas posed on either side of a Buddha and stared sweetly into the darkness. Delicate silk robes fell from one shoulder of each bodhisattva, and down past each round belly. Their sensuous red lips and arching eyebrows conveyed a sense of graceful compassion and peace. Twenty Chinese soldiers entered the cave, and we stood there swaying quietly as the beam of a guide's flashlight drew our eyes up and around the twirls and swirls on the walls and ceiling surrounding the sculptures. Tang paintings covered every inch of the walls where the dancing beam of light fell, bringing forth sailing fairies and banners, flowers, flecks of gold, and lotus patterns from the darkness. The soldiers had traveled considerable distance to see these famous dark temples bored into a small mountain. The 496 caves contain 2,000 sculptures and 54,000 square yards of painting, an immovable repository of ten centuries of Chinese and Central Asian art. The art on display highlights the vacillating intricacy and sophistication of Chinese art as well as varied levels of foreign influences. Painted on the walls were the dances and instruments I'd seen at the Kashgar wedding. The walls also bore the shade of sea green I'd seen on pots in Ürümqi, on banners at Shihezi, and in Turpan tombs. The rhythmic silk patterns Uygur women wear today were painted on the walls of these caves centuries ago.

The leading families of Dunhuang, all "clever in worldly affairs and erudite in Buddhism," according to one scholar, endowed much of the brilliant artwork in the hills here. "The biggest families would have a son who wanted to go off to fight or trade," explained a professor of art at Dunhuang, "so they would build a cave when he left. If he came back safely they'd build another. But when the traffic on the Silk Road slowed down, the big families moved away. The richer the society," he added, "the richer its art."

One early evening a week later I stood on a train platform in a tiny mining village in eastern Gansu Province, far from the world of wealth and art of ancient Dunhuang. Giggling, dirty-faced children and their parents surrounded two men whose own faces were black with coal dust. The men held a long pole on which a monkey did tricks for the laughing crowd. The keepers yanked the monkey to the ground, and one miner took off his cap and passed it through the crowd, but nobody offered money. He announced that the monkey would not perform again until at least one person in the large crowd produced some cash. The hat went around again. Each child gazed up hopefully at his parents as the cap approached, and each parent stared at the next set of parents as it passed by. It was only after the cap had gone full circle that the crowd seemed to realize that nobody had any money to give. And they all turned and shambled away.

Modern Gansu Province is a long way from the wealth the art professor mentioned in Dunhuang. After the Silk Road fell into disuse, bad times came to Gansu to stay. There were bandits and invasions, ravaging droughts, and political upheavals such as a late 19th-century uprising which reduced the population by hundreds of thousands—some say millions.

I got off a slow train through Gansu in the gray steel town of Jiayuguan, 200 miles east of Dunhuang. I stayed in a guest house which was comfortable, but it had been constructed in a small courtyard surrounded by a mammoth stamping machine, ancient blast furnaces, a pig iron foundry, and giant machines which grabbed ore-filled railroad cars and turned them upside down to empty them—all night long. After sitting up through a night of whooshing, smashing, and jangling sounds outside the window, I emerged from bed wondering how to get the iron filings out of my throat.

Jiayuguan was plunked down in the middle of the desert some 25 years ago during a period of such radical industrialization that the Chinese declared their economy would soon catch up with that of Great Britain. Mao Zedong called it the Great Leap Forward.

"We don't call it that any more," an official at the steel mill said quickly.

"What do you call it?" I asked.

"We don't refer to it at all any more," he said.

The city sits astride the Silk Road in a narrow defile between the snow-capped Qilian Mountains and the black Mazong range, a few miles from a hulking, crenellated fortress that used to guard the entrance to Ming China. The mountains and fort were often shrouded in the mill's haze. A few days after I arrived, a violent sandstorm blew in from the desert to the north, turning day into night in Jiayuguan. Bicyclists stopped in the street to protect their faces, and people ran into alcoves and doorways to try and catch a breath.

Three miles from town at a commune, the sandstorm was followed by a shower of hail, which drove the entire bean crop into the ground. The night before the hail, rain floated away much of the commune's topsoil. "Some things haven't changed since Liberation," a commune leader said as we looked at the lifeless beanstalks. "You should see the droughts and the frost."

Long Yuhai, one of the local farmers, sat on a small stool next to an old wooden desk that was propped high on stilts to protect it from the water that enters his house on some days. There was a sewing machine on the desk and the walls were covered with maps, posters, and drawings that were rough approximations of the Dunhuang paintings. There were photographs of Mao, photographs of the young Long Yuhai in a variety of martial postures, an old canteen, and a broad-brimmed straw hat stained by sweat and glazed by sun. Long said he had just passed his 58th birthday.

"I was a shepherd boy," he said. "I went to school for only three months, but I still understood Mao and came to explain him to the people. Then Mao got rid of the thieves, the gamblers, and the opium. Right in this place people lay around smoking opium. They never ate. I helped with land reform and things got much better here until 1959. . . ."

"The Great Leap Forward," I said.

"We don't call it that any more," Long said. "But in 1960 things got very bad, and then in 1961 my mother starved to death right over here." Long began to blink, then looked away from the hard bed in a corner of his house.

No one knows the precise number of people the famine killed in China between 1959 and 1961—as many as 14 million, according to conservative estimates. I asked Chinese between 30 and 60 years old about their parents, and many told me that they died in 1960 or 1961, and left it at that.

At that time Gansu was run by an official named Zhang Chongliang, a man who lied to Zhou Enlai about the horrifying conditions in order to appear patriotic. "We were too good here in Gansu," said Long Yuhai. "We were too good and patriotic, so we ate grass and bark." He talked about the Cultural Revolution, when he was forced to wear a dunce cap and clean out latrines. He began to talk about recent problems. Then he stopped. "Oh," he said. "I just don't want any new enemies—that's all. Things always change."

A few days later, as the long train chugged east through the narrow Gansu corridor, the insipid piped-in music was interrupted by transmission of a "historic" speech by Hu Yaobang, who had been named Communist Party chairman just the day before.

I walked through the train to find someone who was listening, but nobody was. A few years ago each passenger would probably have been standing at attention in the aisles, staring reverently at the nearest loudspeaker. But things, as Long Yuhai said, tend to change.

I found myself scanning the rows of heads for bright scarves or any other sign of the bright, eclectic cultures I'd seen at the oases. In retrospect, the Uygurs and Kazaks seemed all color and twinkling eyes, all shouts and grins. Along the last 600 miles of the Silk Road, I had seen the light flatten out and the colors mute in palpable abatement. The food became bland and basic, and people were more subdued, more plainly dressed.

But one thing was consistent all along the Silk Road: the sound of China working. Whether in restaurants, homes, or factories; in the offices of academics, intellectuals, or political officials, I heard the sounds of whips on the backs of camels or mules and the revving of tractor engines. From Kashgar to Xian, I heard in the background the cranking of small cement mixers, the scraping sound of shovels on the ground, the banging of hammers, or the cracking of rock.

My train coursed through fields now yellow with rapeseed, and then at the top of a rise the city of Xian, the eastern terminus of the old caravan route, came into view. Near Xian I would visit the tombs of the great emperors who had sent soldiers and traders out along the Silk Road and who had welcomed exotic travelers bearing gifts and strange tales from the west. In modern Xian I would also find electric streetcars rolling down wide, paved boulevards. There would be long limousines bearing high-level Chinese officials, who prefer polyester cloth to silk.

The wild west behind me seemed so different. I'd seen soldiers guarding borders once patrolled by Han Dynasty warriors. Cars had seemed out of place in the donkey-filled streets of the oasis towns. I'd traveled the Silk Road through a land of old-fashioned pioneers and proud, tall men, who wear robes and carry silver daggers—a place where nomads gallop up hillsides on horseback just because their ancestors did it that way too.

Whale-backed Muztagata—Ice Mountain Father—breaches at 24,757 feet in the Chinese Pamirs, literally the "high, wide, grassy valleys between mountains." Through them coursed strands of the Silk Road, fabled route of caravans bearing not only silk but jade, tea, spices, and gold. Although motor vehicles have largely replaced camels, doughty Bactrians (above) still serve roadless areas, transporting goods to market and moving herdsmen's camps.

Living off stored calories, the twin-humped animal can travel a week or more without eating. It drinks seldom but deeply, swilling 25 gallons of water at a time. A "lean beast grows fat here in ten days," Marco Polo said of Pamir pastures. Today nomadic Tajik and Kirgiz graze yaks, horses, sheep, and goats as well as camels on the high grasslands.

At the foot of Muztagata (opposite) a Muslim camel driver kneels toward Mecca. Kirgiz centuries ago accepted Islam, which—like Buddhism—entered China over the Silk Road.

OVERLEAF. Curious citizens eye the camera for an impromptu civic portrait in Kashgar's central square. A trading hub of the vast Xinjiang region, the city seems more Middle Eastern than Chinese. Behind the clock tower sprawls Id Kah Mosque, said to be the largest in China with room for 8,000 worshipers. To the right of the shrub-lined plaza, government buildings squat in the haze; to the left is parkland.

Earl Kowall. Opposite: Galen Rowell

Dawn's haze silhouettes Uygur villagers filing to a Kashgar market (left). Afoot and on donkey carts, they travel thoroughfares once crowded with trade caravans carrying cargo from such distant points as Samarkand and Hamadan. Junction of the Silk Road's north and south arms that embraced the Taklimakan Desert, Kashgar served as a gateway for nationalities and religions. The roadside mosque typifies the small shrines that local Muslim families build.

Adobe-like bricks of mud, straw, and salt form Kashgar houses. Workmen (above) strip bark from plane tree poles and erect a framework for a courtyard wall. Higher walls deflect blowing sand. On some roofs piles of camel's thorn protect drying fruit from prying children.

199

S haped like bagels and pancakes, crusty nan awaits hungry customers at a Kashgar bazaar (left). The veiled vendor and her squinting partner are Uzbeks.

Of the city's many ethnic minorities, the most numerous are Turkic-speaking Uygurs, such as the blacksmith and his apprentice sons forging a farm tool (below). Most Uygurs farm fields watered by snowmelt. Others work in state-run crafts cooperatives, textile factories, or carpet mills. One local industry turns out musical instruments.

A Tajik herdsman (opposite), hands gnarled by years of roping horses, seems soothed by the sound of his own music. Sheepskin tambourines, souna horns, and long-necked dutars also lend exotic sounds to Kashgar. In the speech and music of its people, one hears the echoes of many lands and cultures.

201

Earl Kowall. Opposite: Ned Gillette. Overleaf: Bruce Dale

Uygur craftsmen fashion trunks (above) as wedding gifts for Kashgar's well-to-do. Lacquered and brass-trimmed, a trunk may endow a bride's family—or a groom's, if the girl is eager to marry.

Decorative burial markers—shaped like caskets—grace the mausoleum (opposite) of Apak Hodja, 17th-century Muslim leader described as "Kashgar's patron saint." Shrouds protect patterned surfaces from dust. Heads of Apak families got large tombs; their children, smaller ones. Burials were beneath the markers, for Muslim tradition dictates that bodies must touch the ground. Legend holds that Apak's granddaughter Xiangfei rests beside him, but scholars believe her tomb is more symbolic than real. Chosen to be a wife of Emperor Qian Long, she was borne on a litter to Peking—a three-year journey. She died within a year, possibly by her own hand, and was buried near Peking.

OVERLEAF. Celestial Lake, where immortals were said to feast on ripe peaches, lures visitors from Ürümqi, capital of the Xinjiang Uygur Autonomous Region. Blue waters more than a mile high mirror Tian Shan peaks draped in dragon spruce. On icy slopes grows the fabled snow lotus. Renowned for medicinal properties, it is said to have "magic powers that save life on the verge of death." Kazaks use it to treat arthritis.

202

The furrowed face of a Kazak farmer (above) bespeaks Turk and Mongol heritage. Shouldering a scythe to cut hay near Ürümqi—Beautiful Pasture—he has the security of a commune while preserving old ways.

Nomadic life persists in a Kazak camp pitched on a Tian Shan meadow (opposite). Her kitchen an open pit, a mother cooks bread in a greased wok as her youngster hovers nearby. Water heats in a kettle for milk tea—a mixture of black tea, sheep's milk, and butter. Kumiss, fermented mare's milk, also slakes thirst.

The woman saves a pot of coals to warm the damp yurt. On the rack of lashed poles she airs felt bedding and hangs clothes. Before snows come, Kazaks dismantle their domed, tentlike homes and move down the mountain.

Their stage a Turpan courtyard, Uygur dancers swirl beneath a canopied grape arbor (above). Despite a Death Valley climate, grapes and melons thrive in the oasis city astride the Silk Road. Snowmelt from Tian Shan heights flows through miles of karez, or subterranean aqueducts, to irrigate vineyards and gardens.

Seedless white grapes (left) flourish in Turpan's hot, dry summers. City of wine and raisins, it became famous for "mare teat" grapes, introduced about the seventh century. Winery workers (far left) fill almost a million bottles a year.

OVERLEAF. Near Dunhuang in western Gansu Province, the sand mountains are said to thunder when sand slides occur. In quieter times, heedless flocks forage in the shadow of mountains named Ming Sha, or "singing sand."

Bruce Dale (also upper and left). Overleaf: James L. Stanfield

209

HHoneycombed cliffs (upper) near Dunhuang, storied Silk Road oasis, form an extension of the famed Caves of the Thousand Buddhas. In A.D. 366 the wandering monk Luo Zun saw at sunset on Mount Sanwei glittering lights that gave the illusion of countless Buddhas. Inspired, he hewed a grotto in the rock. Over the next ten centuries artisans carved myriad rectangular chambers, covering walls and ceilings with paintings. Statues, some towering close to 100 feet, filled the rooms. A hidden library yielded thousands of scrolls written in Chinese, Tibetan, Sanskrit, even unknown languages.

A Peking art student (lower) copies a Tang Dynasty procession of horsemen, palanquins, and courtiers. Another Tang masterpiece depicts Sakyamuni, Buddhism's founder, riding through a sky strewn with flowers (right). Angelic creatures with streaming ribbons cushion his steed's hooves.

212

Mountains of cotton bear witness to agricultural vigor in China's arid west. At a Dunhuang purchasing depot a modern conveyor vacuums the contents of primitive carts and spews a blizzard of fluff from its nozzle (above).

Workers in Gansu communes toil to make the desert bloom. They cut irrigation channels through sand ridges and plant trees to stabilize banks. In sheltered fields they grow spring wheat, legumes, and potatoes as well as cash crops—deep-rooted cotton, sesame, hemp. Rubber-tired carts pulled by donkeys, horses, and camels trundle goods to market (opposite). Traders brought cotton to China over the Silk Road in the third century. A Buddhist pilgrim to India reported that cotton cloth was made from "thread of a wild silkworm."

215

Clouds of dust blot out the sun, darkening Lanzhou on the Yellow River. When the wind dies, a pall of pollution is apt to linger, spewed from the stacks and towers of industrial plants. Once a stop for Silk Road caravans, the sprawling city of two million serves today as hub for highway, rail, and air routes to northwest China. Petrochemical factories, an oil refinery, and machine works line the river. Hydroelectric dams tap its power and prevent floods. Since the 1960s Lanzhou has cradled China's atomic energy industry. But the land itself accounts for the area's main industry, farming, which occupies some 80 percent of the workers. Loess, wind-borne silt, blankets central China with fertile layers reaching 300-foot depths. Despite little rainfall, the good soil around Lanzhou yields bountiful harvests of melons and other fruits. To preserve precious moisture, farmers mulch cultivated fields with pebbles and sand.

Lowell Georgia (also left and opposite)

The Great Mosque at Xian, its entrance casting a shadow on carved dragons (opposite), resembles a Buddhist temple. Islam took root in Xian, the ancient Chinese capital and eastern terminus of the Silk Road, in the 8th century. The restored buildings date mainly from the 14th century.

The imam, in Persian-style robes (above), stands in the minbar overlooking the prayer hall. Above him an Arabic inscription from the Koran proclaims that "teaching benefits the believers." With the mosque often filled to overflowing, worshipers, their shoes removed, pray on the stones of the courtyard (left).

THE NORTHWARD FLOW OF TRIBUTE

By Robert M. Poole

Photographs by George F. Mobley

Behind the watchman, a window of the guardhouse had been thrown open to the black spring night of Hangzhou, where the Grand Canal begins its 1,100-mile crawl along the eastern coast of China. I was waiting for dawn with Shi, the watchman who makes sure all boats are properly moored and registered on this stretch of water. We passed the time with few words and countless cups of green tea, waiting for sunrise to bring the jolt of noise and movement. It did. As soon as night dissolved at the window, shouts rose from the canal, along with the labored sound of wooden oars slapping on water. Shi pulled his cap on and led me out. There in the soft morning light, sampans edged out of a fog and advanced one by one toward the boat house, much as they have since this part of the canal opened 1,400 years ago. Now as then, peasants nosed their vessels into the soft clay banks and prepared to meet the day.

Two women in long pigtails trudged ashore with shoulder-pole baskets brimful with nuts and disappeared down a cobbled sidewalk in the direction of the market. A man rinsed cabbages close by, and stacked them in baskets. Another emerged, groggy, from a tent on his boat, groped for his black canvas

A solitary junk ripples the sunset waters of Lake Tai.

shoes and pulled them on. He shoved off and sculled downstream, joining the morning rush hour on one of the world's oldest and longest canals.

In the making for at least 24 centuries, the canal curves like a scar across the face of China, covering ten degrees of latitude from Hangzhou (Hangchow) to Peking, roughly the distance from Tampa to New York City. It is one of those Chinese engineering marvels created, in the words of one scholar, by "a million men with teaspoons." He guessed low. Millions dug it.

In its best days, it was called the Bridle on the Dragons because it crossed five major rivers—the dragons—and turned them to the will of man. Though diminished, it still traces parts of its old beat, rising in the garden cities of the south, sliding north across the Yangtze Valley, and creeping past the Shandong mountains before it meets the Yellow River on the North China Plain. There it flags, a victim of too much silt and too little rainfall. Between the Yellow River and Tianjin (Tientsin), short sections remain open. From Tianjin to

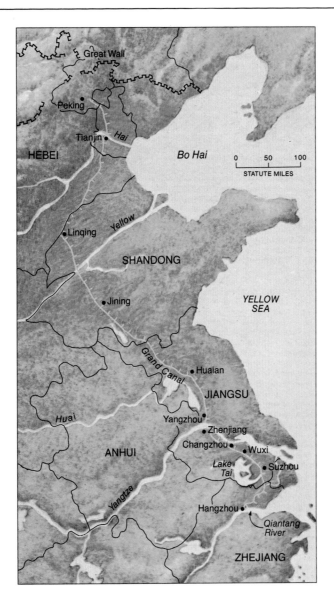

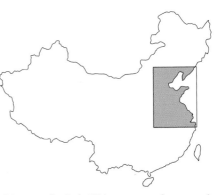

Nature denied China a south-to-north river, so its rulers built their own. Begun about 2,400 years ago, the Grand Canal is still in use over much of its 1,100-mile length. Robert M. Poole followed the old waterway from its southern terminus at Hangzhou to Tianjin, where the canal becomes unnavigable. His two-month journey led from the lush mid-south, where farmers grow two or three crops of rice each year, to China's dust bowl, where the earth barely supports a single wheat crop. Poole interviewed bargemen, artisans, storekeepers, ferry passengers, factory workers, fishermen, and others who call the canal their home.

Peking, the waterway dies, utterly dry. My journey ended in Tianjin.

My plan was to follow the old waterway from the lush green south to the dusty north, staying as close to the canal and its people as possible. I traveled hundreds of miles by cargo barge, train, passenger ferry, fishing junk, tug-boat, automobile, and, at one point, borrowed bicycle. Only my request to ship aboard a manure boat was summarily rejected.

I started in Hangzhou, a city that had stirred poets and enchanted travelers long before Marco Polo pronounced it the noblest and finest in the world. The Venetian traveler marveled at its sheer size, at its huge communal baths, and at courtesans "adorned with much finery, highly perfumed . . . and here in such numbers as I dare not venture to report."

With time, the luxurious baths have disappeared and the ranks of the courtesans have thinned to nothing. But time has not diminished the delicate grace of Hangzhou. I saw it in the city's soft blue mountains, in its bustling tea-houses, in its shade-mottled streets.

From the start, those who came to Hangzhou seemed more interested in commerce and culture than in war. Beset by Jürchen nomads from the north, the Song Dynasty retreated here in the 12th century to establish its capital at a safe distance from battle. Instead of armies, they built palaces and gardens. And as other Chinese fled south to escape the nomads, Hangzhou became the world's largest city, with a population exceeding one million.

From Precious Stone Hill, which commands the best view of Hangzhou, I saw that the age-old beauty endures. I climbed the mountain one afternoon in April, after rain had scattered most of the sightseers who normally crowd the long green ridge overlooking West Lake.

The lake lay half-concealed in drizzle, rimmed on three sides by distant mountains. Swathed in clouds that raced before the wind, the mountains floated in and out of view, as in a dream. On the water, a group of long, low boats drifted, no more than dark shapes on the flat gray lake until, from one boat, a silhouette arose, a fisherman casting his lines. I watched him cast and haul, cast and haul, until he glided out of sight behind an island.

Turn north on Precious Stone Hill and you see another side of the city. Here is the face of working Hangzhou, where the tile-roofed houses of old are overshadowed by brick apartments with balconies and plate-glass windows. New smokestacks rise where pagodas stood. But the old emphasis on commerce remains. In crowded markets and specialty stores one can buy silk parasols and the famed green tea, Dragon Well, grown in the nearby hills.

The canal flows through this commercial district, paralleling East Huancheng Road, an old market street lined with the dappled-bark plane trees that grow all over southern China. I explored the neighborhood one morning, walking downstream from a traditional pharmacy that sells lizard skins and tiger-bone tonic, to a wharf where ten barges were tied up. Stevedores were unloading a cargo the Chinese have venerated throughout history, silkworm cocoons. The cocoons are gathered from the surrounding countryside and stuffed into 44-pound bags, which are shipped down the canal to this point.

Workers hoist the lumpy white sacks on their shoulders here and pile the cocoons on carts, which take them to the silk factories a few blocks away. There the fuzzy covering of the larva is reeled off to make silk thread.

I climbed onto one of the wooden barges still half full of bags. The musty smell of cocoons surrounded me as I settled on a gunwale to watch a man working on the opposite side of the boat. He concentrated on threading a needle, with which he soon began stitching a ripped bag that had leaked cocoons onto the deck. He did not look up, but proceeded at the slow, confident pace I came to recognize as the standard in China. One never gets the sense that people are working against deadlines here; steadiness is valued over speed.

When I looked again, my needle man was three boats away, preparing to jump to the fourth. He probed cocoon sacks and dodged the dogs, chicken coops, potted plants, and hanging laundry in his path. All signs indicated that the members of this cocoon fleet lived on their vessels, a fact confirmed by Ji Shiben, a stocky, square-headed man who invited me over to his barge.

We sat on lumpy cocoon bags in the warm sun, rocking slightly in the wake of passing traffic, while Ji's wife cooked in the cabin. Ji was born on a boat, a third-generation waterman who believes that life on the canals is perhaps the freest in China, where one's work often restricts mobility.

"We're seeing different cities all the time," said Ji, who sat yoga-style, his legs tucked beneath him. He looked at the clear sky. "When I'm floating on the canal on a day like this, it makes me feel good. I think this is the best life."

A few days later, I took my first trip on the Grand Canal, and knew what Ji meant. I felt the surge of anticipation that I imagine Ji must feel each time he sets out on a voyage. I was bound north from Hangzhou with a string of barges that carried 789 tons of cargo—tea, gravel, hemp, and cardboard. Alone in the bow of our pilot boat, I watched Hangzhou disappear, its white plaster cottages and arched bridges gradually replaced by a rolling countryside of yellow rapeseed. Peasants in straw hats moved through green mulberry foliage, picking leaves that would fatten the year's second crop of silkworms.

Boats passed us in both directions, some with sails patched together in crazy-quilt designs of every imaginable fabric—faded fertilizer bags, clear plastic squares, blue-checked cotton, and translucent canvas—all reminding me that the Chinese throw away virtually nothing.

Our barges were lashed end to end with steel cables so that the vessels, towed by a pilot boat at the head of the line, moved as one in serpentine fashion up the canal and around its bends. I worked my way down the line, leaping from barge to barge until I found myself five vessels back in the company of a barrel-chested man in a white shirt and dark pants. He was Zhou Ziai, who has worked as a canal pilot for about 40 years.

Zhou gave me tea and we settled back in the shade of his cabin to enjoy the slow ride. To starboard, three small boats lay low in the water near the muddy bank, sunk almost out of sight under the weight of their cargo of boulders. Unassisted by anything except strong backs and firm grips, workers strained to lift the stones, one by one, from the boats and heave them to the bank above, where other workers would build a wall reaching back down to the water. The shoring up of the dikes could be a picture from a hundred or a thousand years ago. The work proceeds now much as it did then.

My fellow traveler, Zhou, was following the line of the canal with his eye. Perhaps he knew what I was thinking.

"They say this was all made by men," he said. "When I was little, I listened to the old men talk about the history of this place. Sometimes when I'm out here at night, I think of those old men and the history."

It began as early as the fourth century B.C. with the Hong Gou Canal, used to ferry troops between the Yellow River and the Huai River Valley, a distance of some 250 miles. The Hong Gou (Canal of the Wild Geese, or Far-Flung Conduit) eventually would silt up and fall into disuse, but it formed the model for the Grand Canal. The great waterway uncoiled by stages across China's intractable landscape as countless peasants shoveled earth, lifted stones, hauled soil, uprooted trees, and patched dikes in the service of the emperors.

Manpower was the key to such huge projects—manpower and human suffering of staggering magnitude. The most impressive construction in ancient China occurred under the cruelest rulers, such as the Sui Dynasty emperor Yang Di. Yang Di assumed power in 604, reportedly by poisoning his father. He pressed northward with a canal that would connect the Huai River Valley and the Yangtze River, a project his father had launched. The young emperor also extended the canal south from the Yangtze to Hangzhou, laying out the basic route the watercourse still follows across southern China.

Yang Di's project required a labor force of 5.5 million. In some areas all males between 15 and 50 were forced to work with an armed guard of 50,000 watching over them. Those who did not cooperate were punished "by flogging and neck weights" or beheading. Every fifth family was made to furnish one of its members to supply and prepare food for the workers and guards.

Yang Di's canal was finished in just six years—a 1,500-mile, Y-shaped waterway linking south and north China for the first time, an important step in the nation's reunification. During construction, two million workers were *zhe,* an imprecise word which means something like "lost" but does not explain whether the two million fell ill, fled, or died.

The canal was primarily a one-way street—a highway for southern grain sent north to support the emperor and his imperial army. As the waterway grew, so did the cities in its path. Suzhou (Soochow), my next stop after Hangzhou, flourished as a center for shipping, culture, and grain storage in the seventh century soon after the Grand Canal linked it to the Yellow River, some 300 miles to the north. Now an industrial city with a population of about

600,000, Suzhou is still identified with its sister city, Hangzhou, as a place of graceful living and natural beauty: "Above is Paradise," goes an old Chinese saying, "below are Hangzhou and Suzhou."

The phrase seemed apt as I approached Suzhou by rail on an April afternoon. Trees flickered past the window, interrupting the sunlight at regular intervals as we clacked through a marshy countryside thick with greening rice and lavender clover. It is a region where water seems as prevalent as land. The city itself is encircled by canals and stitched through with interlocking waterways that give it the look of Venice. Like Venice, Suzhou is a city of waterfront houses and flying bridges. Boatmen pole and scull their sampans on the black water, threading around each other in the narrow passages between stone embankments. Cottages rise from the mossy banks, as if they are all a piece of the same slab of rock that thrusts above the water. On typical residential streets, many houses show two faces—one for the street, one for the canal.

Walking through the city, one sees remnants of the old grandeur that once blossomed in the gardens of rich officials and merchants. Retreating from the noisy city around them, these men built their own worlds in elaborate private landscapes.

In these gardens, some now restored and open to the public, the Chinese fondness for mental gamesmanship is manifest. Man-made streams suggest miniature rivers. Boulders hauled from nearby lakes are carefully chosen for their shape and texture, then cemented together in mounds resembling mountains. Gnarled trees, twisted by the human hand to look storm-blasted, rise in tiny courtyards at every turn.

Artifice is the operating principle, for the garden designers were simulating wilderness in the heart of a crowded city. So they depended on optical illusion to make spaces seem bigger than they really are: A blue stone pathway curves down a hillside and out of sight by a wall, inviting the visitor to discover what lies around the bend. There he finds a pond spangled with lotus and bridged by walkways winding in several directions. One of these leads by the pond to a dead-end wall in which windows are cut to reveal other scenes of bamboo and pine beyond, beckoning the visitor to continue through a half-hidden passageway to the side.

Just after sunrise one morning, I sat in a bamboo chair and gazed across a green pond in the Humble Administrator's Garden, imagining what it must have been like to live amid Suzhou's literati a few centuries ago. The greatest of these artists, Wen Zhengming, helped design and build the garden I enjoyed. He lived a few feet from the pond, which now rippled with reflections of surrounding pavilions and rocks. Surely Wen and his friends sat here on a morning like this and discussed how one would paint such a scene.

Now the garden is a favorite meeting place for the old-timers of Suzhou, who begin drifting in when the gates open each morning. Most come singly. They stake out positions on a portico rimming the Hall of Distant Fragrance teahouse, where some of them have met each day for 40 years. They go through a routine, rearranging chairs and setting out tea tins, cigarettes, matches, and cups in preparation for the morning. Everything is just so. Attendants soon come round with kettles trailing steam, and fill the cups.

I take a place at a table with four aged workers in horn-rimmed glasses and dark blue caps.

"Take a look at us," says a former factory worker of 85. "We're all old heads. We come here because it is a good, relaxing place to sit." He sips from a cup which proclaims in red letters that he is "Retired With Glory." The old men talk about opera, current events, and "lighter" topics, he says.

Beneath the surface calm, though, there is uneasiness in the garden. Huang Mingcai, an 82-year-old raised on a diet of Confucian ethics, is concerned about changing values. "We have far too many people," he acknowledges, but he questions hard-line policies on birth control. And, like old people everywhere, he wonders what the younger generation is coming to.

"They're cursing and hitting each other in the streets," he says with a pained look. Huang is afraid to go out at night. "In the old days, we had a Confucian moral underpinning to our society. Now it is gone. Because the emphasis is on jobs for all the young people, it means that I have to cook for myself and look after myself when I go home from here."

Elsewhere in Suzhou, new things cause other problems, as the rush to modernization often obscures—literally—the city's age-old beauty. One muggy afternoon in May, I stood atop the Suzhou Hotel and watched a famous landmark, the Tiger Hill Pagoda, melt from view in smog. I shut my hotel windows at night to keep out the pollution. And along the canals, one finds people washing food, dishes, clothes, and night-soil buckets in the same water, despite red-lettered signs warning against the practice.

To its credit, Suzhou is trying to clean up. New gardens rise along the sidewalks. As I left town, an official told me things will be put right within a decade. "You'll hear birds singing on every street, and the town will be full of beautiful flowers and trees."

I swung onto the canal again, this time with three boats lashed into single-file formation, bound for Wuxi, 25 miles upstream. We carried two tons of toothpaste, six tons of automobile batteries, twenty tons of steel, and other cargo. A breeze blew, pulling with it the smell of breakfasts and coal smoke from the tiny boats that danced at their moorings on both sides of the canal.

We passed around a bend, and the home of Xia Tangbao, a woman I had visited two days before, appeared across the coffee-colored water—an old wooden barge tied up at canalside. It had a canvas roof held on by scattered bricks and boards. As we floated by, she did not look up, so all I saw was her gray head leaning into a bank of black coal smoke from her stove. She was cooking breakfast on the afterdeck. At 55, Xia Tangbao is plump and slow-moving, and has never lived on dry land. She yearns for a house, "a place by the canal with big windows so the breezes could come in."

Out in the open countryside, peasant boats outnumbered the barges that predominated in cities, and I began to see fishing huts with nets deployed at regular intervals on the water. Again and again, the nets came up empty, but a crewman assured me that fishing was good. I had not watched long enough, he said. "We have an old saying: 'Ten nets, nine empties; one net, success.'"

At length the canal narrowed and filled with traffic, and I saw the smooth green hulk of Hui Mountain gradually enlarge against the blue sky, signaling our approach to Wuxi.

The town originally was called Youxi (which means "with tin") for the mines that thrived here 2,000 years ago. Youxi became Wuxi ("without tin") when the mines were depleted during the Han Dynasty. Now a resort and manufacturing city of 750,000 people, Wuxi also maintains its role as a major shipping center, a position it has held since the first great grain fleet came sailing up the Grand Canal in the seventh century.

By five in the morning, Wuxi was humming. Entrepreneurs sold sugarcane, books, straw mats, and headboards for beds in the old commercial district by the canal. A woman hawked breakfasts of rice, porridge, greens, pickled vegetables, and *youtiao*. The youtiao, or grease stick, is a favorite food, something like a doughnut, except that it is unsugared and runs in a straight line instead of a circle. The whole meal cost ten fen (about six cents).

Traffic stood still on the water, where passenger boats, barges, and sampans were packed so tightly between the banks that it looked as if I could walk from one side to the other, a distance of 40 yards, without wetting my feet. I hopped a ferry instead, paying the pilot two fen (about a penny) for the two-minute passage. On the other side, I wandered until I came to a stone stairway that led down to the water. Seven or eight people squatted on the bottom step, doing their wash. They beat the dirt out of their clothes with wooden paddles dimpled and worn smooth by time. One woman worked over a shirt: She rinsed it, beat it, rinsed it, brushed it, rinsed it, stamped it with her feet, kneaded it, rinsed it, beat it, kneaded it, rinsed it, beat it, and put it away clean in a metal pan from which she took another shirt, and later a jacket and assorted rags, for washing. In six minutes she had done the whole load.

There was a certain music here, a rhythmical order seen and heard as the washers raised their paddles in the sunlight and brought them whacking down on the bundled laundry by their feet. The order was soon interrupted by a tugboat that pulled in and moored at the steps, transforming the laundry area into a wharf. The washers stood up, holding their dripping clothes.

It was too much for one man. He turned red and jerked the mooring line from a cleat at the tug's bow, shouting at the crew: "Why do you dock here? Why don't you go somewhere else?" A crew member retied the line. The angry washer's shouts were answered by the seven-woman tug crew, now massed at the bow in a show of solidarity. After a few minutes of yelling and arm waving, it was over. The tug left and the washers resumed their work.

228

These conflicts over canal use are nothing new. Two centuries ago the Chinese wrestled with the right-of-way question when the dowager empress Xiao Sheng took to the water with her royal fleet. In deference to her, local officials wanted to clear the canal of ships hauling tax grain to the north. The waterway was too narrow, they reasoned, and the dowager empress should have it to herself. But the local officials were overruled by the emperor Qian Long, who loved his mother but wanted to keep the tribute flowing. He decided the tax boats and the dowager's fleet could maneuver around each other.

North of Wuxi, I followed the route the grain fleets once took up the Grand Canal. On this voyage, my companion was Capt. Li Huaiju, a pilot who has worked on the water for 23 years. He sat at the wheel of a 60-ton vessel. When I asked why he chose a life on boats, he smiled.

"I have always been interested in sailors," he said. "As a young man, I was taken by their uniforms." He gestured, making an imaginary cap brim with his hand, which then swept over each shoulder where the epaulets would be. For 19 years he wore the white hat and uniform of a Yangtze sailor. Now transferred to the Grand Canal, he does not miss the uniform. "I achieved my ideal in the beginning. Now I think of my family."

On days like this, Li also thinks about traffic jams and errant boats, like the one that suddenly strayed across our path. Li jumped. "He's moving too slow." Li's right hand, sheathed in a white glove, pulled back on the throttle. He shouted through a loudspeaker until the boatman rowed out of the way.

It took five hours to cover the 20 or so miles from Wuxi to Changzhou, where Li deposited me, along with his cargo of rubber hoses, screwdrivers, and umbrellas. From Changzhou, I jumped a train to Zhenjiang where, through a series of locks, the Grand Canal meets the Yangtze.

For only 30 fen (about 18 cents), I crossed one of the world's mightiest rivers by ferry. As a foreigner I got special treatment. I walked to a separate window at the terminal and bought a special ticket. I was led to a separate entrance. Chinese passengers stared at me as they waited in line for their tickets. Embarrassed, I hustled alone through my entrance and down a ramp to wait for the sailing of the *New People,* empty except for the crew and me. In a few minutes we had company. The gates opened and about 200 passengers rattled down the gangway, shouting and stampeding and ringing the bells of their bicycles, which were handed to crewmen on the ferry's upper deck. Passengers rode below. An old man bearing a new bed found a place near me.

Soon we were under way, the broad Yangtze spreading smooth and brown behind us, and I was talking to the old man with the bed. He turned out not to be so old, only 53, though a lifetime of tilling the soil had aged him. He had come south from his village near Yangzhou, a full day's journey, to buy the bed for his son. Now he was returning.

"It's for my son's marriage," he said.

"Congratulations," I said. "When is the wedding?"

"He's not planning to get married," he said.

"I thought he was."

"Not yet," he said. "My son is only 20. I am preparing so I'll be ready when the time comes."

Water is the element of the southern Chinese. It serves as their highway and forms a backdrop for their festivals of spring. It nurtures their staple foods—fish and rice. Look around southern China and you will always see someone working in or on the water. Nowhere is this more apparent than in the lower reaches of the Yangtze Valley, where the Grand Canal threads into a network of natural streams and subsidiary waterways that run like filaments of silver through the dark green delta.

Across the river, I drove along the canal to explore this fertile countryside. People were busy in the fields, for it was *sanxia*, the "season of three summers," a time for planting rice, harvesting wheat, and weeding fields.

In the paddies, women stooped in the water, drilling the first rice seedlings of spring into the mud with their fingers. Their hands moved so quickly that I saw only a blur. It looked interesting, so I rolled up my pants and plunged in. To my surprise, it was warm, even pleasing, as the soft mud enveloped my feet. I took a step back and picked up a chunk of turf which held the seedlings. I pinched off a few sprouts, reached down to plant my first rice, and discovered my first mistake. I had walked where the row of rice was to be, which meant that there was only water in the outline of my footprint, where there should have been mud to receive the seedlings. I stopped to fix the mud. I tried again. My seedlings flopped over, disappearing in the water. My rows were crooked. My turf was disintegrating. I was taking too much time. My teacher reminded me that I was planting rice, not doing silk embroidery. I looked back. Peasants who were shoulder to shoulder with me a few minutes before had almost completed their rows. They laughed, and I waded out.

For 100 miles north of the Yangtze Valley, the earth is this way, a moist and sprawling checkerboard of small plots supporting two or three crops of grain each year. Through this region, the Grand Canal runs broad and deep—big enough to carry 600-ton riverboats down to the Yangtze.

I covered this leg of my journey by automobile, rolling along an elevated blacktop road that hugs the canal from Yangzhou to Huaian. It was a hot afternoon in mid-May, but I managed to remain cool on the highway, shaded by tall willows, for which I silently thanked Kublai Khan. He started planting trees along the canal some 700 years ago.

It almost did not happen, this willow-lined canal. When the Mongols roared into China, they found a nation of stay-at-home farmers who sat around watching the crops grow instead of galloping after livestock on horseback. Any self-respecting nomad knew that galloping made more sense.

"Although you have . . . conquered the men of Han, they are no use to us," some advisers told Genghis Khan. "It would be better to kill them all and turn the lands back to pasture so that we can feed our beasts on it."

But one counselor was wiser. "You can have everything you want," he told the khan, urging him to milk the Han for their grain, silk, and silver. "How can you say that the Chinese people are no use to you?" The Mongols took this advice and later began remodeling the Grand Canal (the first serious overhaul in almost 700 years) so they could ship grain more efficiently from the southern breadbasket to their new capital, Peking.

It was a fair arrangement. The north got its rice. The south got political stability and the protection of a strong central government—at least for a time. Both regions benefited from the granaries in which surpluses were stored as a hedge against famine. By 1327 the canal had assumed the route it follows from south to north today.

Throughout the south, I managed to keep the canal in sight. But I had to leave it at Huaian—the dividing line between north and south China—where my hosts routed me around the waterway by airplane, train, and automobile. They did not say why, but I suspect it was because the canal dries up in the north, a part of China that drought and flood have pummeled for centuries.

It shows in the face of Jining, a once-gracious city in southern Shandong Province. The wharves lie idle here, and the Grand Canal squeezes to a trickle, perhaps five feet wide and a few inches deep. Cargo boats lie gripped in mud, waiting, who knows how long, to receive the gray bricks, green drums, and straw mats piled on the docks of the Jining Transportation Company.

"They used to call this place a little Suzhou," said He Weigang, who showed me around the docks. "It was a relatively prosperous place." But new railroads and the lack of rain have taken the canal cargo away. This part of the canal never really recovered from the 19th century, when it was closed to grain traffic during rebellions and floods. People of the region now use it for local transportation and irrigation—when water is available.

Between Jining and the Yellow River, I saw another China, an arid land where villages huddle among trees, their buff-colored houses built of hard-packed earth with thatched roofs, instead of the plaster-and-tile homes of the south. The people are taller, the vegetation sparser.

Driving north from Jining at twilight, I saw something like a sailboat—no, three sailboats—running far ahead of me on the road. I elbowed a companion, who confirmed that I was not hallucinating. Peasants were sailing overland, their sails mounted on masts in their handcarts. As we passed the fleet, I saw one sailor loping along in front of his two-wheeled cart, bracing the front handles in his armpits and running before the wind. His sails were full.

This northern wind is reliable, as plentiful as water in the south. It blows in cold from Siberia in winter, and hot from the East China Sea in summer. Such is the North China Plain, a triangle of land formed by the Huai River Valley, the Yellow Sea, and the Loess Plateau. Nothing on the plain encourages the sort of attachment southern Chinese feel for their land. Wheat grows better than rice here, and oxen or mules replace water buffalo in the field.

Gao Zhenbao prefers mules. "They're faster," he said. Gao should know. For most of his 48 years, he has followed all manner of beast through the fields of the Gao family village northeast of Jining. I caught him ready to plant corn one morning, and he let me follow. We marched through furrows hemmed in by standing wheat. Gao's partner, Song Yutian, went first, leading the mule, followed by Gao and me. I had trouble keeping pace with this entourage, which plowed 150 feet in about two minutes, leaped over a ditch, and laid down more corn at a similar pace on the other side.

Gao and Song talked as they worked, this time about the prospective longevity of their mule.

"He'll be more than 70," said Gao.

"I say 50," said Song.

I asked if they should be talking this way in front of the mule.

"He knows what I'm saying," said Gao. "Look at his ears. He can hear. He doesn't mind. He knows how the world works."

Gao was talking mules, but this is the sort of thing almost anyone in China will tell you about the *people* of Shandong Province: They know how the world works. They are tough, robust, honest, explosive, and willful.

"Shandong people talk louder," said Gao. "And they're not afraid to eat bitterness." Over the years, they have eaten their share. The diet grew so heavy in the 17th century—a time of earthquakes, floods, and rampant banditry—that a local official wondered whether fate was "throwing rocks upon a man who had already fallen in a well."

Those who have survived it all sometimes sniff at their brothers and sisters who have had an easier time of it in the south. I met a Shandong native who dismissed everyone below the 33rd parallel in a word: "Sissies."

From southern Shandong, I drove north along the canal, now silted in for most of its 55-mile course between Jining and the Yellow River. A few small sampans worked along this stretch. From the dikes, I watched the changeful river lolling below me, its seaward movement barely perceptible from this height. Here the Yellow River pulls itself out of the canal's reach, climbing 20 feet above the North China Plain on its heavy bed of silt. To keep pace with that climb, engineers would have to rip out the old canal locks and build new ones every few years. So for the moment, the waters of the river and canal, separated by an earthen dam, mingle no more.

North of the river, the story is much the same. On its 55-mile run to Linqing, the canal is more "dirt road" than waterway, in the words of a Chinese official. The last section I traveled, Linqing to Tianjin, holds a foot or two of water but no boats. It has been useless for navigation for two decades now.

Tianjin once prospered at the Grand Canal's expense. Situated near the Yellow Sea, the city is about 70 miles southeast of Peking. When Mongols established their capital at Peking in the 13th century, Tianjin became its window on the ocean, a receiving port for the tribute grain shipped down the Yangtze, out into the Yellow Sea, and up to Tianjin, a ten-day trip. From there, grain sailed to Peking by canal. This was the alternate route Kublai Khan chose while his Grand Canal was being rebuilt.

As the waterway neared completion, hostility arose between canal proponents and blue-water partisans. They started killing each other. Wang Jiweng, a father of the canal plan so despised by the ocean faction, died on his way to Japan in 1284, probably murdered by sea-route boosters. Long after Kublai Khan's reign, the two contingents were still feuding.

Tianjin won either way, for it faced the canal as well as the sea. As northern China's chief port, it tempted 19th century Europeans to muscle their way in for a share of the lucrative trade.

Now China's third largest city with a population of 7.5 million, Tianjin retains its international flavor. I walked through the old French Concession, where wrought-iron gates sprout fleurs-de-lis and thick Corinthian columns shoulder up turrets and balconies. Across town, I passed a boarded-up synagogue and went into the Kiessling Restaurant, a Russian-German bar and grill in continuous operation since early in this century. "Our chefs can cook anything," said a heavy Chinese waiter in thick glasses and a white jacket. "We've had everybody pass through—Russians, Japanese, Germans."

It is a worldly city, with an outward-looking face one does not often find in other parts of China. Despite all the signs of foreign influence, I saw in Tianjin's people the same enduring qualities of strength and quiet dignity that I had discovered all along my canal journey. Those characteristics seemed distilled in the person of Li Chunai, a sturdy woman who lives in a shack built of salvaged brick and wood, the leavings of the 1976 earthquake that destroyed a large part of Tianjin.

Li Chunai's family of six has a three-room house with cardboard windows, thin walls, and a tarpaper roof. She showed no trace of discontent, and I imagined that she could endure the shack indefinitely, making do as Chinese have done through the centuries.

"My house may be broken down," she said, "but my heart is good."

Later I went outside of Tianjin for a last look at the Grand Canal, the thing that had first drawn me to China. There I found the once-great waterway sprouting weeds. Children dug for water in the dry canal bed, perhaps beneath where an emperor's barge had floated a few hundred years ago.

233

234

Spring fog settles over Hangzhou's West Lake, blurring the distinction between water and sky. Lifted from their earthbound context, pedestrians on willow-lined Bai Causeway might imagine themselves adrift amid the clouds—a notion suited to the city's long association with celestial concerns. Known through much of history as the City of Heaven, Hangzhou's mountains and gardens attracted artist and emperor alike. Mongol rulers so admired the steep-roofed houses (left) that they took them as models for their own palaces and temples in the north. Walkways across the lake bear the names of poet-governors who helped to build a graceful city that time has treated kindly.

Steadfast as the rock on which it stands, Bao Shu Pagoda marks the top of Precious Stone Hill, a venerable counterpoint to the concrete and plate glass of modern Hangzhou. Beyond the high-rises, boatmen work the Grand Canal as they have for centuries, passing under an arched bridge typical of south China (above). The canal, opened here in the seventh century, linked southern rice lands to the imperial capital of Luoyang, transforming sleepy Hangzhou into a commercial center and garden spot. Now a favorite with Chinese and foreign tourists, the city has reopened formal gardens that once were the preserve of merchants and emperors. At a West Lake park called Viewing Fish at Flower Harbor (right), visitors feed a school of golden carp.

237

S*ilk, the fabric of royalty and the prize that once lured traders from afar, fixes the attention of south China to this day. In an enduring rite of spring, peasants take millions of silkworms into their homes, hand-feeding them mulberry leaves until they spin their precious cocoons. The cocoons are then packed on barges and shipped to Hangzhou via the Grand Canal—to be carted to factories by the ton (above). Workers at the Hangzhou Silk Printing and Dyeing Mill (above right), sort the larva cases, then boil them to loosen the filament, which is unwound (right) in long strands. A ton of unprocessed cocoons yields about 240 pounds of raw silk. The woven finished product (opposite) is checked for flaws before export.*

"If one is . . . aching of the brain, smarting of the eyes, troubled in the four limbs or afflicted in the hundred joints, he may take tea," advised an eighth-century Chinese writer. "Its liquor is like the sweetest dew of Heaven." One of the best known varieties, Dragon Well, has greened the hills of Hangzhou for more than 1,200 years. By March, people from nearby villages are in the fields and workrooms, picking and drying the season's first leaves. They work carefully to keep from crumbling the leaves which, when brewed, resume their original shape—a mark of quality valued by connoisseurs.

OVERLEAF. *In a field near Hangzhou, a young woman stands amid ripening rapeseed, a prime source of cooking oil.*

241

Laced with waterways, lavished with gardens and winding lanes, Suzhou retains a reputation as a city of genteel living—a spirit echoed perhaps in the good-natured amusement of a citizen basking in the afternoon sun (right). Because of its many canals, the town sometimes is called the Venice of China, a place where boats glide beneath sitting-room windows. With wood in short supply, concrete serves as an inexpensive boatbuilding material. Air chambers fore and aft help keep such craft buoyant. Traditionalists prefer wood, "spry like a living thing," in the words of one veteran waterman. "Concrete boats," he says, "are cumbersome; they're like lazy people who refuse to labor."

244

学雷锋，树新风，文明经商，优质服务！

ocks and water, the two essentials of Chinese landscape art, dominate Suzhou's Stone Lion Grove Garden. To the cultivated Chinese eye, such contorted shapes suggest mountains, animals, or human forms. Suzhou's gardens, once the haunt of wine-loving poets and painters, now draw a more sober, less poetic clientele. At a table in the Humble Administrator's Garden (left), a retired man, one of many regular visitors, whiles away his morning with nothing stronger than a mug of tea.

Across town (above), shoppers pause before a display of hams and ribs in a state market. Bamboo shoots, part of a meal-to-be, already have been lashed to one shopper's bicycle.

247

Like slow-blooming flowers, delicate objects take shape in the workrooms of Suzhou's most peaceful factories, the Embroidery Institute and the Sandalwood Fan Mill. Artisans (top), using needle and thread, take up to six months to fashion screens like the bird-and-bamboo design (above).

Men and women throughout China still use fans to keep cool and to stir cooking fires. But the exquisite folding fans, like those introduced from Korea in the 11th century, generally are reserved for export. At the Fan Mill (above, right) a craftsman burns intricate designs into slats of Mongolian oak, now favored as a substitute for the rarer, more expensive sandalwood from which the lacework fan (opposite) was made.

Twilight at midday dapples the floor of a bamboo forest near Wuxi. This variety, called hairy bamboo, is harvested for food as well as lumber. Its edible shoots form an ingredient in many Chinese soups and fish or rice dishes.

Webbed with nets, the glistening waters of Lake Tai spread before the town of Wuxi. The lake, once an arm of the East China Sea, abounds with shrimp, crabs, and fish that adapted to fresh water as the bay's mouth silted shut. Today the lake yields some 12,000 tons of food a year.

OVERLEAF. The Grand Canal, clotted with traffic, serves as Wuxi's main street. A forest of derricks on the left bank transfers cargoes between boxcars and barges.

254

F*rom the humid south to the dry north, the Grand Canal crosses a land of contrasts. At Zhenjiang (left), donkeys appear, replacing the water buffalo of the south. Farther north, near Huaian (above), mud-and-thatch houses outnumber the plaster-and-tile dwellings that prevail farther south. And outside of Jining (above), farmers such as this one in a straw hat grow wheat instead of rice. The Grand Canal changes too. "When I was young I used to swim in it," recalls a Jining resident. "Now there's almost no water."*

255

Beneath a towering mound of straw, a Grand Canal bargeman passes the afternoon waiting for a tugboat to haul his home and its cargo to a paper mill two days' journey away. Trappings of home—an upturned wooden tub, potted plants, and a duck—compete for space aboard the craft which, according to the sign, hails from Gaoyou, about 40 miles to the north. Throughout southern China, where canals and streams crisscross the green landscape, many people spend their lives afloat. Between Changzhou and Wuxi, children greet morning from an open-air bedroom on the canal (top). Elsewhere mourners (above) accompany a body on its final voyage.

Web-footed commuters set out for a morning of work near Huaian (opposite): These cormorants have been trained to dive for fish and bring them to tubs their masters maneuver through the canals of the town (above). The boatmen use poles to propel their craft—and to keep their feathered charges moving. Choke collars usually keep the birds from swallowing the catch—until the collar is loosened, so that a cormorant can claim its reward (right).

Old ways and new flourish side by side in Tianjin, gateway port to northern China. A fisherman, using time-honored techniques, dips his hand net from a municipal wharf, oblivious to the bustle of commerce from distant lands. On these piers may be found cargo boxes bearing labels from Japan, Poland, Germany, and the United States.

Dutch envoys, arriving in Tianjin in 1655, marveled that "all the boats which go to Peking, whatever their port of origin, call here, and the traffic is astonishingly heavy." Today, towering cranes thrust into the sky, replacing the "sturdy walls . . . with watch-towers and other defence works" that commanded the city in the 17th century.

At the Xingang Shipbuilding Factory nearby, workers weld the plates of a modern, ocean-going vessel—while wearing bamboo hardhats.

THE TORRENT OF LIFE

By William Graves
Photographs by Bruce Dale

When it came time to board the ferry the pig got on first. Captain Huang has certain priorities. Aboard his *fanchuan,* or sailing junk, cargo always loads first and passengers find seats after that.

The pig was a large one on its way to market, strapped securely on its side to a wooden packboard and laid flat on deck. When the fares were collected the owner dutifully paid out 30 fen—about 18 cents—10 fen for himself and 20 for the pig. Then we were off across the spectacular Xiling Gorge section of the great river known as the Chang Jiang, or Yangtze as foreigners call it. Captain Huang skillfully compensated for the powerful current by pointing his boat almost directly upstream to catch a following wind.

On the return voyage, as I talked to Captain Huang about his river, I asked him why he charged twice as much for a pig as for a human passenger. He looked at me as if I had lost my senses.

"Because," he answered patiently, "a pig takes up twice as much deck space as a seated passenger. I have been ferrying pigs and people across the Chang Jiang for almost half a century, and I have never had any complaints." He shook my hand then as I stepped ashore and wished me well on the

Out of the misty mountains surges the Yangtze, carving its awesome gorges. By Herman Wong.

remainder of my voyage up the Chang Jiang (Long River). The voyage had begun hundreds of miles downriver at Shanghai and would end upstream at the historic city of Chongqing (Chungking). "It is a very great river," Captain Huang said as we parted. "You will find no greater one in all the world."

The immensity of Captain Huang's river and its importance to China are difficult for an outsider to understand. From its source high in western China's Qinghai-Tibet Plateau, the Yangtze flows east and south for more than 3,900 miles, a distance greater than that of any river in the world except for the Amazon and the Nile.

In the process the Yangtze cuts China in two, spans nine provinces, drains an area of some 695,000 square miles, and affects the lives of more than 300 million Chinese—one out of every 14 people on earth.

The effects are not always beneficial. During the summer of 1931, massive floods along the lower Yangtze engulfed neighboring cities, took 145,000 lives, and displaced 28 million people. Though hundreds of miles of dikes now border the lower river, the Yangtze still overflows after periods of heavy rain at terrible cost in lives and property.

Overshadowing all else is the Yangtze's role as China's great central highway. In a country where land transportation is still underdeveloped, the Yang-

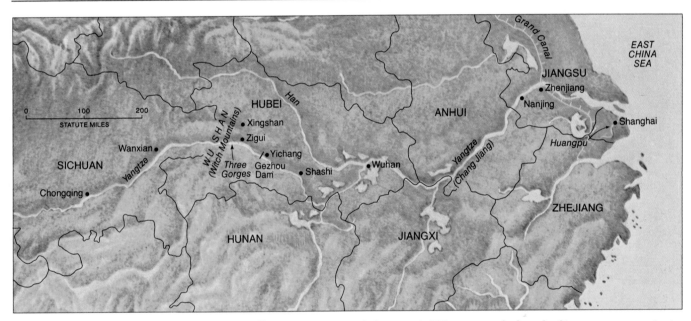

William Graves traveled over 1,000 miles along the Yangtze—from its mouth on the East China Sea to its confluence with the Jialing River at Chongqing (Chungking). Like a great dragon, Chang Jiang—the Long River—undulates through nine provinces on a 3,900-mile journey to the sea. Born in the high Tanggula Mountains of Tibet and Qinghai, the Yangtze falls 16,400 feet over the length of its upper course. On its middle passage between Sichuan and Hubei, the river winds through soaring gorges to the lowlands of eastern China. Widening and often wandering through scenic lakes, the river loops and turns northeastward for its final swing to Shanghai and the sea.

tze links east and west and at its lower reaches serves as the main thoroughfare for movement of China's goods and people. Though no accurate records exist, cargo on the Yangtze accounts for an estimated 60 to 80 percent of China's total inland shipping.

From the 19th century, the Yangtze Valley has served as a highroad of conquest as well as a key commercial region. Strategically, control of the great river basin has helped in control of China. In 1842 a British force moved 200 miles up the Yangtze and forced the Chinese to accept the Treaty of Nanking (Nanjing), which opened five ports to foreign trade. The anti-Manchu Taiping army moved downstream in a fleet of boats in 1853, winning territory as they went, including the city of Nanjing. Well into the 20th century, foreign gunboats found the broad river a convenient and relatively secure means of penetrating the heartland. The Yangtze served as an escape route for Chinese refugees when Japanese invaders forced the Nationalist government farther and farther inland. Transported first to Wuhan, the uprooted government was eventually chased upriver to Chongqing, where it settled until the end of the war. The capture of Nanjing by Communist forces in 1949 signaled the end of Nationalist Chinese power on the mainland.

As befits one of the world's great rivers, the Yangtze goes by half a dozen different names. As a young stream high in the Qinghai-Tibet Plateau, it is known to the Tibetans as Dri Chu—Female Yak River. Chinese there call it Tongtian He, or Going Through the Heavens River, and lower, bordering Sichuan and dropping through Yunnan, it is known as Jinsha Jiang, or River of Golden Sand. Chinese occasionally add the prefix *Wanli* to Chang Jiang, making it Ten Thousand Li River. Only along its lower reaches does the river go by the name familiar to foreigners—Yangtze.

T
he city the world regards as the gateway to the Yangtze actually lies some distance from the river. Shanghai, China's major port and largest metropolis, spans the Huangpu, a tributary of the Yangtze, about ten miles above the confluence of the two rivers. In my exploration of the Yangtze I started at Shanghai and proceeded down the Huangpu to its junction with the Yangtze, then followed the latter upriver.

About a quarter of all China's oceangoing cargo travels the great waterway between Shanghai and the sea. The Huangpu's channel is so shallow that some freighters such as giant container ships must unload downriver and barge their cargoes upstream to Shanghai.

What the Huangpu lacks in depth it more than makes up for in sheer volume and variety of traffic. Early on my first morning in Shanghai I strolled the old Bund, the great waterfront avenue now known as East Zhongshan Road, to watch the city and the port come to life.

On land, Shanghai's first stirrings take the form of a stately ballet—the rhythmic, slow-motion calisthenics practiced by many urban Chinese and known poetically as *taijiquan*—boundless fist. Well before sunrise hundreds of Shanghai residents gather along the waterfront on their way to work to practice taijiquan individually or in organized groups. Here and there Western forms of exercise compete with the classic Chinese. At one point on my walk I suddenly found myself involved with two young Chinese boys in what quickly developed into a furious three-handed game of frisbee.

Ashore or afloat, Shanghai displays endless color and variety. As dawn touches the river, the great waterway erupts with perpetual sound and motion. The effect is of a vast and leaderless symphony orchestra tuning up for a performance. There is the drumroll mutter of heavy diesel barges snaking up and down the river on long multiple tows, the shrill piping of tugs, the brassy fanfare of shuttling ferries, the occasional chime of a ship's bell aboard a sailing junk, and the deep-throated chorus of oceangoing ships bellowing for right-of-way amid the confusion.

Ironically, Shanghai's bustle and energy are threatening its very existence. Not long after my morning stroll I met a group of local geologists who informed me gravely that their city is sinking.

"Fortunately, it is a slow process," one of the group explained, "but some parts of Shanghai are sinking by as much as several centimeters a year. Our problem, you see, is size. We have 11 million people and more than 8,000 factories. Such a city requires immense amounts of water—in this case groundwater. So much has been pumped out from under Shanghai that the city is slowly subsiding." He shook his head sadly.

"As you know, Shanghai means literally 'on the sea.' But it appears we are sinking *into* the sea instead."

One proposed solution is to pump water back underground and shore the city up hydraulically. A better long-range solution would be to disperse some of the residents and factories beyond Shanghai's metropolitan area, which now measures more than 2,200 square miles.

In fact, however, Shanghai is doing just the opposite. Not far from the city, at Baoshan along the Yangtze, a gigantic steel mill is rising that will absorb not only water but thousands of workers. Meanwhile, to keep floods from its door, Shanghai depends on a network of dikes and, one suspects, several million prayers during the worst of the summer typhoon season.

After two days in Shanghai, I boarded *Dong Fang Hong No. 12* for the voyage upriver. Dong Fang Hong means "The East Is Red," the title of a revolutionary song praising Mao Zedong. Despite Mao's posthumous demotion the phrase Dong Fang Hong still symbolizes the revolution and thus is popular as a name for a wide range of products manufactured in the People's Republic.

Dong Fang Hong No. 12 is one of the more massive products: 5,500 tons of aging but sedulous river steamer, with a length of 371 feet, twin diesel engines, a cruising speed of 15 knots, and a capacity of 2,000 passengers. There are many such ships in the Dong Fang Hong fleet that serves the Yangtze, but only *No. 12* has Hu Fushen.

Hu is a likable gentleman of 51 years, more than half of them spent as a riverman on the Yangtze. As a boy he shipped aboard barges and junks, later worked as deck crewman on tugs and ferries, and finally rose to become chief steward of *Dong Fang Hong No. 12*'s second-class passenger section, the highest grade of accommodations aboard ship.

As a foreigner I had no choice in the matter; I was automatically assigned to the best section and charged accordingly. Hu welcomed me at the gangway of the Dong Fang Hong terminal in Shanghai and escorted me to a small, neat cabin on the top deck overlooking the bow. Soon afterward *Dong Fang Hong No. 12* cast off, and in about two hours we reached the junction of the Huangpu and the Yangtze.

It was like putting out to sea. As the banks of the Huangpu slipped behind, we entered a vast and featureless expanse of water that seemed to have no boundaries. As far as the eye could see there was neither land nor any suggestion of it, only the great caramel-colored ocean that is the lower Yangtze.

"It will grow narrower soon," Hu said as I surveyed the scene from the rail. "Downstream the river is even wider, about 30 miles at one point, but here it is only 25." He smiled with pride. "The Yangtze is a giant among giants."

For the next 200 miles Hu elaborated on his theme with an inexhaustible repertoire of stories, legends, facts, and superstitions, all relating to what the Chinese regard as the earth's mightiest river.

From Hu I learned that one must never turn a fish over on one's plate while eating aboard ship. "Upside-down fish means upside-down boat," Hu warned. "Rivermen are very superstitious." Similarly, the sight of a *jiangtun*, or river pig, as sailors call the increasingly rare Yangtze dolphin, is a guarantee of rain or fog on the river within three days.

Though I never put the overturned fish theory to the test, I did see a jiangtun one morning far upriver near the city of Wuhan. It appeared during a stretch of good weather that was forecast to continue several days, but the next evening torrential rains swept the river, adding to already serious flooding below Wuhan.

Second only to his love of the Yangtze was Hu's pride in *Dong Fang Hong No. 12*. During the 200-mile voyage to Nanjing he showed me over parts of the ship and gave me a short course on the economics of river travel.

"It is the best form of transportation in China," Hu declared. "From Shanghai to Nanjing, for example, you can go for as little as four yuan [$2.40] if you travel fifth class. That is not luxury, of course—merely a seat on a wooden bench on one of the lower decks, sometimes near the engine room if the ship is crowded. But the train fare from Shanghai to Nanjing is somewhat more, and the baggage allowance on the train is only 44 pounds. On a riverboat you are permitted 66 pounds of almost any kind of baggage free of charge—clothes, furniture, bicycles, lumber, vegetables, live poultry, anything. On both the train and the boat, you must buy your food separately from your ticket, and the food on both is good." He swept a hand majestically across the Yangtze. "But what train on earth offers such a view?"

The answer is none, if one considers the enormous diversity of that view and the insights it provides into the daily workings of China. The very slowness of the boat adds to the ease of observation. During the 36-hour run between Shanghai and Nanjing—seven times longer than the train trip—I made note of the various cargoes I saw bound upriver and down, mostly aboard massive barges fashioned of tapered logs in a style little changed since man first plied the Yangtze many centuries ago.

The barges were lashed in ranks side by side or strung on long tows, hauled in either case by tugs or other barges powered by diesel engines. Barges headed downstream often traveled alone, their helmsmen displaying astonishing skill in maneuvering through the hazards with no power other than their arms and the river's current.

Virtually everything China grows or makes travels the mighty Yangtze. In the space of an hour I noted cargoes of steel pipe, oranges, cement blocks, live geese, herds of pigs, straw baskets, earthenware jars, sugarcane, baled cotton, charcoal, casks of wine, apples, tanned hides, and coffins.

One of the most common types of cargo traveled on its own—cedar and cypress logs lashed together in giant rafts, some nearly half the size of a football field. Each raft had a great sweep oar at bow and stern and usually a cabin amidships for the crew to sleep in.

Some 50 miles below Nanjing we passed the intersection of the Yangtze and the Grand Canal. Several hours later we reached Nanjing, my first port of call on the Yangtze. I said goodbye to Hu, who was bound upriver all the way to Chongqing, the farthest point that river steamers can navigate.

Few cities in all of China symbolize the country's historic agonies and triumphs more dramatically than Nanjing. The city, whose name means "Southern Capital," dates back at least 2,400 years, though archaeological evidence suggests that the site was inhabited as early as 6,000 years ago.

In its long history Nanjing served eight different dynasties, including the glorious Ming for a short time, as a center of power and splendor with few rivals anywhere in the world. Then, in December 1937, invading Japanese troops changed Nanjing's image almost overnight. It became a monument to mass murder, torture, and destruction. The toll in civilian lives alone was 150,000. Few Chinese today will discuss the Rape of Nanking, as the world came to call it. Japan is now China's leading trading partner. Official histories of the city totally ignore the subject and concentrate instead on the villainies of the Kuomintang, who returned to their former capital of Nanjing in 1945 and governed there until Communist forces seized the city in 1949.

In time Nanjing recovered, and has become something of a showcase for Chinese skill and technology. No foreign visitor can escape a tour of the celebrated Nanjing Bridge, a long, graceless double-deck structure that represents an engineering milestone in the People's Republic. The Chinese view it as a symbol of their self-reliance.

More impressive to Western eyes is Nanjing University, one of China's best, with a faculty of over 1,600 and an enrollment of 4,000, including students from 17 foreign countries. One of the latter is Randy Stross, a 26-year-old native of Denver, Colorado, who was doing doctoral research in Chinese history when I met him.

According to Stross the educational facilities at Nanjing are commendable, while the quality of daily life for Chinese students is mediocre at best.

"Foreign students live two to a room in the dormitories," he explained, "but Chinese students live eight or more in the same size room. As foreigners we have unlimited washing privileges, while the Chinese get one ticket a week to the local bathhouse.

"Of course," he added, "we pay for the extras. As a foreign research scholar I pay 2,500 yuan a year, or roughly $1,500, for tuition. The Chinese students pay nothing, and in fact some of them get a small subsidy if they're really poor. But the differences are still hard to live with. One of the big things is food. We get roughly the equivalent of an American diet, with meat and chicken, while the Chinese get the bare minimum. I play for the university basketball team, and the Chinese members get an extra allowance of food as athletes. But their energy level is still so low we can only practice about half as long as an American team does."

For some 700 miles above Nanjing the Yangtze runs wide, flat, and monotonous. Above the city of Yichang the river changes drastically in shape and character, thanks to an age-old barrier called Wu Shan—Witch Mountains. Here over ages the Yangtze has laboriously carved one of China's great natural wonders, the spectacular Three Gorges.

The Chinese are struggling to tame the Yangtze with yet another great barrier, Gezhouba, or Gezhou Dam. Chinese engineers have been discussing the idea for decades. Now at last it has become a reality.

To reach the new dam I flew from Nanjing upriver to the city of Wuhan, then later caught *Dong Fang Hong No. 34* the rest of the way to Yichang.

Wuhan is actually three cities in one, combining the former municipalities of Wuchang, Hanyang, and Hankou. The result is a sprawling metropolis of four million inhabitants bordering both banks of the Yangtze.

In a sense Wuhan is a fortress city, forever besieged behind a great rampart of dikes by the unpredictable Yangtze. Wuhan has good reason to fear the river; during the catastrophic floods of 1931, the city lay drowned under many feet of water for close to three months at an appalling cost in lives. For a time Jin Shilong thought his would be one of them.

He is now 75, a strikingly handsome man with snow-white hair, gentle manners, and a wry sense of humor. I met him at the Hubei Flood Prevention Agency, where he has held the post of senior engineer for the past 20 years. At the time of my visit the Yangtze was overflowing its banks both above and below Wuhan, but the city itself remained dry and apparently secure.

"It was the same way for a time in 1931," Jin recalled. "The river was not much higher than it is now, but the old-fashioned dikes simply couldn't hold it." The dikes gave way just before six o'clock on the morning of July 27, and within seconds Wuhan's narrow streets became millraces of death.

"There was no warning," Jin said, "only a sudden great wall of water. Most of Wuhan's buildings in those days were only one story high, and for most people there was no escape—they died by the tens of thousands." Unquestionably Jin would have been one of them had he not been employed as a railroad clerk, so junior that he had to work the night shift.

"I was just coming off duty at the company's main office, a fairly new three-story building near the center of town," Jin told me. "When I heard the terrible noise and saw the wall of water coming, I raced to the top story of the building." He was marooned there for 70 days, until the water receded in his part of town. From time to time he was supplied with food and water by rescue boats making the rounds of the few survivors.

I asked Jin why one of the rescue boats hadn't removed him to safety and he gave me a look of surprise.

"Safety? But I was already in the safest possible place! The flood covered an area of 32 square miles, and it was a long voyage to the nearest land. Meanwhile I was in one of the tallest and strongest buildings left standing. At that time no one knew whether the water would subside or rise even higher."

Finally, after two and a half solitary months, Jin was able to leave his refuge. He did so determined that neither he nor Wuhan would ever again suffer such a tragedy. He became a flood-control engineer and helped to rebuild his city's defenses, literally from the ground up.

During a brief tour of some of Wuhan's enormous earthen dikes, I asked Jin if the new Gezhou Dam upriver below the Yangtze gorges would provide additional protection from floods.

"No," he answered, "the dam is not high enough, only 230 feet. It is mainly for hydroelectric power, which we need almost as badly as flood control. But there is talk of a very high dam, perhaps 656 feet, to be built somewhere in the gorges themselves. That would take at least ten years, but if it happens Wuhan's troubles will be over and I will no longer be needed here." He smiled. "But by then I will be almost old enough to retire."

Another resident of the Yangtze may soon retire, thanks to Gezhouba. The giant sturgeon, which can weigh three-quarters of a ton or more, used to swim in countless numbers nearly 2,000 miles upriver from the mouth of the Yangtze to spawn and then return to the East China Sea.

"Regrettably those days are over," Dr. Cao Wenxuan told me at Wuhan's Institute of Hydrobiology. Dr. Cao is Assistant Director of the Research Office of the Institute, a branch of the Chinese Academy of Sciences respected throughout the world for its research on freshwater aquaculture.

"The sturgeon's traditional spawning grounds lie far above the new dam and the gorges," Dr. Cao continued. "It is impossible to transfer fish of such size safely around the dam, and unless we can establish new spawning grounds below Gezhouba very soon, the sturgeon may well disappear from the river. Fortunately, the sturgeon is a unique case. None of the other 270 or so species of fish in the Yangtze is strong enough to battle the powerful currents in the gorges. Since they have never migrated to the upper part of the river, the dam will not affect them."

Fortunately indeed, for commercial aquaculture on the lower Yangtze produces about 660,000 tons of fish a year, one-sixth of China's total catch from both salt and fresh water.

Just upriver from the city of Yichang, massive Gezhouba stands 919 feet thick at the base. The concrete and steel colossus extends a mile and a half across the Yangtze below the river's magnificent Three Gorges. So vast is the dam and so sheer the walls of the gorges that the level of the Yangtze will be raised an average of 65 feet for a distance of more than 60 miles upriver. At the time of my visit to Gezhouba, which takes its name from a sandbar in the river, only a few hundred more yards of the Yangtze remained to be dammed. Engineers were planning to open the recently completed sluice gates and divert water from the last remaining section of riverbed so the dam could be built across it. With a representative of the dam's construction office I toured the immense structure and absorbed enough statistics to fill an engineering manual. When completed, with all 21 giant turbines running, the dam will generate an average of 14 billion kilowatt hours of electricity a year—three times China's *total* electric energy supply in 1949. Huge locks at either end of the dam will accommodate ships up to 10,000 tons.

Unlike the Great Wall and the Grand Canal, whose primitive construction techniques called for millions of laborers, Gezhouba's partially mechanized work force numbers fewer than 100,000 under normal conditions. Yet the majority, like Che Songnu, still work with their hands.

I met her during our inspection tour at the base of the dam, where she was assembling wooden forms for pouring concrete. Amid a rolling cannonade of dynamite blasts along the cliffs upriver, I learned that Che Songnu is 29 and that she comes from a village almost 400 miles away in Hubei Province. Though she has a husband and five-year-old daughter at home, she has worked at Gezhouba since construction began in 1971, and plans to stay until the dam is completed.

I asked Che Songnu how often she was able to see her daughter.

"Only once a year," she answered, "but it is a long visit, nearly six weeks."

Such a vacation is almost unheard of in China, and I asked her how she managed it. "By working extra," she replied. "Usually I skip my one day off a week and work some holidays as well. In a year's time it adds up to six weeks, and I am allowed to take them all at once." She smiled politely at the construction official and added, "Gezhouba is a very special place."

For a look at the Three Gorges before their lower level disappears forever beneath 65 feet of water, I chartered a tug to carry me upriver to Chongqing. The individual gorges of the Yangtze are divided into three major groups: Xiling, Wu, and Qutang. Much of the excitement of traveling there will be gone once the dammed water rises to obliterate the rapids and whirlpools.

Nothing prepares a traveler for his first view of the Three Gorges. The walls of Xiling Gorge just above Gezhouba soar abruptly from the surface of the river on either side like the nave of some vast natural cathedral. The gorges so often are shrouded in mist that local dogs are said to bark in terror at a glimpse of the sun.

One glimpse of the Yangtze itself is enough to strike terror into the heart of many a traveler. From a leisurely pace both above and below the gorges, the river thunders through its great notch in Wu Shan at speeds up to 17 miles an hour. Even veteran rivermen dread the three great hazards caused by such power and velocity: *xuanwo,* whirlpool; *jiliu,* rapids; and most terrible of all, *shuipao,* or water cannon, a type of giant vertical spout that can capsize a small river steamer.

Happily for me our tug captain and crew had spent most of their lives navigating the 127-mile stretch of river within the gorges. Not only did they know every feature of the river itself, they were familiar with the history and legends that have supplied the various gorges with their unforgettable names. During the five-day voyage upriver through the gorges, the crew singled out the most famous ones: Yellow Cat Gorge; Lantern Shine Gorge; Windbox Gorge; Soldier's Book and Sword Gorge; Ox Liver and Horse Lung Gorge. Some gorges earned their titles from legendary events that had occurred in them, while others are said to have been named for their physical appearance. One of the latter is Ox Liver and Horse Lung Gorge, but try as I could I saw no anatomical resemblance.

"Aha," said Capt. Zhang Yuanzhi, "perhaps that is because you have never seen an ox's liver or a horse's lung."

I admitted I hadn't and asked if he had seen them himself.

"No," he confessed, then pointed a finger triumphantly toward the gorge. "But I am told they look exactly like that!"

It was in Xiling Gorge that I encountered the ferry captain, Huang, who gave me my memorable lesson on transporting pigs across rushing torrents.

Along the entire navigable length of the Yangtze, few areas are more dangerous than the Qingtan Shoal of Xiling Gorge at low water. Here in the dry season of fall and winter the Yangtze reaches its maximum rate of 17 miles an hour, and here many a river vessel has come to grief.

At Qingtan, as in other critical areas of the gorges, anchored barges equipped with giant winches and steel towing cables assist ships headed upriver without power enough to battle the current on their own. Wang Zongli used to provide the same service by hand.

Wang is a former tracker, one of those hired in times past to haul barges and sailing junks upriver through the gorges. The trackers worked in crews, sometimes as large as 200 men, harnessed to long towlines of braided bamboo extending from the bow of the boat to the shore.

Where the shoreline consisted of nothing but sheer cliffs, masons centuries ago carved out narrow galleries for the trackers, often high up in the vertical faces of stone. Today one can still see the galleries and marvel that human beings not only could pass along them crouched almost double, but that they could haul tons of ship behind them at the same time.

Here and there among the galleries one can find deep grooves in the jagged stone, attesting to centuries of wear by braided towlines.

I met Wang in the town of Zigui, where our tug moored overnight. Most upstream traffic in the gorges still stops during the hours of darkness, despite lighted buoys and other navigational aids.

Wang is an amiable gnome, standing less than four and a half feet tall and weighing roughly 120 pounds. Beneath his shapeless tunic is a wiry frame that carried its owner through 18 years of incredible hardship and danger.

"It was not an easy job," Wang declared with notable understatement. "I began as a tracker at the age of 16 and worked till I was 34; after that the strain began to tell. We worked long hours, winter and summer, but winters were the worst. The towline would freeze solid as an iron bar, and ice in the galleries could cut through the thickest straw sandal. We always started before daylight, usually without breakfast, and simply stuffed handfuls of cold rice into our pockets to eat along the way."

Once during winter Wang lost his footing and went into the river. He would have drowned in the icy water if two fellow crew members hadn't jumped in and pulled him out. Twice he did the same for others and a third time he tried but failed—the man's body was never found. For such fearful risk and effort the trackers were paid next to nothing, a fact Wang still regards with bitterness.

"The distance from Zigui upriver to Wanxian is 140 miles," he said. "With a fully loaded junk the haul took about a month, though of course in some places we could ride aboard ship with a following wind.

"For the whole month's work we were paid three silver dollars in addition to our food, but we had to furnish our own towing harness and sandals. Nowadays I earn more than that in a single week as crewman aboard a tug. And danger is no longer my companion. As for trackers, the winch barges and tugs have almost put them out of business. From a thousand or more in my day there are less than a hundred trackers left in the gorges, though many barge and junk crews still haul their own vessels. Soon the river level will begin to rise and cover many of the galleries. I will not be sorry to see them go."

My last day in the gorges began early, as we cast off and headed upriver toward the city of Chongqing. Sunrise cobbled the sky astern and brushed the great peaks on either side with an array of colors to match the poetry of their names—Peak of the Gathering Cranes, Peak of the Flying Phoenix, Peak of the Emerald Screen, Peak of the Lion With the Silver Badge.

Tendrils of mist laced the surface of the river, and high overhead a solitary fishhawk creased the early morning wind. At such times it is easy to accept the ancient legend that the peaks are goddesses who came down to earth and fell so deeply in love with it they refused to return to heaven. Then the last of the great battlements of stone slipped behind, and within hours the Yangtze broadened once again into the downriver approaches to Chongqing.

I have nothing against that city, but it was an anticlimax. China, after all, is full of teeming cities, but throughout that vast and infinitely varied land there is only one Yangtze and one Wu Shan. Where the two come together even goddesses are apt to lose their hearts, and a mere mortal has no chance at all.

Chongqing nonetheless is a pleasant and hospitable city, despite its reputation both for searing cuisine and an equally fiery temper. There are relatively few bicycles in the central district because the streets are so steep they have to be stairstepped. Chongqing lies in southeastern Sichuan Province, an area isolated by mountains and typified by the Chinese proverb: "Sichuan—first to rebel, last to yield." Such legendary valor symbolizes Chongqing's role as the Nationalists' World War II capital—their fog-wreathed western redoubt that the Japanese never managed to occupy.

Chongqing has made good use of at least one of its wartime mementos, a system of caves dug into the hillsides on which the city stands above the Yangtze and Jialing Rivers. They were dug as shelters from heavy Japanese air raids. They also shut out Chongqing's fearful summer heat.

The caves are now used as storage areas—and in some cases small grocery shops and restaurants. One afternoon I took refuge from a late autumn heat wave in an establishment with the irresistible name of the Yellow Flower Paradise Cave Teahouse. The shop is owned by the Yellow Flower Garden Road Collective. Xiao Li is one of the owners and principal attractions. She is a lovely young woman with graceful manners and a shy smile. As she served me a steaming glass of fragrant tea, she explained that her whole family belongs to the thousand-member collective. The teahouse was opened seven years ago to provide jobs for young people like Xiao Li after they graduate from school. Serving tea is a worthwhile occupation, but it has its limits. I asked Xiao Li if she had other ambitions. To my disappointment she gave me the standard reply I had heard countless times in China. "It is an honor to be a waitress for the people," she said, "and that is what I will remain—unless, of course, I am needed somewhere else."

I remarked that the teahouse was a notable improvement over the use the caves had been put to in the past. Xiao Li looked puzzled, and I mentioned the Sino-Japanese War and the bombing raids that had claimed several thousand lives among her people.

She smiled then, apparently convinced that I was teasing her, and I decided to let the subject drop. I was astonished that an educated young Chinese should know—or at least acknowledge—so little of her own city's history. Later I reflected that Xiao Li and her generation have troubles enough without borrowing the agonies of the past. With any luck the Yellow Flower Paradise Cave Teahouse will continue to serve tea and never again have to provide refuge from the miseries of war.

Chongqing represented the end of my journey, not by my choice but by decision of the government in Peking. Like many areas of China today the upper reaches of the Yangtze are still closed to foreigners, except for scientists or mountaineering expeditions.

By all accounts the region is worth exploring, for the Yangtze is born at an altitude of 16,400 feet in one of China's most remote and beautiful areas—the Tanggula Mountains on the border between Qinghai and Tibet.

Nourished by countless glaciers and shaped by mountain gorges, the river traverses the plateau region of southwestern Qinghai, descends to Yunnan, then cuts abruptly north to Sichuan and its meeting with Chongqing. One day, I hope, the area will be opened again to all foreigners, and the entire length of the Yangtze can be explored.

The evening before I was to fly back to Peking and the United States, I took a walk through one of Chongqing's small parks located high on a hillside overlooking the river. Below me Chongqing resembled a great floodplain of light, washing down the slopes and ravines into the valley of the Yangtze.

I stood there until darkness fell. I could no longer see the river, but rows of lights along the waterfront indicated several moored ships. I wondered if *Dong Fang Hong No. 12* might be one of them and if my friend Hu was aboard, preparing for the return voyage downriver.

I could picture him the next morning, welcoming overseas passengers aboard and helping them get settled in their cabins. Doubtless he would entertain them with stories about the river and at some point he would surely declare that the Yangtze is not only a great river but a giant among giants.

I have to confess I agree.

J unks with quilted sails glide across the Huangpu River, inland harbor of Shanghai. A tributary of the lower Yangtze, the Huangpu joins the larger river in a confluence about 20 miles wide. These fanchuan, *or sailing junks, resemble those that traded with India six centuries ago. Chinese junks of that era were some of the world's biggest ships. Junks today carry most Yangtze cargo. Although China's network of railways and roads has greatly expanded, rivers still serve as important arteries of commerce. The Yangtze transports some two-thirds of all goods shipped on China's inland waters.*

A river of people flows along Nanjing Road in the heart of Shanghai. Here in the 19th century foreigners built a city-state that served them as both port and pleasure spot. Now, with a population of more than 11 million, Shanghai is China's largest metropolis and its industrial leader.

As the Shanghai day begins, early-bird shoppers throng a market (above) in the old French Concession of the foreign settlement. The best vegetables will be snatched up before lunchtime. Americans would recognize most of the array— spinach, potatoes, celery, onions, cauliflower, tomatoes, sweet potatoes. Others sound exotic: sheepfoot onion, jiaobai (the stem of a wild rice), ivory radish.

Merchantman and tug, junk, and ferry churn the waters of Shanghai harbor, China's busiest port. On a typically bustling day, close to a hundred ships and thousands of smaller vessels may jam the 37-mile waterfront along the Huangpu River. Large ships usually anchor near the mouth of the Yangtze and transfer their cargo onto lighters. Fully loaded deep-draft ships cannot navigate the shallow Huangpu, Shanghai's channel to the sea. The port lies some ten miles inland.

About a third of the oceangoing ships that dock at Shanghai are foreign. Of all the goods that pass through China's ports, one out of every four tons is handled on Shanghai docks.

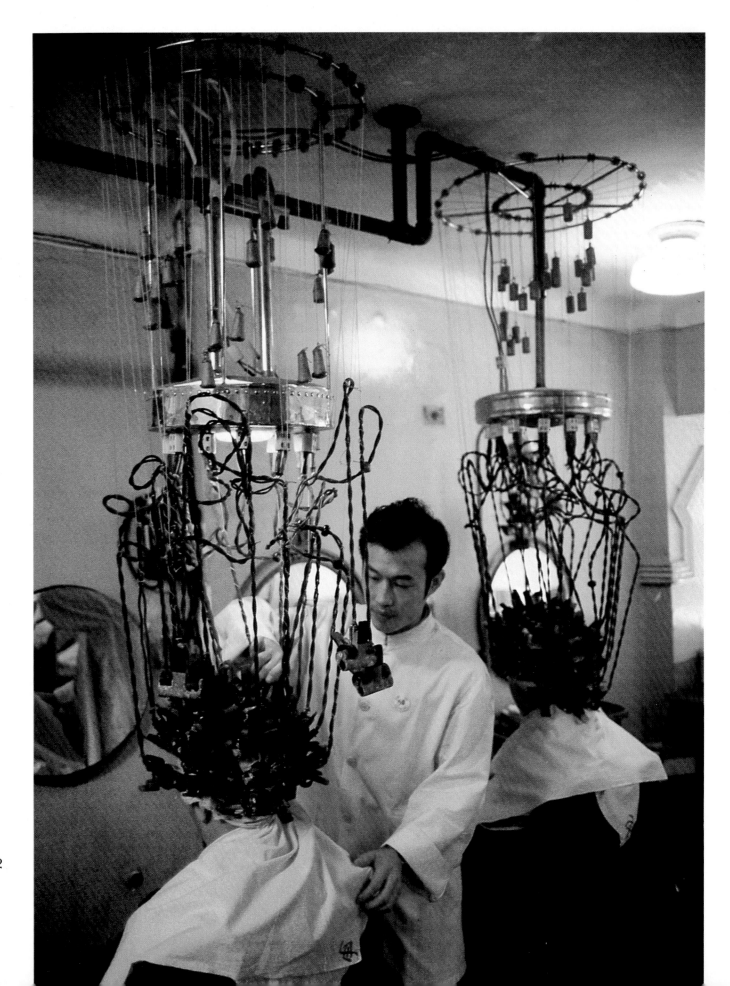

Overleaf: George F. Mobley

Western ideas find their way into Shanghai, long China's most cosmopolitan city. Table tennis, an import played here on a makeshift table, is one of China's leading sports. Beauty shops have revived the permanent—by an antiquated process. Elderly English readers (left) abound, many of them alumni of missionary schools run by foreigners until 1949.

OVERLEAF. *By early morning light a train of barges nears the crossroads of the Yangtze and the Grand Canal.*

283

Baskets brimming, a mother walks to market along the Nanjing-Zhenjiang road.

More modern conveyances travel Nanjing's Yangtze bridge (right), built in the 1960s. Here, where the river is nearly a mile wide, nine piers support a double deck. Lengthy approaches were built to allow sufficient clearance for large ships. On the lower deck, railroad tracks span the river for 4.2 miles; the upper-level highway and its approaches total 2.8 miles. Six other bridges now cross the Yangtze, the river which long divided the country. There was no bridge at all over the Yangtze until 1957, when one was completed at Wuhan.

Commerce and learning converge at the ancient trading city of Wuhan, as do the rivers Yangtze and Han. Passengers streaming from **Dong Fang Hong No. 45** (opposite) carry cumbersome loads of bamboo furniture bought upriver near Chongqing.

Traditional curved roofs look down upon a modern dormitory of Wuhan University. The guitar-playing student at a dormitory window (left) is one of 3,500 students at the university—and one of a tiny minority in China. Only about 4 percent of the nation's high-school graduates can expect to enter an institution of higher learning (compared to almost 40 percent in the United States). Chinese college graduates now get academic degrees, which were banned for years as symbols of social elitism.

A flashing harvest of silver carp rises from a Yangtze-linked lake near Wuhan. Twice a year workers at the South Lake State Fish Breeding Farm wade into their fish and haul out some 150 tons. The silver carp is a major product of this region. The fish are shipped to market alive and flopping, like the one cradled in the arms of this jubilant fish farmer (opposite). Chinese scientists claim the new upriver Gezhou Dam will have little effect on the carp and most other Yangtze fishes. But the giant river sturgeon will suffer. The dam bars the sturgeon from its spawning grounds far up the river.

OVERLEAF. Night does not end the day for workers on the Gezhou Dam, which, when completed, will be the first harness on the Yangtze. When workers began to build in 1970, they favored the slogans of Chairman Mao over the principles of engineering. Two years later, work stopped and designers started over. Returning with more plans and less ideology, they began anew China's largest modern project. North China, which has over 55 percent of China's cultivatable land, has only 7 percent of the country's flowing water. A major goal of engineers is to transfer the impounded waters of the Yangtze to the arid north.

Overleaf: Huang Taopeng, China Pictorial

Manpower pulls
a junk against the current. The junk's
crewmen lean on sweeping oars (above)
or get help from the wind. But, in stretches where the river shows its might, the
men must get out and haul, digging sandals into rock. Until recent years, boats
were pulled upriver by scores of trackers
straining on bamboo hawsers sometimes
half a mile long. Urged on by drum and
gong, at times by lash and cane, the trackers strained, while in the boat men prayed
to the gods of the wind and exploded firecrackers to try to ward off the menacing
gods of the rapids.

OVERLEAF. A ship gingerly wends its way
through Wu Gorge. Shrouded in poetry
—Peak of the Flying Phoenix, Peak of
the Gathering Cranes—the 127 miles of
gorges display their beauty but hide their
dangers in fog and turgid flow. Beneath
this splendor lies a graveyard of ships.

295

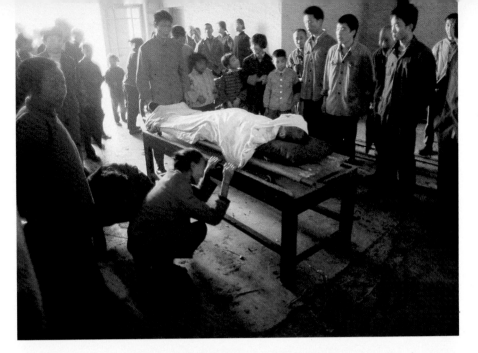

Grief shows many faces at a crematorium in the old river town of Shashi. A funeral procession files through the Little North Gate (opposite) with flowery paper wreaths that hark back to times when the cortege leader carried a long white streamer known as a "soul cloth." In those days all the dead were buried in coffins. Sometimes mourners strewed paper money along the way to placate the ghosts that were thought to haunt the road. They would often place a pot of rice in the grave and scatter tea leaves upon it. Today mourners view the body in the room where it will be cremated (above, left). Outside, a young woman bears a photograph of the man for whom she grieves. Her white hair ribbon and black armband are badges of grief. Most people in the cities and larger towns adhere to China's official policy, which calls for cremation and meager rites, but the burden of grief remains as heavy as ever. As always, it is eased by the arm of a loved one.

The Chinese penchant for mythmaking is so strong that officials describe a copiously leaking aqueduct (right) as a scenic waterfall. Nature and myth are often intertwined in China, and almost every natural phenomenon has one or more legends associated with it. The squirting rock spring (above), in the western mountains of Hubei Province, may be an exception: it is revered simply for its beauty. Traditional folklore values water as the "essence of jade," and the Chinese term for scenery or landscape is shanshui, which means "mountains and water."

Steep or sandy, the banks of the Yangtze are replete with vignettes of river life. Families, shuttling from shore to shore, make a living by ferrying and small-scale farming. The boat on the left (above) carries bales of hemp, a state monopoly. From the boat on the right come sweet-potato vines destined for pigs. Where banks are steep, boat passengers must hike up steps that may number in the hundreds. The oranges and tangerines awaiting transport on the terraced bank came from the green-mantled slopes of the Three Gorges.

OVERLEAF. Twilight calm settles upon the Jialing River and the sparkling fringes of north Chongqing. The city climbs a promontory wedged between the Jialing and Yangtze; the rivers meet at its eastern tip. Once the capital of Nationalist China, Chongqing serves as a hub of commerce for the western provinces.

Book browsers crowd a streetside lending library in Chongqing (above). Such stands, financed by local educational and cultural bureaus, flourish across China. Children gather to thumb through adventure comics; as with most selections, these tend to trumpet the party line. A few non-political works find their way onto shelves. They include tales from ancient lore—and a sprinkling of Western classics, such as Snow White.

A self-proclaimed dentist operates from a sidewalk stand (right). His private practice treats those seeking quick service. The government offers more professional care, yet turns a blind eye to competing entrepreneurs.

Art students test their talents on one of Chongqing's many stone-stepped lanes (opposite). Throughout the city, stairs plunge from the hill's summit to the rivers below. Moisture from Chongqing's perpetual fog often makes the steps slippery.

BY RAIL TO THE MONSOON JUNGLES

By Shirley Sun
Photographs by Jodi Cobb

To the Chinese, especially the Chinese in the north, Xishuangbanna is a land of endless fascination. The name conjures up images of a tropical paradise, the home of wild elephants and peacocks, golden monkeys, and slender, lacquer-haired women in close-fitting blouses and ankle-length sarongs. These Dai people, say the Han Chinese with envy, think nothing of adorning themselves with jewelry and wild flowers to make themselves more alluring.

"It will be raining in Xishuangbanna," my friends in Peking warned, when I announced my plan to make the long train journey down the length of China to the Dai autonomous area. It was early May; the monsoon rains might already have begun. From the vantage point of Peking, where gritty desert sands clogged my throat, it was hard to imagine a tropical land of diluvial rains. Nevertheless, I prepared quickly for the journey south.

A remote pocket of Yunnan Province on the border with Burma and Laos, Xishuangbanna was almost inaccessible for centuries. Until local roads began to run south in the 1950s, a journey there from Kunming, the provincial capital, could take a month. Today one is still at the mercy of sudden

In a village near Dali, a Bai mother feeds rice to her baby.

downpours and uncertain road conditions. Malaria (which the Dai called the "evil vapor") devastated Xishuangbanna as recently as the 1950s. Although health programs have nearly wiped out the disease, I swallowed the little white anti-malaria pills just in case.

The train from Peking to Chengdu departs daily at 8:57 a.m. The young conductor, Zhang, appeared earnest and serious in his dark blue cotton uniform. In the center of his cap was the red logo of the railway workers. Another young trainman, Cao, who had a smooth, pale complexion and clear eyes, showed me to my compartment in the "Sleeping Coach with Cushioned Berth" car. The only first-class car on the train, it contained eight compartments with two double-decker bunks in each.

Almost all foreigners travel by "soft sleeper," which is nearly as costly as air travel. Some Chinese travel by "hard sleeper," but most of the hundreds of passengers on my train could afford only "hard seat." They sat up all the way,

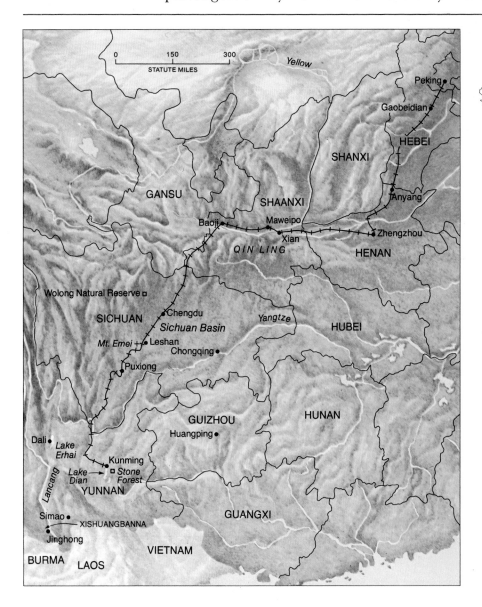

In her train journey southwest from Peking to China's tropics bordering on Burma, Laos, and Vietnam, Shirley Sun traveled through six provinces. From the vast dry, loess region of the north, she crossed into Sichuan, long called the "Heavenly Kingdom" for its fertile soil, and now one of the last refuges of the giant panda. The last stop was in mountainous Yunnan, a province whose climates range from cool-dry in the north to seasonally torrid or torrential on its southern borders. Along the way, the author met members of several of China's 55 minority groups, nearly half of which are represented in Yunnan.

day and night. These cars are usually so crowded that many passengers must stand. Foreign tourists almost never travel on "hard seat," or even on "hard sleeper." Those who try meet great resistance in obtaining a ticket.

My compartment was luxuriously decorated. The berths were covered with pale blue brocade, over which Cao had placed a cool straw mat for summer. Deep blue crushed velvet curtains and white lace curtains hung from the window. On the table was a small fern in a porcelain pot with a cracked-ice pattern. Beneath it in a wire holder stood the ubiquitous hot water thermos bottle. The Chinese constantly replenish the hot water in their tea mugs, making countless cups from one pile of tea leaves.

Rousing music came over the loudspeaker as the train moved slowly out of the station. I settled into my seat. Sunlight streamed through the lace curtains. Cao looked in with a smile. Was it too warm in the compartment? Should he pull the shades? He was quietly attentive to my comfort. He looked young. But, he said, he had been working on the railway for over ten years and had spent many years on this route.

Soon I had another visitor. It was the manager of the dining car, dressed in a soiled white jacket. What preference did I have in the cuisine? Did I prefer Peking or Sichuan cooking? Sichuan, most definitely! I had looked forward to the hot, pungent dishes which are among the great cuisines of China, and I was delighted to be able to enjoy the food while journeying to the province.

Parched, flat fields passed by my window. Occasionally I saw grazing sheep. The train stopped at a small station, Gaobeidian, where many passengers got off to stretch their legs and buy the local specialty: dried bean curd in long threads tied together on top with a straw knot. I bought a bunch for 20 fen (12 cents) and tasted a strand—very salty. At other stations I jumped out to buy pickled vegetables and marvelously fat dried red dates.

I took the bean curd strands to the chef and asked him to make something with them. Using sesame oil and spices, he prepared a cold dish that had a smooth consistency and a fragrant aroma. He also prepared four other dishes: braised fish, sautéed bean sprouts, cubed chicken with greens, and diced ham with eggs. My dining table, set with blue and white porcelain, was an embarrassment of plenty, contrasting starkly with the stricken landscape outside. In the fields grew stunted wheat, one foot tall, due to be harvested in a month. I was told that there had been very little rainfall in this region since 1973. Still, farmers toiled on the sun-scorched earth, working right up to the edge of the railroad tracks. For their back-breaking labor, they would eat dried sweet potatoes and coarse grains. Their diet contained very little rice. And here on my dinner table were delicious dishes that I had not ordered and could not finish.

It grew stiflingly hot by midafternoon when the train pulled into Anyang station. The small nondescript brick stations we had been passing all looked the same. One couldn't tell them apart except for their signs. The black characters gave this one great significance. We were in archaeological country, the land of the royal house of Shang, nearly 4,000 years old, the first dynasty to leave behind its own recorded history.

We sped through the central plains of Hebei, Henan, and Shaanxi, traditionally called "the cradle of Chinese civilization" from the ancient settlements and royal capitals established there. It was hard to reconcile the grandeur of the past with the barren loess landscape before my eyes. Where were the hallmarks of former empires? Where were the splendid palaces, temples and walled cities? Little remains on this scorched yellow earth.

The unrelenting forward motion of the train sucked me into the darkening landscape, engulfing me in shadows. I fell into a fitful sleep, awaking intermittently as the train lurched to a stop at nameless stations. Perspiration soaked my pillow and the mat beneath me. Shafts of light from the stations filtered through the window, casting eerie silhouettes on the compartment walls. I poured another cup of the salty Laoshan mineral water which I had brought as an alternative to the boiling hot water in the thermos. The liquid cooled my throat and soothed my stomach, if not the dream chamber of my mind. History and legend converged in my subconscious as phantom images of buried cities, legendary sages, and emperors loomed forth.

High green mountains sparkling with dew met my eyes the next morning. Left behind was the dry, yellow earth of the north. Before dawn, we had passed Xian and Maweipo, where in 756 the fleeing Tang emperor, Xuan Zong, was pressured into allowing his soldiers to strangle his beloved concubine, Yang Guifei, for suspected treachery.

We were now on the most difficult stretch of the terrain between Baoji and Chengdu. From the third century B.C. to modern times, Baoji had been a strategic outpost controlling the Qin Ling mountains, which separate north from south China. The track over this 416-mile stretch through rugged mountains was completed only after engineers had blasted out 303 tunnels and built 994 bridges. As our train entered a dark tunnel almost every mile, we were continually hurtling in and out of darkness.

The high mountains historically formed a natural defense for Sichuan Province. In 1938, the Chinese Nationalists moved their wartime capital there to Chongqing to protect it from Japanese invasion. A popular song for travelers who braved the journey to Sichuan was written in the eighth century by Li Bo, one of China's greatest romantic poets:

> *Eheu! How dangerous, how high!*
> *It would be easier to climb to heaven*
> *Than walk the Sichuan Road. . . .*

On the afternoon of the second day, we passed into lush Sichuan. Flowing rivers, verdant foliage, and wooden farmhouses with black-tiled roofs, enclosed by thick bamboo groves, speckled the countryside. The bamboo's leaves fanned gently in the breeze. Fields of bright yellow rapeseed and golden wheat were ready for harvest. Farmers worked in wet rice fields that were separated by rows of mulberry trees. This was the land of the "Heavenly Kingdom," its basin made fertile by an irrigation system built two thousand years ago and most recently renovated in the 1970s.

For more than 2,000 years, Chengdu has been the economic and cultural center of the Sichuan Basin. It was established as the capital of the state of Shu in the fourth century B.C. During the Han Dynasty, Chengdu prospered; its lacquerware, gold and silver handicrafts, and brocade were known throughout China. After the fall of Han, it became the capital of the kingdom of Shu, but little remains of its former splendor. The Jin Jiang, or Brocade River, in which lengths of silk were once washed, has turned gray and muddy.

Most of Chengdu's ancient walls have also been destroyed, either in centuries of warfare or during the Cultural Revolution. The old palace in the heart of the city was demolished in the 1960s to make way for a gargantuan Soviet-style exhibition center. A statue of the late Chairman Mao Zedong towers three stories high in front of it. Officials from the Cultural Relics Bureau told me matter-of-factly that they had contributed a few days' manual labor to the demolition of the city walls. I wondered how these men, whose job it is to protect antiquities, really felt about having taken part in the destruction of these irreplaceable structures.

Bustling crowds filled the streets of Chengdu. Peddlers and shoppers congested sidewalks and alleyways. The stands were decked with many articles: colorful blouses, skirts, scarves, combs, and ribbons. Flower vendors on bicycles sold fresh gladioli. Enterprising tailors lined one street. Every morning, seven days a week, they would set up their treadle sewing machines. With hands and scissors seeming to outspeed their machines, the tailors could cut and sew up a blouse or a pair of pants for a customer in one day. Depending on their speed, they could make one or two hundred yuan a month ($60-$120), more than twice the salary of many factory workers.

The produce markets were the most crowded. People stood shoulder to shoulder. Piles of vegetables were stacked up on the side of the street: sweet potatoes, tomatoes, eggplants, string beans, and *wosun*, a light green, crispy, fragrant vegetable, shaped like a bamboo shoot. Stands displayed meats and eels, a favorite delicacy. With the eel's pointed head nailed to a board, the butcher would make a slit down its center with a sharp knife, rinse it in a tub of water, and present it to the customer in a flash.

It used to be said that in the whole world, China had the greatest number of teahouses, and that in all of China, Chengdu had the most. But teahouses were closed down during the Cultural Revolution because their enjoyment was considered a decadent, bourgeois habit. Now in Chengdu they have made a surging and boisterous comeback. I saw open-air teahouses on almost every block. Tea drinkers recline and chat for hours in large bamboo armchairs that permit air to cool their backs.

Different teahouses offer different kinds of entertainment. One might feature flower-drum musicians, another, a butterfly harpist, and yet another, a favorite storyteller. During the day the Chess Garden serves over a thousand chess aficionados. In the evening it becomes a rousing teahouse with sing-song storytellers accompanied by music. Twenty-five fen (15 cents) buys a cup of hot tea with unlimited hot water refills. The stemmed cups have lids to keep the tea hot between unhurried sips.

The night I was there, elderly men made up most of the audience. Some hummed along with the music, some smoked long-stemmed pipes, others spat. Nimble wrists waved fans to and fro to circulate the hot air. The performer, Cao Gurong, a local favorite, was dressed in bright pink and heavily made up with white powder and cherry-red lipstick. She was basking in her triumphant return from a debut in Peking. She sang the role of the heroine of a love story and tantalized the audience with her graceful movements and alluring eyes. Shouts of "hao—bravo" came from her most ardent fans. They were visibly transported by her music and beauty, and I was moved by the radiant happiness on their old furrowed faces.

I eagerly sought out the innumerable little snacks for which Sichuan is celebrated. At Lai's Dumplings, a spacious spot with square wooden tables and stools, I lined up to buy a ticket—12 fen (7 cents) for a bowl of four meat-filled dumplings, and another 4 fen (2 cents) for a dish of sesame sauce—and then again at a large window to obtain the dishes. I shared a table with an old man. Seeing me eat with relish, he said that he had been patronizing Lai's ever since it was just a humble peddler's stand nearby, but that during the Cultural Revolution the quality of the rice dough and stuffing had declined and the dumplings had become less tasty. Learning that I was from abroad, he became curious. "How much do you make a month?" he inquired.

"Just enough to get by," I replied, as I usually did to this frequently asked question. It was not my intention to be evasive, but telling the amount would have given him the misleading impression that Americans were super-rich.

Next I visited Chen Mapo Doufu Dian, the home of the best-known Sichuan bean curd dish, a variation of which is served in Chinese restaurants the world over. The dish was first made some 120 years ago by a pockmarked woman named Chen, who made such delicious bean curd that the dish was affectionately named after her as Pockmarked Mama Chen's Bean Curd. The restaurant remained in the family for four generations—until 1957. Since then it has been managed by the city and run with a staff of 50 workers.

Despite its fame, the restaurant is old and worn, with a dirt floor and wooden tables and stools. A huge mound of steaming rice was piled in a bin facing the entrance. A stack of chipped wooden chopsticks in a container hung from the wall. I had come during off-hours and the place was empty. Flattered by my interest, the chef welcomed me to the kitchen and showed me where they made their own bean curd daily. They had to start at midnight, first soaking the soybeans to soften them and then grinding them into paste.

"We select only the very best soybeans," he said.

He just happened to have ingredients left to make one portion of the mapo doufu. I watched intently as he took out a huge cleaver and began to mince garlic and a piece of pork, and chop green scallions into diagonal sections, all with amazing speed. No food processor needed here! Soon a few people gathered around. A stocky middle-aged woman appeared and briskly ushered me out to the dining room. Was I planning to open a restaurant and serve the dish? I learned later that she was from the Chengdu Food and Beverage Department, which manages all the restaurants. I assured her that while I was an admirer of Sichuan cuisine, I was lacking in the culinary skills to reproduce the dish. Still, she asked me to wait in the dining room. A group of foreigners had come here before to watch the chef cook and had opened a restaurant abroad, she said. Now they had to be careful.

Shortly, the mapo doufu was served, glistening in a heavenly reddish-brown, aromatic, and pungent sauce. I savored its hot, spicy taste. The minced pork was soft and tender and the bean curd remained in small, unbroken cubes. It was without a doubt the most superlative dish of mapo doufu I had ever tasted. I asked the chef what herbs he used. "None at all," he replied proudly. "That's how simple it is. Only salt, red pepper, and peppercorns."

While eastern Sichuan is densely populated, the western part is thickly forested and mountainous. Its bamboo forests are the final refuge of the giant panda. For more than half a million years, pandas roamed the regions north and south of the Yangtze River. But human encroachment on their natural habitat has shrunk the panda population to about 1,000, now limited to Sichuan and the southern edges of Gansu and Shaanxi. Worried that the pandas might become extinct, the Chinese government invited the World Wildlife Fund to participate in a joint research and conservation project in the Wolong Natural Reserve.

About 100 pandas live in the Wolong Reserve, one of eight panda reserves in Sichuan. It is the largest in area with about 770 square miles. According to Chinese folklore, ten dragons from the East China Sea were flying over this region between the Qinghai-Tibet Plateau and the Sichuan Basin. Overwhelmed by its natural beauty, one decided to settle down and eventually turned into a mountain, which the people named Wolong, or Reclining Dragon. The other nine dragons became mountain ranges nearby.

The drive to Wolong, about 150 miles northwest of Chengdu, takes many hours because of the rough road. Once at the reserve, I was surprised to find two communes inside its borders. Most of the commune members were of Tibetan descent. Smoke curled up from the chimneys of the low stone and wooden houses on both sides of the road. Patches of vegetables under cultivation stretched from the roadside halfway up the mountain.

Early the next morning, we drove up the Balang Mountain, past black-turbaned Tibetans grazing goats that climbed agilely over the steep cliffs to reach for leaves. Pink and white wild rhododendrons bloomed in tall trees high up the slopes. The mist cleared away, revealing vistas of snowy peaks ahead. As we climbed up to a height of 12,500 feet, tufts of clouds hovered below the peaks against a gloriously bright blue sky.

On a grassy slope, a professor from the Chengdu Medical College lectured to a group of students on wild herbs. Across the way, in an emerald green meadow spotted with alpine flowers, villagers dug for medicinal herbs which the commune would then buy.

At dusk, the villagers came down from the mountains. The men carried hoes, and the women and children carried baskets on their backs filled with leaves to feed the pigs. The women wore long blue cotton dresses tied at the waist and silver earrings and bracelets. Many had intermarried with Han Chinese and no longer spoke Tibetan.

I met a large, extended Tibetan family. The grandparents, who were probably in their forties, looked healthy and robust. They lived with their seven children, two daughters-in-law and grandchild. The Tibetans are very proud of their large families. The family planning policy, in force among most Han Chinese, has not been imposed on China's minority groups.

I asked to take a picture. The family posed smiling and, pointing to my Nikkormat, said, "Give us a picture!" They made the motion of a print coming out of the camera. Ah! Even in this remote corner of the world, they have seen the magic box that spits out pictures! When I explained that my prints would have to be processed, they quickly put their hands to their faces and walked off, saying, "If you don't give us the picture, you can't take it."

I asked Yin Deren, the administrator of the reserve, about the people living at Wolong. "We are a nature and a people's reserve," he replied. "It is unusual to have a commune inside a nature reserve, but these people have always been here. We tried to move them out, but it wasn't possible, so we are educating them and giving them economic incentives not to hunt. Every peasant receives 5 fen (3 cents) a year for protecting one *mu* (.16 acre) of forest land."

Yin spoke with respect of Dr. George Schaller, the eminent animal behaviorist, who was doing field research at Wolong for the World Wildlife Fund. "He does not demand luxuries. When he finds panda droppings, he picks them up with his hands and puts them in his pockets"—Yin made fists of his hands and stuck them into his pockets, protruding them—"and brings them back to study."

With Hu Jinchu, a Chinese biologist from the Nanchong Teachers College, and research assistants, Schaller has camped for months in the mountains to record the pandas' patterns of eating, sleeping, playing, and mating. I met him soon after he had come down from the mountain. A tall, lean man tanned by outdoor living, Schaller spoke quietly but forcefully about the need to protect the mountain ecology.

"Plants and animals take care of themselves," he said. "The thing is to leave them alone. It's really people we have to manage. You must draw a line beyond which people can't go, and be firm. This is the first time in many years that China has been politically settled enough so that it can accomplish things if it sets its mind to it.

"So far we have captured and collared only three pandas," he continued. "The collars have mounted radio transmitters that tell me where the pandas go after we set them free. This information will give us an idea how much area a panda uses and how much bamboo it needs to consume."

A sense of peacefulness pervades Wolong. It takes time for the place to reveal itself. I regretted I could not stay the weeks or months necessary to encounter a panda in the wild. I had only a few days, but was grateful for those. At Wolong, I heard the murmur of the mountains, the roar of the river, and saw the beauty of wild rhododendrons. I made friends with the children. On the morning of my departure, the children came down the mountain from all directions and smiled as they waved good-bye.

I was determined to buy a second-class ticket for the 24-hour trip to Kunming. Unable to do so through the hotel, I went to the railroad station and joined the long queue. At last I boarded the train and found my "hard sleeper" in car three. Triple-deckers were lined up closely throughout the car. Mats and blankets covered the leather bunks. The accommodations were far from deluxe, but spacious and comfortable compared to the congestion in the "hard seat" sections.

As the train moved slowly out of the station, music and announcements came over the loudspeaker. "Welcome aboard! Please do not spit at random. Put cigarette ashes in the ashtray." The passengers had brought their own tea cups. They had also brought along their own towels and had hung them up side by side on a rack near the train window. A whole row of these flowery towels looked like a colorful field of patchwork. An attendant came through the car carrying a big metal cauldron and filled our cups with hot water. The train's disc jockey played "Jingle Bells" and "Rudolf the Red-Nosed Reindeer," and I had to remind myself it was May.

By evening we passengers were well acquainted. We ate watermelon seeds and chatted; many smoked. Steam curled up from the big cauldron, blotting out our reflections in the windows.

The Chengdu-Kunming line, which crosses over the eastern edge of China's most forbidding mountain terrain, was not completed until 1970. It passes through 427 tunnels and over 653 bridges. Many workers died in the attempt to cut paths through the sheer rock. Near Puxiong is a cemetery in memory of those who sacrificed their lives to the railway. Row after row of tombstones stand forlornly on a hill.

Shortly before ten o'clock, an attendant came through our car calling, "Get ready for bed! Lights out at ten!" The passengers climbed into their berths. Almost as soon as the lights went out, sounds of snoring filled the car.

In the morning we passed through open red-earth country. Across the endless expanse of blue sky, iridescent white clouds billowed, some smooth silk, some puffy cotton. We had reached Yunnan Province.

Forested mountains cover most of Yunnan. Only 5 percent of the land is cultivated. Members of some 25 minority groups, with their own cultures and languages, account for about one-fourth of the province's 30 million people. Yunnan's plant and animal life is also diverse; most of China's species can be found there in climates that range from alpine to tropical.

Kunming, the capital, is beautifully situated on a high, fertile plateau surrounded on three sides by gently rolling mountains. Southwest of the city, colorful patched sails skim the surface of Lake Dian, a shimmering body of water some 25 miles long. Broad avenues, pastel buildings, and parks filled with trees and flowers give the "city of eternal spring" the atmosphere of a relaxed southern outpost.

In the park beside the lake, red geraniums, hydrangeas, jasmines, and primroses bloomed next to thick clusters of bamboo. Women leisurely played mahjong on stone tables under the warm sun. Near the park, a creek ran alongside yellow earthen houses with white roofs and upcurving eaves. Naked children splashed in the water. A man fished with a net attached to two long bamboo poles. Old men smoked under trees by the bank. The sky was clear and luminous. The air and light transformed prosaic surroundings and made them glow. How far I had come from gray, drab Peking, where one might not see the sun for weeks!

Over 2,000 years ago, a highly skilled bronze-making culture flourished near Lake Dian. Tomb excavations at Shizhaishan have uncovered thousands of artifacts, including weapons and drums full of cowrie shells that were used as currency. They have also unearthed objects of silver, jade, and turquoise. Vividly realistic scenes of action—warfare, hunting, and ritual sacrifice—give us a rich pictorial account of this people's distinctive life-style.

Early one morning I set out for the Stone Forest, a 200-acre park of fantastic-shaped rock pillars. I had hoped for solitude in the primeval stone forest 75 miles from Kunming, but its fame is so widespread that it has become one of China's favorite tourist spots. T-shirts, towels, and scarves are all emblazoned with its name.

I followed a stream of people along the narrow paths through the crevices in the rocks. It would be easy to lose one's way in this labyrinth. Looking up, I saw one rock perched precariously on another. Its name was Hanging by a Hair. Many people rushed past me to reach the highest point in the forest, the Viewing the Peaks Pavilion. At last I came to a steep flight of steps and, pulling myself up with both hands, reached the top. What a breathtaking view, a vast sea of gray, craggy peaks and high cliffs, each one dramatically different in shape—nature's giant sculpture garden!

The rock pillars were formed millions of years ago when rainwater dissolved and split the thick limestone. Marine fossils found in the limestone indicate that earlier still the region had been under a deep sea. The Stone Forest is the home of the Sani people, a branch of the Yi minority group, the largest in Yunnan. Sani villages come right to the forest's edge. Out of Sani rice fields rise the strange formations, rock islands among neat rows of seedlings.

A few minutes outside Kunming, the famous Burma Road winds along high precipices through the red-earth country. With barely enough room for two cars abreast, China's World War II lifeline is still western Yunnan's major thoroughfare. Convoys of heavily laden trucks speed along the tortuous 600-mile stretch inside China. A friend who worked in Lashio, Burma, at the time, recalls: "As soon as the war with the Japanese broke out in 1937, the Chinese started to build the road from Kunming to British Burma. The provincial government would round up countless men and put them to work on it—with their bare hands. There was almost no equipment. When the road was opened in 1939, war materials from the U.S. were shipped to Rangoon, and from there sent by rail or truck to Lashio. That ended in April 1942 when the Japanese reached northern Burma." Bypassing Lashio, the road was reopened in early 1945, in time to supply the Chinese Army for the last months of the war.

From the road I saw vistas of green fields and rolling plateaus beneath brilliant skies. Farmers bent over, transplanting rice seedlings to the irrigated fields. Next to the rice fields, golden wheat was almost ready for harvest. It was mid-May. After harvesting the wheat, farmers with water buffalo would plow the earth and turn it over in clumps. Then they would plant rice. On incredibly steep hills I saw shadowy figures moving. Farmers were planting where it seemed that a man could barely stand without falling.

There is no train southwest from Kunming, so I had little choice but to fly to Simao, the jumping-off place for the Xishuangbanna area, my final destination. The flying time is only 40 minutes, but my trip stretched to more than 10 hours. The daily flight takes off only when the weather is fair both in Kunming and Simao. Our plane was scheduled to depart at seven in the morning, but weather delayed it.

That afternoon when the sun came out, I decided to go to the airport. "There are still five clouds in Simao and they are too low," an attendant told me. I couldn't help wondering who was assigned to count the clouds.

A group of Dai people squatted near the landing field. The women wore sarongs and sandals and had large towels draped around their heads. They had been waiting at the airport for three days. They said they had boarded the plane the day before but then had been told to disembark because the weather had changed again in Simao.

Our plane finally took off at 3:30 in the afternoon. Beside me sat a man with a beautiful goldfish in a large tin cup, which he held adoringly. Luckily the clouds had lifted when we reached Simao.

Early the next morning we set out for Jinghong, the administrative center of Xishuangbanna. We drove over lush mountains and past rain forest so dense that light barely filters through. Within this primitive forest—one of the few remaining in China—live elephants, wild oxen, gibbons, boa constrictors, and a third of China's bird species. Although the Chinese have set up reserves to protect 500,000 acres of this forest, from the road I could see acre after acre of stubby, scorched tree stumps—the result of primitive slash-and-burn farming still practiced in Xishuangbanna.

We stopped at Manjinglan, a village about 15 minutes from Jinghong. Beyond the rice fields, silvery clouds hung below the tops of the green mountains. A cluster of wooden houses built on stilts rose above the deep mud. On one porch, a mother bathed her young daughter and combed her long hair.

I climbed up to the house of Yu Jiao, the accountant of the village, and took off my shoes as is the custom. The house was spacious. The living room measured about eight persons' lengths across.

Yu Jiao, the mother of two young children, was a small, delicate woman about thirty years old, but she looked ten years younger. She wore a lime green cotton blouse with pink-flowered trim, a long sarong, and a silver belt. Her daughter was dressed in the same style blouse, skirt, and belt, and wore the same upswept hairdo.

"Her belt is not real silver, though," Yu Jiao said. "The silver one is stored away because we're afraid she might lose it."

While we chatted at a low table, the geese beneath the house squawked loudly and impatiently, trying to get through the fence. Yu Jiao asked her little boy to let them out. He was hovering over his new, prized possession, a transistor radio that the family had recently purchased for 150 yuan (about $90).

"He wanted it so much and pestered us constantly until we bought it," the mother said.

The family had built the house with the help of the village builder, an elderly man who was also visiting that day. They had obtained a permit to cut trees from the forest and float the logs down the Lancang River. Twelve good swimmers helped transport the logs to the village on a raft. When they raised the roof beam, the family invited their neighbors to a feast.

The clothes of Yu Jiao and her husband hang on a post near the bedroom to signify that they will live together always. Among Dai people, the man marries into the woman's family, the opposite of the Han custom. "My husband's relatives sent him to my home the day of our wedding," Yu Jiao told me.

A peal of thunder interrupted our conversation and rain pelted down. I looked up at the small opening in the middle of the roof, expecting rain to pour through, but not a drop fell in. We were safe and dry. The builder told me he had built 30 houses in this village in the past 10 years. He uses no plans but builds according to his knowledge and the amount of wood available.

I noticed that his brown, leathery skin was tattooed with circles and swirls. "If you were not tattooed, no woman would have you," he laughed, speaking of his generation. "Even if you did have a wife, she would think that your plain skin was like a woman's and would laugh at you. I was tattooed when I was 13 and got very sick. My whole body became swollen and I threw up for days."

The old man said that in his youth he had served for 20 years in the village temple, where he learned to read and write Dai. "There were 39 monks at the time and only 50 families in the village. The families who could spare a son from work in the fields sent him to the temple to be educated. We took turns going from house to house begging for food from the villagers. Because of their strong faith, the people would give their best food to the temple. Even if they had nothing to eat, they would give something. During festival days we would eat very well." He laughed, remembering the days of plenty.

"Not many villagers are believers now. Our temple is empty. It was closed in 1963 and later much of it was destroyed by the Red Guards. But the nearby Mange village temple still has some Buddhist deities, and monks come by bus from neighboring towns to worship."

It was indeed raining in Xishuangbanna. My friends in distant Peking had been right. From my room in the Jinghong guest house, I could hear the rain falling on the flowers in the garden. It gushed into the Lancang River, which becomes the Mekong farther south. I knew the villages would be knee-deep in mud.

Crickets had managed to crawl through the crack under the porch door. They jumped on the floor, and onto the table and bed. Flying ants hovered around the ceiling light. The *bihu*, a wall lizard, darted about swiftly and silently, flashing out its tongue to catch insects. Hundreds of tiny ants appeared on my neatly made bed. I crushed as many as I could with my hand and swept them off the sheet. I checked under the embroidered green silk spread. Then I lifted the mosquito net from its hooks and lowered it, switched off the light, and climbed into bed.

It was sweltering inside the net. An army of cicadas buzzed and rasped staccato. And then it came, that inevitable dreaded drone and hum of a mosquito. I climbed out of bed and turned on the light. Satisfied that there was no mosquito, I lay down again. Insidiously, the droning started all over.

By morning all was quiet. The rain had stopped. The myriad creatures of the tropical forest were still. I went down to the garden which overlooked the rushing Lancang River. Purple bougainvillea, fuchsia, and jasmine were heavy with dew. Bunches of bananas hung from the trees. Mangoes and papayas as large as watermelons were still green. I had come to Xishuangbanna during the off-season, just after the lichees and before the mangoes.

Trains like these carry hundreds of millions of Chinese and two-thirds of the nation's freight each year. With more than 30,000 miles of track linking Peking to all the provincial capitals except Tibet's, railroads are China's primary means of transportation. Thirty years ago, China's modest railroad system had fallen into chaos. Of the 13,000 miles of track built since the late 19th century, war and neglect had badly damaged half.

Shirley Sun traveled into Sichuan on the Baoji-Chengdu line, the first to link the province to the rest of China. Formidable mountains made construction an engineering feat: One-third of the 416 miles of track had to be bored through solid rock. A 1970 extension of this line sped the author on to Kunming. Some 653 bridges like the stone arch Strip of Sky (above) link the rails over the 674-mile stretch. As a result, many remote minority areas are now accessible.

In 1876, China's first experiment in railroad-building—a short stretch between Shanghai and Wusong—was so opposed by the local people that they tore the tracks up. Fear that the rails would "throw the elements into disharmony" was a factor in halting construction for the next quarter-century. In the early 1900s, foreigners built railroads mainly to serve their own commercial interests. From the treaty ports, the rails went inland only as far as necessary to sell goods and load up on raw materials. The result was almost no railroad lines in the south and southwest.

323

In China, railroads run on time and make the briefest stops at stations, just long enough to take on ice (opposite, top left), or for passengers to buy a snack from a railside vendor (right). Loudspeakers in every coach and compartment broadcast endless music, interspersed with announcements and news bulletins. A disc jockey (opposite, top right) operates the audio center on each train.

Foreign visitors and high-ranking Chinese officials dine, or breakfast Western-style (opposite, bottom), in cars complete with white tablecloths, shiny cutlery, potted plants, and attentive service. They will then return to the old-fashioned comfort of their "soft sleepers." Since the late 1970s, the Chinese have added nearly 100 new passenger trains to their railway system. With 945 million tickets sold in 1981, it is probably the world's most intensively traveled.

324

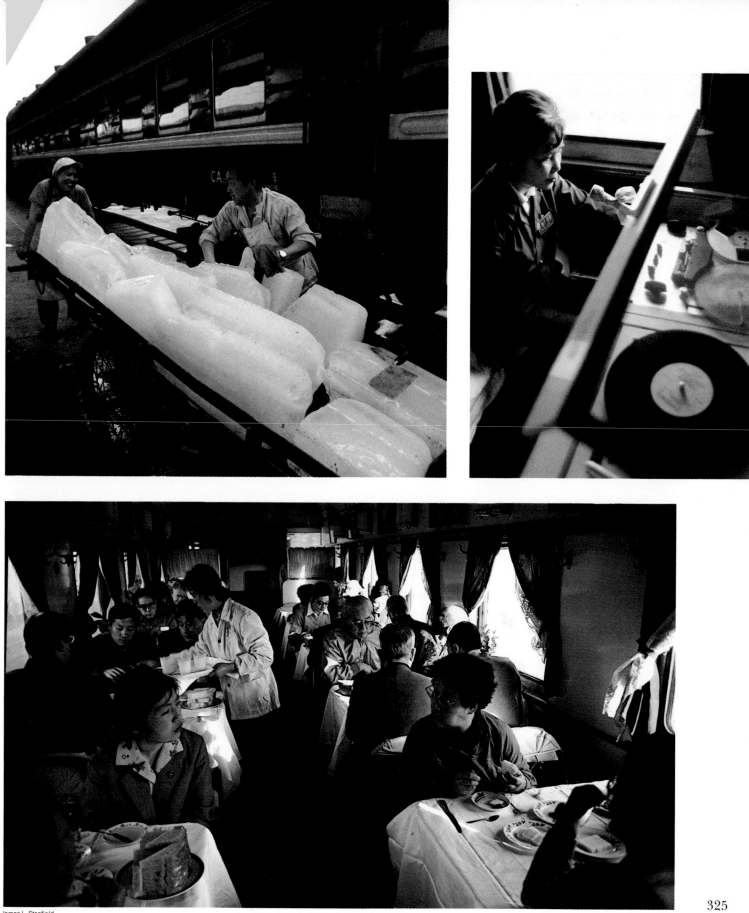

James L. Stanfield

325

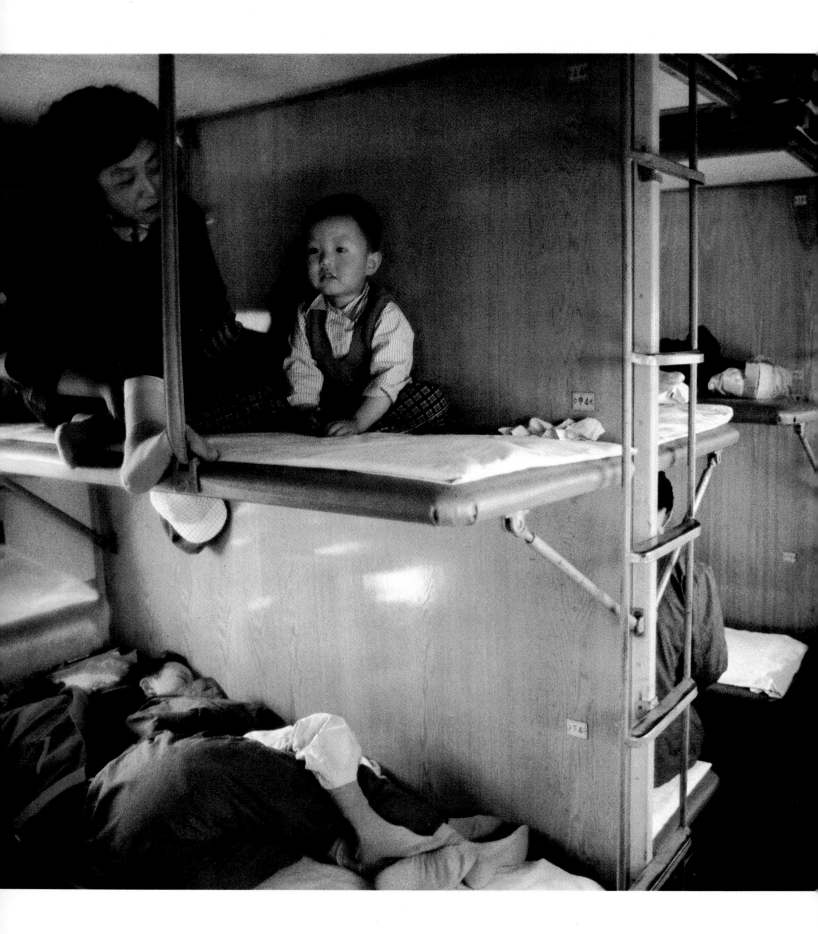

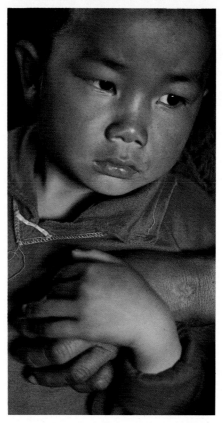

On trains, most Chinese travel by "hard seat" (above) or, if they can afford a ticket, by "hard sleeper" (far left), doorless compartments with six padded bunks in three tiers—and no privacy. If no berth is available, a person may have to sit up on a small flip-down chair by the window. Doubling up with mother is another alternative, that of this rosy-cheeked young boy (left). "Hard class" passengers bring their own food or buy it from attendants who circulate with snacks and drinks. Other attendants continually mop the corridors. At the ends of each car, passengers wash up in uncurtained areas with small sinks.

327

A rare glimpse of a panda in the wild. Only about a thousand pandas remain in the high bamboo forests of southwest China, a small corner of their prehistoric range. Here in Sichuan's Wolong Natural Reserve, scientists study the enigmatic creatures, which are both bear- and racoon-like but may belong to neither family. By finding answers to such questions as how far pandas roam and how much bamboo they need to eat, the Chinese and the World Wildlife Fund hope to save the panda from extinction. Another curiosity: Pandas claw trees (left). Why? No one knows.

But the panda is only one of Wolong's rare creatures. In mist-shrouded mountains (opposite), where climates range from subtropical to alpine, live golden monkeys, white-lipped deer, and other animals found only in China.

329

B illboards like this (left) on the main street of Chengdu, Sichuan's capital, remind Chinese that birth control is serious business. One-child families reap rewards including income subsidies and priority housing. The birth of a second child may eliminate the privileges; a third can incur economic penalties for the family, and put the child at the bottom of the waiting lists for schools. During the 1970s, China's birthrate halved while Sichuan, with 100 million people, reduced its birthrate even further.

In Chengdu, the southwest's second-largest city, a bamboo forest dedicated to Xue Tao, a famous Tang poetess, lures three members of the younger generation (above). The children are potential beneficiaries of China's uphill effort to improve living standards by cutting population growth to zero by the year 2000.

331

A*pricots, peaches,
and apples fill a market (far left) in
Chengdu. Vendors along the city streets
sell everything from geese to bamboo bas-
ketware. A corner shop may steam meat-
filled buns (above) or offer any of 200
other snacks for which the city is famous.
Vegetables (left) go into peppery dishes in
the many restaurants. Bounty from some
of China's most fertile land makes Sichuan Province increasingly prosperous
and self-sufficient.*

*Sichuan is a testing ground for Chi-
na's efforts to liberalize the economy. Private plots of land, free markets, and
sideline businesses are all encouraged.
Bonuses and incentives promote a policy
of "work more, get more."*

333

lderly pilgrims (left) climb Mount Emei, a famous Buddhist mountain in Sichuan. In temples along the 39-mile trail to the summit, the old people, mostly women, burn paper money as an offering to Buddha for long life. (A local guide humorously attributes their longevity to the good exercise of this yearly climb.) With provisions to last them a week or so, a group of women at the base of the mountain (bottom left) prepares for the climb.

"As if the immortal spirits had come down to thrum their lutes," wrote a poet of Mount Emei in 1886, as he stood at the Twin Bridges (opposite) below the Elegant Sound Pavilion. There one can "clearly hear the voices of two waters"— the Black Dragon and White Dragon Rivers—as they come together and cascade onto a giant rock eroded to the shape of a heart. Pilgrims and tourists stop here to rest and listen.

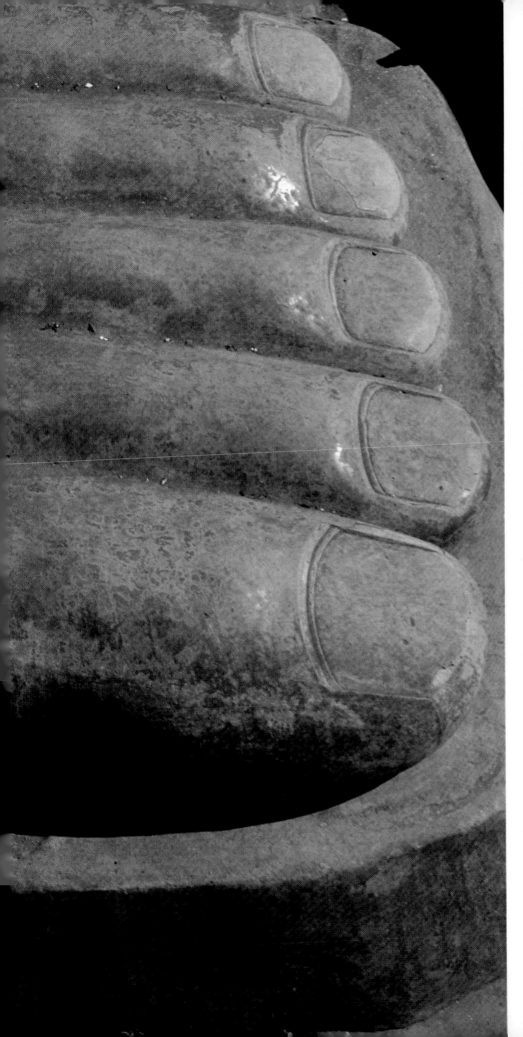

A 231-foot sitting Buddha (above), the world's largest, overlooks the convergence of three rivers at Leshan. The statue was carved out of a cliff in the eighth century in the hope that its benign influence would protect boatmen from the dangerous currents. An ingenious drainage system inside the Buddha channels off water and prevents weathering. From its head at the cliff's crest, a path winds down to the Buddha's foot (left).

337

The still waters of a canal mirror earthen thatched-roof houses in Kunming, capital of Yunnan Province. Dry, cool temperatures and a luminous atmosphere make the "city of eternal spring" unusual in China. After dinner, people stroll the broad avenues or smoke in their doorways (right), reveling in the long twilight. In the early morning, Green Lake Park, near the city's edge, teems with joggers, cyclists, people exercising—and, later, skating enthusiasts.

Although its history goes back 2,000 years, Kunming only began to grow into a modern city during the Sino-Japanese War, when large numbers of Chinese fled to the southwest, bringing dismantled factories and universities with them.

A young Sani girl (left), member of the Five Pines Production Brigade, strings hemp around stakes set in the dirt. Other women will weave the fiber into a beige fabric from which the blue-trimmed Sani garments are made. The Sani are a branch of the mountain-dwelling Tibeto-Burman Yi, the largest minority in Yunnan. Like other minorities, the Sani have autonomous areas within the province. Wooden carts (top) drawn by water buffalo haul Sani loads. In most of China, the horse is still the main short-distance hauler (above).

But in the south, the water buffalo does most of the heavy work.

OVERLEAF. The Stone Forest, limestone formations in fantastic shapes, sprawls out from the Sani village. Legend says that one of China's eight immortals shattered a mountain to make a labyrinth for lovers to court in.

The characters on the city wall (opposite) say "Dali," ancient capital of the Bai people, one of Yunnan's oldest minorities. Today a small city of mixed population and little importance near the Burma Road, Dali was once the capital of Nan Zhao, a powerful and cultivated kingdom that ruled Yunnan for five centuries. Formed from six small Bai kingdoms, Nan Zhao established itself in the mid-700s after beating back imperial Tang forces in two decisive battles. In one battle, 60,000 Chinese died—out of an army of 80,000. The Mongols conquered the kingdom in the 13th century and moved the province's capital east to Kunming.

Today most of the million or so Bai live in the Dali-Bai autonomous district. Official policy gives them and the country's many other minority groups the "freedom to maintain or transform their customs and habits." But official actions promote transformation, and the large numbers of Han Chinese that live in minority areas advance that goal.

At one Bai village, an official (above) weighs brigade workers' loads. The straw and other gleanings will be used for baskets, thatch, and fuel. The village's 16 production teams grow rice, maize, and wheat, most of which the commune keeps. Families can raise livestock and grow vegetables in private plots and sell them to the state or at the district's many fairs.

To Bai villagers, raising the roof beam calls for ritual and celebration. A moment of prayer (far left) dedicates the building. Smearing cock's blood on a post (left) warns away bad animals and spirits. A simmering pig's head (above) assures prosperity, as well as a pungent dish of broth for all assembled. Other customs include throwing coins baked in bread from the roof to show continuing wealth, and splashing the house with water to "waterproof" it.

OVERLEAF. Bai women and children watch firecrackers at the ceremonies. Blue and white embroidered headdresses with short fringes are married women's; those of unmarried women have long fringes. Some material for traditional clothing is now factory-made in Shanghai so minority women will have more time for fieldwork. The state encourages marketable handicrafts only.

347

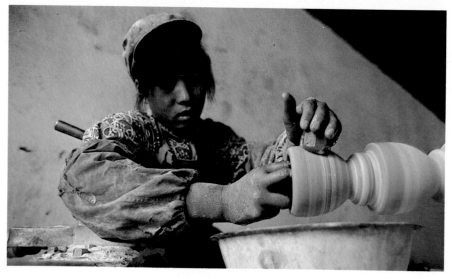

With heavy slabs of marble on their backs (right), Bai workers descend from a quarry in the Cangshan range, just as their ancestors did a thousand years ago. At the bottom of the steep path, one worker helps to free another from her load (top). A factory worker (above) fashions the stone into a vase.

Fine texture and beautiful markings make Dali marble famous throughout China. The word "dali" actually means "marble." "White jade" marble glistens on the bridges, balustrades, and stairways of Peking's Forbidden City as well as on many other palaces and temples. The natural designs in Dali marble inspire craftsmen to create landscape scenes, bas-reliefs, and tiny gardens.

Fishermen in inner tubes (right) keep a day-long silent vigil on Lake Erhai, awaiting their catch. Dali's 25-mile scenic stretch of water and the crystal-clear light of this mountain region also attract artists (above) from other areas. Some 18 rivers flow into Lake Erhai from the Cangshan range. Pumping stations raise the water level to irrigate nearby fields. Near the lake and on a small island in its center, archaeologists have found the tools of a Neolithic people who lived there several thousand years ago.

OVERLEAF. Three Buddhist temple pagodas at the foot of the Cangshan date from the Tang Dynasty. The Ming restored them after an earthquake, and they were thoroughly repaired in the late 1970s.

I
n tropical Xi-
shuangbanna, a wooden house on stilts
keeps a Dai family above the damp earth
and away from animals. A single room
serves as living quarters; curtains section
off a sleeping area. Women prepare
meals on the platform or in the open shed.
Families keep their pigs and chickens beneath the huts.

Dai mothers bathe their children in
streams near the Lancang River (above).
Among Dai, even small girls wear the
traditional ankle-length sarongs, if they
wear anything at all.

Nearly half of Yunnan's 750,000 Dai
live in the Xishuangbanna-Dai autonomous district, a rich basin at the province's southern tip. Dai (or Tai) people,
who total more than 50 million, also in-
habit Thailand, Laos, Burma, and Vietnam. The Dai first appeared in the
Yangtze Valley about two thousand years
ago, but were gradually pushed south by
the Han Chinese.

Rubber trees cover some 650 acres at Xishuangbanna's Tropical Plant Institute. Transplanted from Hainan Island, the trees are part of an experiment to find out where in Yunnan they can flourish. Tapping (above) produces about an ounce of latex a day from each slash. The Plant Institute seeks commercial uses for the region's thousands of tropical plants. From the cananga blossom comes an aromatic essence; from the upas tree, a lethal poison.

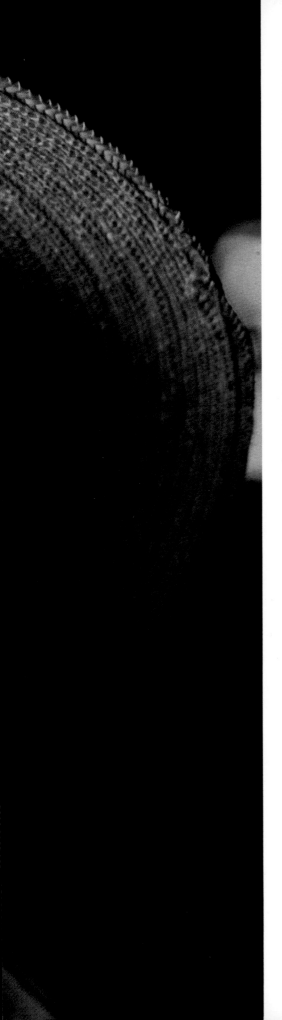

A *Dai matron's gold teeth signal beauty and prosperity. She and her fellow village women (above), all in straw hats and sarongs, harvest the rice near Jinghong, Xishuangbanna's administrative center. The Dai call their region Sip Song Panna, meaning "twelve thousand irrigated fields." The fields grow mainly wet rice, but also tobacco. Water buffalo still do much of the plowing, although increasingly threshers, small tractors, and other farm machines are used. Plantings in and around the villages produce abundant harvests of mangoes, bananas, pineapples, and grapefruits.*

OVERLEAF. Saffron-robed Dai boys attend school at the Manli village Buddhist temple, reopened in 1980. Since the post-Mao liberalization, religious practice in minority areas is making a modest comeback. Historically, the Theravada branch of Buddhism influenced all aspects of Dai life. Monks chose children's names, educated the boys, attended the sick, and appeased the spirits. In return, the villagers supplied monks with food, firewood, and cash, and respectfully shielded the heads of the holy men with umbrellas when they walked in the sun.

Behind the Manli temple nod giant fronds of bamboo. Villagers used such buildings as granaries during the Cultural Revolution, which often helped to preserve them. In temples like this some 13 centuries ago, monks spurred the development of a Dai written language and a rich and enduring literary tradition.

361

B oys at the Manli temple school (above) recite scripture and learn to read and write. It is unlikely that most of the boys will stay long enough to become monks. Although villagers are permitted to practice religion, they are discouraged from proselytizing. At another recently reactivated temple near Manli (right), monks in red caps preside over several Buddhist images that were saved from destruction.

Chinese photograph (also upper and opposite)

Four boys (opposite) perform in the reed-pipe festival of the Miao people in Huangping, Guizhou Province. Their large bamboo pipes, fitted with brass reeds, create a sound akin to bagpipes. The pipes are made especially for such gala occasions when the whole countryside turns out for music, buffalo fights, and horse races. Girls wear lace headdresses and intricately worked silver jewelry, along with their finest embroidered dresses (left). The Miao, found in three south China provinces as well as in Laos, Thailand, and Vietnam, are a tribal, mountain-dwelling people whose customs and dialects survive. Too young to participate much, three Miao children (above) enjoy a snack.

PEOPLE OF THE HIGH PLATEAU

By Roy Reed

Our Toyota Land-Cruiser crept to a stop beside the meager fire and the blackened teapot. The man hunkering by the fire invited us, with some dignity, to hunker with him. He was bare to the waist in spite of the wind from the purple mountain, in spite of the cold river frothing, Colorado-wild, at his feet. His eyes were black. His hair was black and hanging to his shoulders. His skin was bronze.

"Indian," I thought. "He looks like an American Indian."

His name was Tenzin. As he talked and kicked the yak-dung fire, and as he filled our cups with yak-butter tea, Tenzin's authority and rough-handed confidence stirred my memory.

The Chinese government had recently changed its policy to allow Tibetan farmers and herdsmen to dissolve their state-controlled cooperatives if they wished. Tenzin's cooperative had voted to dissolve, and he had taken as his family's share 30 yaks and 127 sheep. It was while he talked of his herd that he teased my memory.

"Originally," he said, "they were the cooperative's." He took a drag on his cigarette. "Now, they are mine."

A monk worships in the Jokhang, Tibetan Buddhism's holiest temple. By Thomas Nebbia.

We were in the sparsely settled mountains 60 miles northwest of Lhasa. Tenzin's gaze moved slowly, proprietarily, across the rocky slopes and the valley and the wild, shimmering sky. Then I remembered where I had seen his tameless eyes. I used to cover the White House as a reporter. Someone once gave President Lyndon B. Johnson a pillow for his place in Texas. The message embroidered on it said, "This is my ranch and I do as I damn please."

"This is my ranch," the eyes of Tenzin said, "and I do as I damn please."

I spent five weeks, practically the whole of a Himalayan summer, traveling among the people of Tibet. I visited in their houses, tents, schools, factories, hospitals, and government offices. I drank tea with them in mountain fields, beside caravans, in dusty markets, and in the holiest temples of Tibetan Buddhism. I talked with rug makers and officials, herdsmen and one-time noblemen. Everywhere, I found them to be warm, gentle, proud, and fierce. In

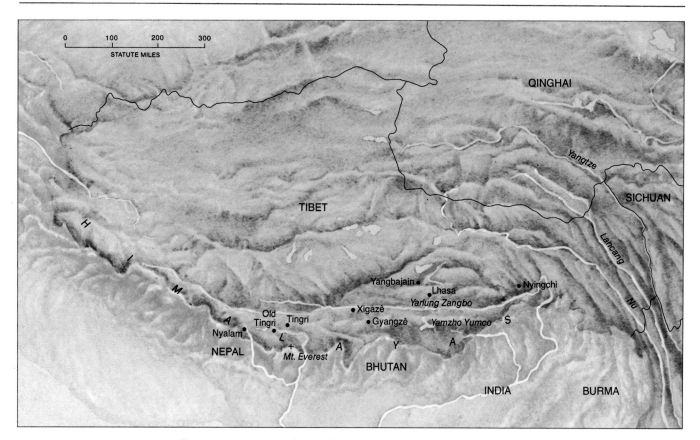

Roy Reed toured Tibet from the bustling towns of the central valleys to the quiet slopes of the Himalayas. His journey took him from the golden temples of Lhasa to the gray mountain village of Nyalam, near the Nepalese border. The author visited herdsmen in the vast countryside. He walked the narrow streets of Gyangzê, an ancient market town some 50 miles from the Bhutan border. And at Xigazê he looked upon the fast-flowing waters of the Yarlung Zangbo (or upper Brahmaputra) River, which, some 400 miles east, begins its fall to the Bay of Bengal.

Roy Reed's visit preceded the political protest sparked by Tibetan monks in Lhasa in 1987.

this latest round in a centuries-long client-state relationship with the Chinese, the Tibetans still eat their own food, drink their own beer, wear their own clothing, pray to their own gods, and go their own mysterious way.

For all my preparation, I could not really see Tibet in my mind. Central Sichuan, the last of the more or less known world, gave no clue. The Ilyushin prop-jet climbed out of Chengdu airport and headed west, and as we left western China, I jotted in my notebook, "The fields of Sichuan are as green as England and as flat as the Arkansas delta."

Central Sichuan, like England and the delta, is comfortable to the Western taste. I had lingered there to savor the lush air and the wonderfully spiced foods. Then into the unknown, the highest, strangest, farthest place on earth.

I had assumed that I would watch from the plane's window and plot my drift from one world to the other, from lowlands to foothills to high plateau. But the gods tease the traveler. The mountains of the ancient China-Tibet frontier are covered with clouds much of the day. When we landed at Lhasa's airport, lurching quite suddenly through the cloud blanket, it was as if we had traveled through time, and the former world had faded in my senses.

A caged bird chirped in the luggage rack. I could make out a muddy pond at the base of a mountain, and alongside it a strip of vivid green. The green in these high valleys seemed far more precious than the lazy green of Sichuan. I was to learn during the coming weeks that every weed, every pulse and breath, is more precious in Tibet.

Tibet is almost twice as big as Texas. Most of it is a plateau ranging upward from 12,000 feet. Mount Everest, the highest point of our planet, rises 29,028 feet on the border with Nepal. Life here, in all forms, is sparse.

When I stepped from the plane, I was struck first by the blinding blue of the sky, then by the chill. Poplars rippled near the runway, and the splashes of light so dazzled me that I could barely discern the green in the leaves. The encircling slopes were impenetrable purple in the cloud shadows and not just brown but bright brown in the sunlight. The date was June 26; the temperature was in the low 60s. A steady breeze from the mountains made the air feel like the air of March in the Ozarks.

The altitude distorted my consciousness. I walked 200 yards up an incline, panting and dazed. I hastened to the car and inhaled oxygen. Most visitors, I learned, stay close to their canvas oxygen bags. Before the week was out, I was stricken with altitude sickness—dizziness, headaches, and diarrhea. In ten days, my face was red and peeling from the unobstructed sun.

We drove into Lhasa in late afternoon during what I mistakenly thought was the rush hour. I soon learned that rush hour lasts all day in the capital of Tibet. Wheeled vehicles were rare until the Chinese took over in 1951. In the newly paved streets, trucks, army jeeps, and official cars compete with bicycles, dogs, goats, sheep, cattle, men, women, and children. Chinese law punishes more severely a driver whose car strikes a pedestrian or a cyclist if he has not sounded his horn. Drivers, therefore, speed through the crowds with horns blaring enthusiastically, never touching their brakes.

When the horns stop, late at night, the dogs take over. China tried to get rid of city dogs, flies, birds, and other nonproductive creatures several years ago. The campaign never caught on in Tibet. Tibetan dogs roam freely in city streets and rural pastures. Some are offspring of the Tibetan mastiffs that Western travelers have always feared. The few Europeans who visited Tibet in the old days often carried clubs to fight them off. A friendly Tibetan in Gyangzê (Gyantse) stood guard over a sleeping mastiff while I walked through a gate. "He may not recognize people," he said. I lay awake one night in Lhasa and listened to a dogfight nearby, and afterward for half an hour the dogs of Lhasa commented on the brawl from every quarter of the city.

The population of Lhasa is about 100,000. A third or more of those are Han Chinese brought in, often reluctantly, to work for the government. The figure does not include numerous soldiers of the People's Liberation Army, who work at common labor in normal times but are ready to help quell any signs of political unrest. The soldiers will be here indefinitely, but Peking claims it is replacing the Han cadres with native Tibetans.

New Lhasa has wide streets, traffic lights, and gray, barracks-like buildings. It covers about a square mile. A state-owned department store sells food, soda, piece goods, toys, electronic gadgets, and other 20th-century necessities. The shelves are as plain as those of a Southern country store. Mainly Tibetan men and women toil in a few small factories that produce rugs, shoes, and small-scale industrial goods. New Lhasa, the creation of the Chinese, is an architectural bore.

Old Lhasa is another story. As soon as I could get away from the guest house in the Chinese section, I walked down the People's Road toward the old quarter. The wide, poplar-lined avenue dead-ends after half a mile at the Barkhor, the heart of old Lhasa. The Barkhor is a narrow, circular street perhaps half a mile round. It begins and ends at the front door of the Jokhang, the ancient temple that is the central shrine of Tibetan Buddhism. Clamorous with commerce and worship, the Barkhor is the St. Peter's Square of Tibet.

I first saw it in the late afternoon. Hundreds of people were in motion, all walking clockwise to keep their right side facing the holy center. An old woman whirled a prayer wheel as she walked. A young man murmured the common Buddhist mantra, "*Om mani padme hum*—Hail to the jewel in the lotus." A dozen pilgrims prostrated themselves in the dirty street and edged toward the temple like inchworms, a body-length at a time. On the sidewalks, people sat on stools selling their goods: *tsampa*, the ground barley that is the staple of every Tibetan house; *chang*, barley beer; tea seasoned with salt and rancid yak butter, which gives it a pleasant cheese flavor; hats, shoes, clothing, and all kinds of handicrafts.

Men, women, and children crowded round to try to sell us brass Buddha figures, silver-handled knives, wood-and-silver tea bowls, rings, bracelets—anything that might be exchanged for cash or some Western item of value. Few succeeded, but all went away with a hearty smile.

One insistent young man sold me a bracelet. His hair was tied in a swelling crest. He carried a long knife on a belt with a silver buckle. His off-white coat, made of homespun wool, was worn in the traditional fashion with his right arm bare and the sleeve tucked into the belt to form a pouch. His boots were homespun wool of red, green, and yellow. He looked like a buccaneer, and bargained like one. Money finally changed hands and he thrust the note into the pouch of his coat. Then he gave me a warm grin, looked me squarely in the eye, and slapped me on the shoulder. I knew I had been conned by a master.

I spent about two weeks exploring Lhasa and the surrounding country-side. I went to bed every night exhausted by discovery. The downtown guest house where I stayed was an aging accommodation with slip-covered chairs and a cold-water tap that operated an hour in the morning and an hour at night. Showers were in another building and by appointment. The bed, which sported a brightly colored quilt, was the only comfort. (The only guest house that matches Western standards is about five miles outside of Lhasa.)

On the day I met Tenzin, the herdsman, I saw hot water wells drilled into the valley at Yangbajain (Yangpachen), about 60 miles northwest of Lhasa. The government is harnessing geothermal power there for electricity. The project is experimental, but the government has high hopes. About 1,000 Tibetans and Han Chinese were working there during my visit. The hot wells were producing enough electricity for the work camp and a few communes nearby. Qian Shanbei, a Chinese engineer, told me that river water was Tibet's real strength. Tibet has about 20 percent of China's potential waterpower, he said, and on these fast-flowing mountain streams are at least 500 small hydro-electric generating plants. I saw several of those, each—when kept in repair—providing electric power for a single village.

I visited the great Buddhist centers of Lhasa that survived the Chinese takeover and the Cultural Revolution of the 1960s and early 1970s: the Potala, home of the Dalai Lamas and the governing site of all of Tibet's religious rulers since the seventh century, towering above the city from Red Hill; the Jo-khang, once shut down by the Red Guards but now, since the government tolerates religion again, a place of worship with a few lamas praying and burning yak-butter candles; the Drepung Monastery outside the city, once a community of thousands, now virtually a museum tended by a few dozen lamas; the Norbulingka, the Dalai Lama's summer palace, now a museum and park.

Tibet had more than 3,700 monasteries and temples before the Chinese came, according to friends of the Dalai Lama. Almost all have been destroyed. A Chinese foreign affairs officer stationed in Lhasa told a friend of mine that he could count 13 major monasteries still operating at some level. A number of small community temples are scattered through the country. I saw the ruins of several dozen temples as we drove along the main highways.

At the Drepung, an old monk talked to me of the special powers that some lamas are said to have. He said he knew one who could "trance walk," covering the boulder-strewn countryside in a trance with huge bounding steps at the speed of a fast car. He told of another who could produce "mystic heat" and dry wet towels with his body on a winter night, outdoors. I later learned that heat-producing feats had been tested by Western scientists, who observed temperature rises of up to 15°F in less than an hour.

At the traditional Tibetan hospital, a few blocks from a modern Chinese hospital, I met an old physician who told me of doctors so sensitive that they could touch a string extending through a window and tell what thing or creature was tied to the other end. I must have looked doubtful. He turned to a young Chinese woman in our group—a woman I don't think he had ever seen before—and studied the pulse of both her wrists for five minutes. Then he said to her, "I think you have a problem with your heart." She nodded, apparently amazed, and said, "Yes, that's right."

On the sly, late one afternoon, I visited a funeral rock that was off limits to foreigners. It was a 40-foot oblong boulder raised at one end to make a level surface. I saw ravens picking the bones of a corpse that had been cut up and left there before dawn. The rock was pockmarked, perhaps from years of pecking by the ravens. I was told that a body left before dawn will be picked clean by daylight. The Tibetans call this "sky burial" and believe that it hastens the soul to its next incarnation.

Prudently pessimistic, the Chinese have made little effort to change the funeral practice. They have tried, unsuccessfully, to change other Tibetan ways. For example, the government tries to discourage people from urinating and defecating on the street. But many people still do so whenever the urge overtakes them.

I saw a naked boy of about ten hitching a ride on the back of a bicycle. He hopped off opposite the department store, at the busiest intersection in town. He stood at the curb for a long time with his hands clasped behind his head, just watching the people go by. No one paid him any attention.

The government tried to train the Tibetans to grow wheat in large quantities, and nearly ruined thousands of fragile acres before giving it up. The Tibetans still eat barley, as their fathers did.

I visited an agricultural research station. The manager showed me dozens of splendid experiments with crops. I came away with the impression that the Chinese overseers were simply marking time while they fretted over how to persuade the Tibetans to adopt new methods. I was reminded of Faulkner's old Bayard Sartoris, who spent his days fretting over the cunning, intractable field hands he had inherited after the fall of the slave system in Mississippi.

To my surprise, I saw house sparrows. I heard one chirping under a rope of prayer flags on the windy crest of a 16,000-foot pass. On the funeral rock at Lhasa, unconcerned among the huge ravens, a dozen sparrows pecked at pieces of bone. I was awakened every morning by the gossip of sparrows outside the government guest houses in Lhasa, Gyangzê, Xigazê (Shigatse), and Tingri. The high, thin air of Tibet will knock a lowland man to his knees, but this humble bird thrives. The sparrow is a perfect simile for the common Tibetan—cheeky, undefeated, quick, firmly at home and full of swagger in one of the world's most hostile climates.

The last thing I saw the day I left Lhasa was the Potala. The huge red and white palace had been my first sight every morning as I turned over in bed. I had watched it disappear at night, resisting the darkness. I had seen it defy the mists of dawn, and I had watched thunderclouds swirl and come apart against the golden turrets. Now I was leaving without seeing the mysterious palace in a small, special way that I had wished. Twice, I had been driven up Red Hill for guided tours, and they had been instructive. I had especially enjoyed a tiny, cavelike room called Chogyal Draphu. A guide told me that it was one of the few remaining rooms of the original building. It was lighted by yak-butter candles. The ceiling was arched and dark from smoke. Several Buddha images were crowded into the room, which I could cross in three or four strides. The ancient Buddhists had considered it the best place in the world for meditation. I remember standing alone for a moment wrapped in the yak-butter smoke, overcome by a history so remote from me that I could only marvel.

I had wanted very much to slip away and go back to the palace. From street level to the roof was a climb of a thousand feet, a daunting task for an oxygen addict. Most men know they will never climb Everest, or sail across the Atlantic. The least I could do in tribute to the heroic tradition was climb to the roof of the Potala. Now I had missed the chance. Or so I thought. I had not counted on the vagaries of travel and the obstinacy of the bureaucracy.

We left Lhasa at midmorning on a crisp, sunny July day. Beside me at the wheel of the Land-Cruiser was Lin, a Chinese Army veteran, a genius in dust, mud, and flood. Sitting in back were John Holden, a Minnesotan who spoke fluent Chinese, and Ma, a Lhasa Muslim who translated from Tibetan to Chinese. Lin and Ma were employed by the government agency that had arranged our trip through the mountains and over the frontier to Nepal.

On the dusty road that morning we passed hundreds of workers in fields of vegetables, barley, and rape. Many were women with hoes. They wore long black wool skirts, black jackets, and red head scarves. At noon, they huddled around teapots and small fires.

We met a few dozen motor vehicles, mainly army trucks and jeeps, and scores of wagons drawn by horses, yaks, mules, and goats. We saw houses of stone and gray adobe with sod roofs, most in compact villages but here and there tucked alone into the shelter of a bluff. We saw caravans of yaks and burros crawling the mountains, sometimes so far above us that even the hairy yaks were mice against the purple mystery.

375

As we gained altitude, the fields became smaller and wrapped with terraces. We rounded a steep curve at 12:15 and made two simultaneous discoveries—the first snow peak of our trip, high in the west, and a truck hurtling down the middle of the narrow gravel road. Lin swerved to the edge of the abyss. The truck driver grinned as he swept past. Several days later on the same mountain, we saw a truck overturned and its load of grain spilled in a hairpin curve. We hoped it was the same driver.

We inched upward in first and second gear. The noise of Lhasa was miles behind us. Up here, the silhouette of a single eagle or the squeak of a lonesome mouse was enough to catch my full attention. We stopped for half an hour at the top of a 16,400-foot pass about 75 miles southwest of Lhasa. The air was chilly, perhaps 50°F. This was a favorite place of pilgrims. In spite of the government's coolness toward religion, the pilgrims had stacked stones in cairns all over the ridge and strung ropes for hundreds of small flags to carry messages to the gods. Behind us lay the ridges and valleys that had led faithful Buddhists for centuries to the temples of Lhasa. Ahead of us, far below and to the west, lay the big lake, Yamzho Yumco (Yamdok Yutso).

I stood gazing at Yamzho Yumco and heard the sparrow chirp among the flags. At the same moment I smelled, wafted on the wind, burnt yak butter. Yak butter is burned everywhere in religious ceremony, in temple candles, at roadside cairns. The scent rises from ancient greasy stones and breathes from faded silk *tankas,* or banners. Rub against the clothing of a Tibetan and you come away smelling faintly of yak butter and smoke. Then in your imagination mix the scent of smoke and butter with the peatlike fragrance of burning yak dung, and you glimpse the Tibetan soul. It is a soul that accommodates fierce violence and devotion to life. Ma told me about the *dop-dop,* a fraternity of free-wheeling monks who organized brutal gang fights with rival dop-dop. They often volunteered for wars against foreign invaders. The survivors of fights and battles would return peacefully to their duties in the monasteries.

We ate lunch that day on a blanket beside the lake. The boys and men of a tiny fishing village sat peering and smiling, and Lin gave them tidbits. Many of them carried wool slings. Almost all Tibetan countrymen carry knives and slings—Davids ready for Goliaths, like the Tibetan soldiers of centuries past who used slings with deadly accuracy. A British expedition from India, led by Col. Francis Younghusband, came up against slings, flintlocks, and broadswords in 1904. Competing with Russia in the "Great Game" over Central Asia, Britain had been seeking ties with Tibet, which had long been closed to foreigners. When the Dalai Lama refused to receive a British emissary, Younghusband marched over the Himalayas to open Tibet by force. The Tibetans tried to block his advance with a stone barrier, but the British killed 600 of them. Then at the *dzong,* or fortress, in Gyangzê, ferocious Tibetans held the British under siege for seven weeks, and only the arrival of reinforcements allowed Younghusband to break through. He continued to Lhasa, where he finally secured trading rights. Strangely enough, after such a beginning, the Tibetans and British eventually developed a warm friendship.

By midafternoon we were climbing again. Above the road were abrupt rock crests and sheer slopes of snow. We rounded a curve and there, not a mile ahead, was a glacier. The snow and ice lay like a rumpled horse blanket on a ridge. I counted ten rivers plunging out of it.

I found it hard to believe that people survived here. The grass was pitiable and the wind blew constantly. But not more than two miles down the road we came to a nomad's black tent of woven yak hair. Two men crouched by a fire. They immediately passed the tea bowl, like the whiskey bottle in a backwoods store. Women and children brought yak cheese. After an hour, Jigme Dorje, the man in charge, finally made the supreme gesture of hospitality. He went into the dark tent and, searching in a corner, found a ragged shank of dried yak leg on the dirt floor.

"We killed it last November," he said.

In summer, Jigme Dorje's work begins at dawn. He opens the pen, a stone rectangle, and takes the sheep to search for grass among the boulders. Then he builds a fire with twigs and yak dung. The nine inhabitants of his tent, members of eight scattered families, all part of a wide-ranging production brigade of 350 people, arise from their rugs and gather round the fire. Their first meal is like their second and third, mainly tsampa. Sometimes they mix it with yak meat and make a stew. Always there is yak-butter tea. Jigme Dorje and the other men and boys spend the day watching the sheep and weaving boot soles of wool and plant fiber. The women and girls work at the tent, weaving cloth and making butter and cheese.

In winter, Jigme Dorje and his wife and comrades tighten the circle. They move to a sheltered spot and pile sod around the tent to keep out the harsh winds. They wear heavy sheepskin over their wool garments. The sheep and yaks are brought to the pens and kept alive with hand-cut hay. There is little to do except weaving. They have no radio, no books, not even a watch. Of course they have no television. Lhasa has the only television station in Tibet, and only a few houses and government buildings have receiving sets.

I saw no lines of worry in Jigme Dorje's face. His only regret was that he and his wife had no children. He was 28; he seemed to feel no pressure to advance, no pull to the city, no itch for a "better life." I thought of my grandfathers, who were never at home away from the comforting fragrances of soil and barn. I embarrassed him by asking whether he liked the way he lived. He laughed. "Yes, I am satisfied with it," he said. "I grew up this way."

I ate the dried yak meat. It was stringy and smoky, like Texas barbecue. Someone passed the tea bowl. The fire felt good, even at midafternoon in July. I sat quietly for a while. The contentment of Jigme Dorje seemed as precious as grass in this wild vastness.

377

The Buddhists, in their regard for life, dislike killing animals. I was curious about the yak meat.

"First," Jigme Dorje said, "we bind the legs of the animal to make it kneel. Then we stab it in the heart. We say a mantra while we kill it."

A mantra?

"Om mani padme hum."

I had heard it often in the temples and streets of Lhasa. Here in the high, shimmering wilderness, where life was an afterthought, "Om mani padme hum" was a form of thanks to the beast. Jigme Dorje understood the commonality of life, that it coursed through the yak as it did through him, and that both shared it with the grass. He also understood that the commonality was severely tested here, because life was as thin as the air.

Back down in the valley of the Yarlung Zangbo (Yarlung Tsangpo) a few days later, I saw firsthand the rites of Tibetan Buddhism. The Tashilhunpo Monastery in Xigazê is the traditional home of the Panchen Lama, historically the second most revered figure of Tibet after the god-king, the Dalai Lama. The present Panchen Lama is married and living in Peking. In spite of his apostasy, or maybe because of it, his monastery continues as one of the last great living religious communities in Tibet. Tashilhunpo once had 5,000 monks; now it has 575. Many support themselves by farming. Each receives 10 yuan ($6) a month pocket money. The last novice was admitted 22 years ago. But the monastery lives.

The lamas made me welcome and admitted me to several services. At one, worshipers filed through an upper room of the temple and paid small sums to have sutras, or scriptures, read for them and their families. At another, a dozen of the leading lamas gathered in a small room near evening and chanted incantations. They wore elaborate costumes and headdresses, and they blew horns, rang bells, and beat drums to punctuate the chants. Worshipers of all ages inched along past the altars and the Buddha images and left grain and butter as offerings. Some wore traditional Tibetan woolens, others Chinese caps and blue jackets. I was told that 300 worshipers a day come to Tashilhunpo, and as many as 3,000 on holy days.

Much of the daily work at the monastery consists of repairing damage done by the Red Guards. One lama estimated, for example, that 90 percent of the sutras of Tashilhunpo had been destroyed. I found five lamas in a workroom carving wooden blocks to reprint them. The Buddhist faithful are accustomed to such patience. Tashilhunpo has been here 500 years and they figure, against all the evidence of recent history, that it will be here another 500.

I spent several days in Gyangzê and Xigazê, sizable towns that serve the relatively productive central valleys west of Lhasa. The Chinese are working to modernize both towns, especially their tourist facilities. I climbed the high hill to the Gyangzê dzong, now mostly a ruin, where the Tibetans had besieged Younghusband. I visited the excellent rug factory at the foot of the fortress hill and watched women weaving rugs by hand, using native wool and vegetable dyes. I loitered in the old markets of Gyangzê and Xigazê, and once, when I sat and rested in a dusty street, an old woman brought me tea and talked to me in Tibetan.

No Westerners are permitted beyond Xigazê without special government approval. We had that approval. But word came in Xigazê that the monsoon had washed out the Friendship Bridge over a high gorge on the Nepalese border. That meant it would be difficult to reach Kathmandu.

West of Xigazê, we saw no more tourists and few Chinese. We spent the first night at Tingri in a guest house with hard cots and outdoor toilets. We left after breakfast and sped westward down the gravel road. We were well into the foothills of the Himalayas. Our goal that morning was to see Mount Everest. But the clouds had hidden it by the time we arrived at the nearest point on the road, the village of Old Tingri.

I complained to an old man named Tsiring Peyma that I had come from the other side of the earth to see Jomo Langmo (the Tibetan name for the mountain) and that it had hidden itself. He said with a twinkle, "You did not come with a true heart." We returned to Tingri.

I pondered that overnight and tried again. We left the next morning before the moon had set. Rabbits and foxes were still working the ditches. We had been on the road an hour and a half and smoke was just starting up from the villages. Lin drove faster.

Daylight began to break as we came near Old Tingri. We fixed our eyes on the southern peaks and saw that clouds were moving in. We passed a dozen yaks and a sleepy herdsman beside a small lake. Then we rounded a bend and someone exclaimed. Everest, 45 miles to the south, stood white against the sky.

Tibetans believe that Jomo Langmo is the home of five sister goddesses. The residents of Old Tingri used to walk to her base to worship in a temple there, but the temple was destroyed after the Chinese came. The worshipers don't go there any more.

We studied the snow face for an hour. It was an old woman's, lined with rock. Once a duck rose from a lake and etched its silhouette on the peak. A woman in Old Tingri had told me that the abominable snowman lived on the wilderness slopes. The government officials had said it was not true, but I preferred to believe. I thought, as I stood gazing, "They have destroyed the temple. Now they will destroy the snowman. And then they will destroy Tenzin, the rancher, who does as he damn pleases."

Once, along the road to Nyalam, we stopped at the edge of a thousand-foot cliff and looked into a small valley. The floor was all green and yellow, barley and rape, bisected by the foam of a river. On the other side, a mountain rose straight from the valley floor and upward until the dark enormity became the sky. It looked like the wall of the world. Far down at the base, at the end of the valley, sat a village of such perfect symmetry that I wondered whether it had been there, brick and rock of the world's wall, from the beginning of the mountain. I knew as I drew away that I would never enter this magic valley. I went unhappily to the end of my road.

At Nyalam we had come nearly 450 miles from Lhasa. The river crossing into Nepal was only 23 miles down the mountain. Officials at Nyalam told us that nothing had been done to replace the washed-out bridge, and that another bridge between Nyalam and the border was also missing.

Could we use a rope bridge? No, the officials said; it is too dangerous.

The Nepalese government wants to help us; could we have a helicopter come from Kathmandu? No.

Back at Xigazê we met Tenzing Norgay, the Sherpa who conquered Everest with Edmund Hillary in 1953. He told us of two other border posts where we could reach Nepal without crossing a river. No, the officials said.

We returned to Lhasa in a dark rain. Once, we were caught in a flash flood roaring down a mountain, and Lin had to wrestle the Land-Cruiser through boulders in three feet of water.

Having once said good-bye to Lhasa, I found myself back there against my will. I would have to backtrack still farther, to Chengdu, and that meant a wait of several days. Then, as July drifted by, I found myself again absorbed in the warm, untamed life of Lhasa. One afternoon, on impulse, John Holden and I climbed to the top of the Potala without our government escorts. We barged past a surprised workman guarding the entrance and explored on our own some of the hundreds of mysterious rooms, with their funeral stupas, countless statues and images of the Buddhas, brilliant silk hangings, and dark, candlelit passageways.

The Potala is a palace the size of a small town sitting hundreds of feet above the river and the streets of the capital. Legend says it has a thousand rooms, but a series of guides and experts assured me that no one knows. The palace is the traditional home of the Dalai Lamas and their courts of noblemen and lamas. This was the power center of the Tibetan theocracy. More than a hundred lamas—teachers, scholars, advisers to the Dalai Lama—lived in the palace before the Chinese came and turned it into a "national primary cultural protected unit," or museum.

Songtsen Gampo, the greatest of the early Tibetan kings, built the beginning of what is now the Potala in the seventh century. Through the years, fire and rebellion destroyed all but a small portion of the original. In the 17th century the fifth Dalai Lama, Lobsang Gyatso, rebuilt the palace in its present form, sprawled across the top of Lhasa. The stone for the massive walls (some appear to be ten feet thick) came from nearby, but the timbers had to be brought from southeastern Tibet, near Bhutan, where the altitude is low enough to grow large forests. Since the Tibetans did not use wheels, the trees had to be carried several hundred miles to Lhasa on the backs of peasants. The Chinese, as part of their campaign to discredit the old theocracy, say that thousands of workers died in the building of the Potala. I do not doubt it.

The Potala contains countless chapels and altars that still attract worshipers every Wednesday, the only day the Tibetan public is allowed in. A typical chapel has one to a dozen images or statues of Buddhas and a number of metal vessels to receive the coins, bits of grain, yak butter, and other small offerings of pilgrims. Usually there is at least one picture of the 14th Dalai Lama.

In the West Great Hall, about 100 feet long and 75 feet wide, the Dalai Lama used to sit on a throne at one end and preside over official functions while his more important lamas sat on the floor in front of him. Other halls contain the stupas, or tombs, of most of the Dalai Lamas. The stupa that houses the salt-preserved body of the Great Fifth is the largest. It rises 49 feet in the shape of a bottle. It is wrapped with gold (110,000 ounces of it, according to a Chinese pamphlet) and studded with precious stones.

July 30 was a holy day. The celebration carried into July 31, and that night was our last in Tibet. Late in the evening, John and I plunged into the circling throng in the Barkhor.

We had almost finished our last walk around, perhaps the last time either of us would see the fabled street, when we were overtaken by a rain shower. We joined a small crowd under an awning. John made friends with a young man who had walked and hitchhiked illegally from Sichuan Province to pay homage to his Tibetan roots. He sold John a butter bucket, with hearty laughter and hard bargaining.

I stood watching the rain and the people. A striking girl stood just beyond the awning. The rain fell on her black hair and glistened on her high cheekbones. I got her attention and, with awkward sign language, urged her to come into the dry. She apparently mistook my intentions. She ducked her head and moved farther into the street.

John laughed. He nodded toward a young man, a handsome fellow with smoldering eyes and a silver dagger on his belt. Unknown to me, he had been quietly courting the girl. My signals to her had goaded him. The government discourages open courting, but that campaign has had the same success as the one to rid Lhasa of dogs. The young man stepped briskly into the street and took the girl by the arm. She smiled full into his face, and they walked away.

We left the next morning. The plane climbed east from the valley, and I studied a mountainside off one wingtip and thought of love in the Barkhor, and a herdsman smoking beside a fire, and an old monk murmuring a mantra. I also thought of a woman I had seen on the high road to Nyalam. She was washing her hair in a stream. She turned toward us as we passed, and then lifted her head and turned away. Her hair rippled at her waist. I thought of stopping. I reached to touch Lin's shoulder, but hesitated. I looked again and she still knelt by the water, fierce and far away.

Where peaks soar five miles above sea level, the flight from Chengdu to Lhasa crosses the Himalayan ranges of eastern Tibet. Among these ranges rise some of Asia's great rivers, to cut mile-deep parallel gorges as they flow southward. With the world's highest snowline, an average 19,000 feet, and more than 17,000 glaciers, such mountain barriers isolated Tibet for centuries. Only caravans on rough trails traveled the icy wilderness. Since 1954 a 1,550-mile, Chinese-built motor road has spanned passes, canyons, and rapids to link Sichuan and Lhasa.

Earth's highest mountains, these are also the youngest. More than a hundred million years ago this region formed the bed of a vast sea. Beginning some 50 million years ago, the shifting of continental plates carried India to a collision with the Asian plate, buckling up the Himalayas. Repeated upheavals folded sea sediments into the rising terrain. The Himalayan peaks, even the top of Everest itself, are marine limestone, made of the shells of billions of tiny sea creatures. In the last million years these mountains have risen 10,000 feet, faster than any other land area on earth. And, as the Indian plate pushes, they still rise, about an inch every five years.

Galen Rowell. Left and overleaf: Thomas Nebbia

Stairs once reserved for a god-king and his court take citizens of a new Lhasa into the Potala (above), the citadel of Tibetan Buddhism. From its dramatic site on Red Hill (right), looms this palace whose origins go back 1,350 years. In rooftop apartments, the 14th Dalai Lama lived in cloistered splendor until his 1959 flight to India. Tibetans believe him to be the present incarnation of Chenrezi, the all-seeing, all-embracing, compassionate aspect of Buddha. As head of a feudal theocracy, the Dalai Lama ruled a society in which one-quarter of all males were monks. Often monks studied to become lamas, or "teachers." Many were recognized as powerful "living Buddhas." Now all but some 1,000 monks have left Tibet or returned to secular life.

OVERLEAF. A hall exuberant with Buddhist motifs leads into the labyrinthine fortress, where some 1,000 rooms, 10,000 shrines, and 200,000 statues are preserved as a museum.

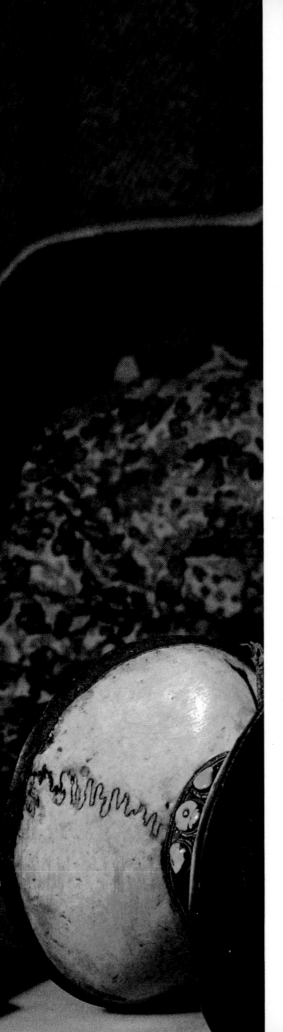

Fred Ward, Black Star (also left)

From a human skull Tibetan Buddhism contrived a sacred vessel now on display in the Potala. It held a ritual offering of consecrated beer or tea, believed to transform evil into good. The drum, made from two skulls, and the bell, bearing motifs that symbolize compassion and wisdom, accompanied cymbals, trumpets, and the chanting of prayers in the ceremonial music of Tibetan lamas. The skulls suggest the impermanence of the human body, seen as only one of many habitations of the spirit on its round of reincarnations. The spirit's goal is nirvana, the blissful union with the highest wisdom, which brings release from the cycle of life, death, and rebirth.

In a chamber of the Dalai Lama (above), a golden robe, a tea set, and an ornate couch evoke his presence. In such surroundings this most revered of living Buddhas often assumed the cross-legged, lotus position, like the lama figures in the wall painting.

389

Thomas Nebbia

Harold A. Knutson

Thomas Nebbia

Galen Rowell

Galen Rowell

Galen Rowell

"Commerce and devotion" drew a variety of people to Lhasa, observed the Abbé Huc, a 19th-century French traveler in Tibet. Today's visitors follow the same lures, and, in a changing land, hold fast to traditional dress and manners. On pilgrimage, nomad women from Qinghai Province congregate near the Jokhang temple (opposite). The women braid their hair in 108 strands because Tibetan Buddhism holds that 108 sacred qualities constitute an enlightened mind. Among them are wisdom, compassion, and sensitivity. The headdresses of silver, amber, turquoise, and coral represent personal or family wealth—secure, portable, and negotiable.

On a Lhasa street, a woman wears facial patches soaked in herbal broth, an old remedy for headaches and other internal disorders (top, left). A jeweled charm box adorns the neck of a woman of Xigazê (top, right). In old Tibet both men and women wore these reliquaries, consecrated by lamas, and containing amulets, prayers, or images believed to protect the wearer from harm.

Tibetans love headgear. A pilgrim who waits to enter the Jokhang (middle, right) wears a felt bowler similar to the hats worn by the women from Qinghai and by many other Tibetans. Such hats came to Tibet with the British in the early 20th century. With her sheepskin chupa turned fur side in, a resident of a commune near Nyingchi displays a hat typical of southern Tibet (middle, left). A young Lhasa jewelry seller (bottom, left) models her wares for tourists and pilgrims. Her headdress is in the style of nomads from eastern Tibet, as is that of a man in festival attire (bottom, right), who decorates his braided hair with tassels of yarn.

391

Galen Rowell. Right: Harold A. Knutson

A cross flagstones polished by the bodies of millions, a prostrate pilgrim inches toward the Jokhang, Lhasa's cathedral of Buddhism. Religious symbols and banners embellish the temple's main entrance (right). For 13 centuries pilgrims from all over Tibet have journeyed to the Jokhang, traversing the road around the old city of Lhasa by repeatedly measuring the length of their bodies, suffering to earn their way to a higher reincarnation.

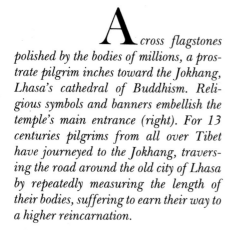

In the burning yak butter of a votive lamp, the fervor of Tibetan Buddhism glows, tended by a monk at the Jokhang. Of a community that once numbered in the thousands, only nine monks remain, curators paid by the Communist government.

At Drala Lugu, a small temple near the Potala, a draped Buddha wears safety pins placed by supplicants who pray for sharpened mental powers (below). Contributions of labor and money from worshipers rebuilt Drala Lugu after the Red Guards damaged it.

Ancient books rest on library shelves in the Drepung Monastery built in 1416 near Lhasa. Carved wooden covers hold sheets handwritten in gold or silver ink or printed with wooden blocks. Titles lie beneath brocade flaps. Every monastery once owned sets of the 104-volume Kanjur—the words of Buddha—and scores of sacred commentaries.

Thomas Nebbia.   Left and overleaf: Galen Rowell

Spinning his prayers on the wind, a holy man begs for alms and endlessly turns his prayer wheel (above). Inside its cylinder, coiled strips of paper bear chants and invocations, called mantras, which Tibetans believe soar soundlessly toward heaven.

On pilgrimage to the Jokhang temple, chupa-clad nomads from the grasslands of northern Tibet make camp on a Lhasa street. The nomad life—tenting in seasonal pursuit of pastureland for the herds—traditionally included visits to holy places for religious festivals. Today the government encourages herdsmen to build houses in permanent settlements, and to treat sacred occasions as "relics of a superstitious past."

OVERLEAF. A rainbow emblazons the golden pinnacles of the Potala. From this palace emanated the power that ruled all Tibetan life.

396

397

Pastures that lie 13,000 feet above sea level nourish a young shepherd and his flocks (opposite). Once nomads depended wholly upon their animals. Sheep gave meat and skins, and sometimes carried burdens. From yaks came butter, meat, milk, wool to make tents, and skins to make boots and boats (left). Hides and furs bought goods such as tea and grain. Today footgear may come from a faraway factory, and even yaks work for the state (above). Red-tasseled to scare away demons, they plow a commune field.

401

The regalia of a harvest festival keeps tradition alive for members of the Red Star Commune, near Lhasa. The silk-tasseled hats and costumes in Tibet's sacred colors of red and yellow are replicas of royal court attire of old Tibet. The arrows, tied with ceremonial scarves called khatas, rest in a quiver which typifies the Tibetan love of bright, intricate design. Once such costumes belonged to the lord of a great estate. For festivals he unpacked them, and his servants and serfs donned the finery to parade, race, and challenge each other at sharpshooting.

In the old days, wealthy nomads and nobles alike prized elegant saddles and trappings and bred fine ponies and horses. Rousing games and competitions marked many occasions. At a New Year celebration in the 1940s, a Western visitor stood in an excited crowd to watch horsemen gallop past, standing in their stirrups. As they swept by a hanging target, the riders "swung up their matchlocks and shot into the bull's-eye. Before they had reached the next target, twenty yards away, they had exchanged their muskets for bows and arrows. Shouts of joy acclaimed the mounted archer who hit the mark."

403

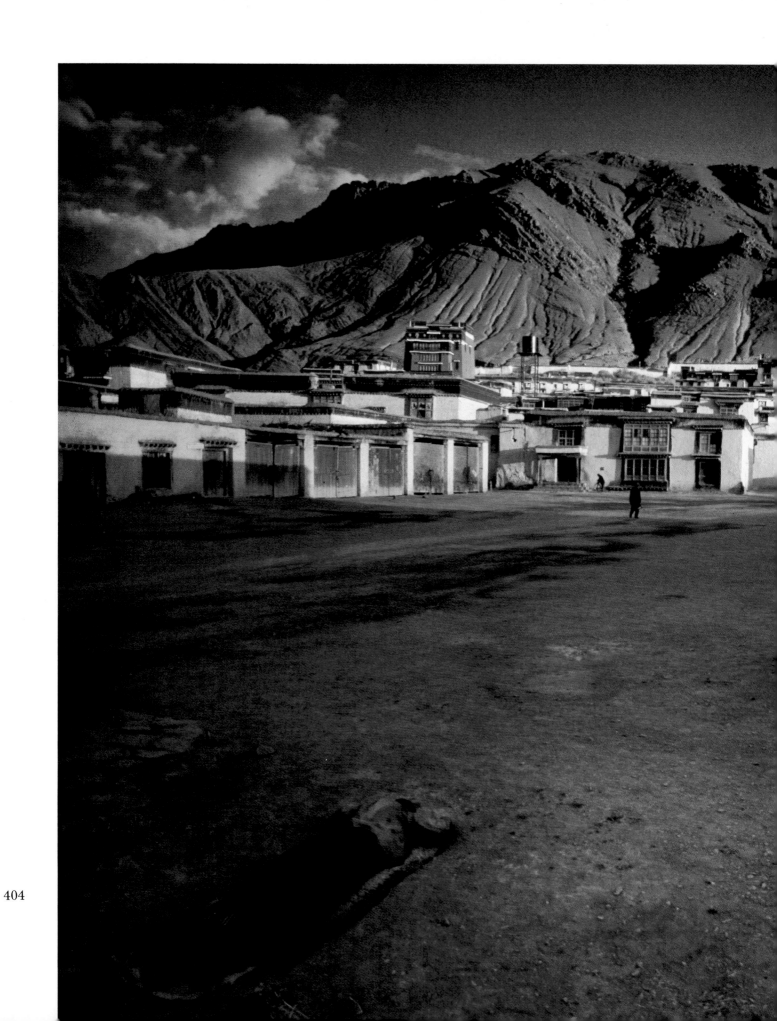

Galen Rowell (also left)

Harold A. Knutson

Dawn breaks as a prostrate pilgrim approaches Tashilhunpo, a monastery near Xigazê. Founded in the 15th century by the first Dalai Lama, Tashilhunpo some 200 years later became the seat of the Panchen Lama, Tibet's second-ranking authority. Outside the monastery gates, a holy man prays with rosary and prayer wheel (above). Inside, inlaid chunks of turquoise form a swastika on a temple floor. An ancient symbol in many cultures, to Tibetan Buddhists the swastika signifies truth and eternity.

Among the most venerated of Tibetan deities is Champa, a Buddha of the Future. Tibetans believe that Champa waits in heaven for a coming age when every sentient being will have earned deliverance from suffering. Then Champa will appear, to preside over the world. His gold-plated, bronze image at Tashilhunpo is 87 feet tall. The figure wears a crown and earrings to show its sovereign rank, and bears on its forehead the mark of divine wisdom. Champa's gesture bestows "the gift of religion."

As a wine-robed monk on the monastery roof sounds a gong for assembly, the faded crest of a yellow hat signals the fallen fortunes of the Gelugpa, or Yellow Hats, once the wealthiest and most powerful of Tibet's monastic orders and the sect headed by the Dalai and Panchen Lamas. Other important groups wore red headgear. In times past, Tibetan valleys and hillsides rang day and night with sounding gongs and trumpet calls of Red Hats and Yellow Hats.

OVERLEAF. An ancient art form serves a modern ideology as Tibetans and Communist Chinese mingle beneath a billowing tanka. The painting on cloth hangs in celebration of the 30th anniversary of the "Peaceful Liberation" of Tibet by the Chinese. It decorates a wall on the grounds of the Palkhor Monastery at Gyangzê, where most of the buildings were razed by Red Guards. Left standing was the 15th-century, nine-tiered chorten, in which worshipers moved past thousands of sculptures, paintings, and hierarchal images of Buddhist ideals, ascending finally to a canopied chapel—the plane of highest wisdom.

Once the "Monastery of the Shining Crystal," the buildings at Tingri stand in ruins (opposite), demolished during the Cultural Revolution. A British traveler of 1924 marveled as his eye traced the harmony of rock and architecture that climbed to the ice-draped pinnacle of the mountain, 17,000 feet above sea level. Then villagers lived under the economic and religious domination of the fortress-monastery. Now Tingri commune members, bearing wooden plows on their backs (left), set off for a day's work in the fields.

Other workers ride in carts (above) across terrain which, until the 1950s, had never known a wheeled vehicle.

OVERLEAF. The moonlit summit of Mount Everest rears beyond a swath of mist and snow swept by a ceaseless west wind. At 29,028 feet, Everest's crest is the highest point on our planet. Tibetans call the mountain Jomo Langmo— "Goddess Mother of the World."

411

TOWARD THE COLD FRONTIER

By Thomas B. Allen
Photographs by Jim Brandenburg

Wind rattled the platform of oil well J2-46 as the team leader explained why the drilling had stopped. A Russian-made cooling pump had broken down. The Chinese pump, a better one, had not yet arrived. His excuse capsuled some of the history and some of the problems of China's northeast frontier. Failure is often blamed on the Russians, who had come during the 1950s as "elder brothers" and, by 1960, had left as enemies. Since then, the Chinese have been working hard to supplement and update Russian technology with their own.

The team leader, Jiang Shuicheng, was a pioneer, sent to these oil fields in the early 1960s, when there was little here for the wind to rattle. Men and women dragged equipment and supplies through snow and mud across road-less plains. Crews lived in tents, in a region where the temperature can fall to minus 25°F. When the first wells came in, the place was named Daqing—Great Celebration—and Mao Zedong proclaimed, "In industry, learn from Daqing." One of the lessons was that China had to go it alone.

Daqing remains the symbol of the struggle to industrialize. The struggle is markedly concentrated in the area China calls the Northeast, but the West

Fiery steel flows at Anshan in China's hard-working Northeast.

has long called Manchuria. To modern China that name recalls the despised Manchu (Qing) dynasty, which ruled for more than two and a half centuries until it disintegrated in the early 1900s. And the Northeast was Manchuria under humiliating occupations by Russians and Japanese.

"China is a machine," said one official, "and the machine is only warming up." In the Northeast, where men and women are working to translate slogans into a better life, I too sought more than patriotic words. Many people helped me on what became a journey beyond the slogans. I traveled by plane, train, car, bus, and, for one short stretch by hay wagon, through a land of forest and factory, city and marsh, moviemaker and lumberjack. On a frontier thrusting toward the future, I saw men making steel and women making bricks of mud. I saw fields where machines and people harvested side by side. On that jouncing, ox-hauled wagon, I lay back in the sun-warmed hay and saw military jets scribing contrails.

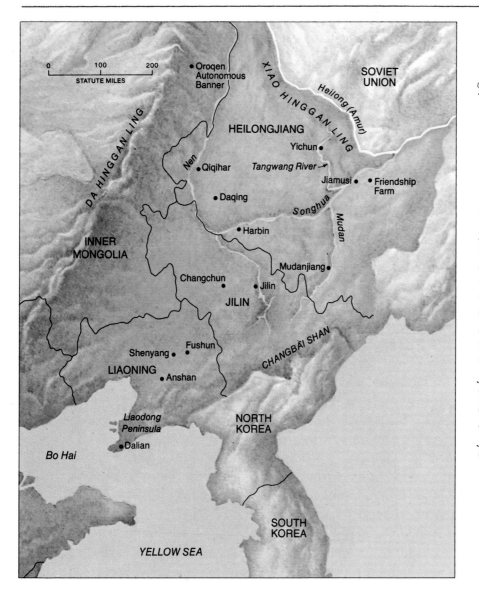

Thomas B. Allen traveled through three provinces that thrust like a prow against the borders of the Soviet Union and North Korea. His journey to the Northeast began as the harvest moon rose over the fields of the Friendship Farm and as autumn blazed in Yichun's forests. Near Mudanjiang he saw the fading of a commune; in Daqing the booming of an oil town. From Russian-built Harbin to Japanese-built Changchun, he saw Chinese at work on land long in foreigners' hands. His journey ended at the port of Dalian, which once served Russian and Japanese imperialism but now serves a nation trading with the world.

I did learn from Daqing. My teacher was team leader Jiang Shuicheng. We climbed down from the drilling platform, crossed the potato field surrounding the derrick, and entered one of the wooden sheds that house 30 of Jiang's 50-man drilling crew. Five live in this one, about 20 feet long, 8 feet wide, and barely 6 feet high. Two tiers of bunks are built in. The only other furnishings are a couple of benches, a scarred table, and small padlocked cabinets. The workers get their meals from a nearby kitchen unit and bring the food back to eat here. As we talked, we could see our breath, but steam heat would not be piped in until much colder weather arrived.

The other 20 crewmen of J2-46 live several miles away in family housing. They commute by bike or in the back of a truck. Women work in the refineries and petrochemical plants scattered over an expanse that also includes more than two million acres of farms—a rural metropolis of 700,000. "Women," Jiang said, "have to work close to the places where they live so they can still take care of the children and keep house."

While most of the people live in the two-room, mud-walled houses typical of the countryside, future housing looms in clusters of six-story apartment buildings under construction. Each building has 24 apartments, some two-room for couples with children, some three-room for couples with children and elderly parents. In each lobby a built-in mailbox unit contains 18 boxes. The leader said they would have to do; no 24-box units were available.

As giggling, whispering children followed, I wandered around a neighborhood of small houses. I was welcomed at several. In one I met a woman named Liu. On her fingers she proudly ticked off some of the family's possessions: two bikes, five wristwatches. Beaming, she showed me her treadle-operated sewing machine and a black-and-white television set. She works as a nursery school teacher. Her husband works in a machine shop. Along with other tent dwellers of the 1960s, Liu's family built their house and thus pay no rent to the administrators of Daqing.

A 12-year-old son and 9-year-old daughter share a bedroom which doubles as the living and dining room. In the parents' bedroom, snapshots are arranged around the mirror or clustered in large frames. Goldfish swim in a bowl on the dressing table. The sewing machine sits on a window ledge. Between the rooms, a wide hallway serves as a cooking and storage area.

Liu's household brings to life China's effort for the so-called "four modernizations." Pamphlets, posters, and billboards proclaim the need to modernize agriculture, industry, science and technology, and defense. But people joke about the *real* modernizations. For some, the modernizations are a bicycle, a watch, a transistor radio, and an electric fan. For others, they may be a color television set, a tape deck, a sewing machine, or a refrigerator.

I went to a Daqing workers' club. In the cement-floored auditorium, workers and their families filled the 800 seats. The crowd applauded earnest performers on a bare stage. Each of three ballets told a story of people dying for the motherland. A stout man in a gleaming white Palm Beach style suit and heavy makeup sang "Family Planning Is Good," the story of a young married couple. They had been saving for a refrigerator, but she got pregnant. The baby was a girl. The singer pantomimed extreme unhappiness and sang on. The couple felt they had to try again, contrary to the official one-baby-per-couple policy. The singer showed even more unhappiness, for the second baby was also a girl. Only now, with two girls and no refrigerator, do the husband and wife decide that "family planning is good." Much applause.

The show ended as a woman in a long black dress sang "A Toast," China's No. 1 song in a national poll. It celebrates the downfall of the Gang of Four and promises, "For the four modernizations we will give our all."

The journey from the oil of Daqing to the forests of Yichun zigzagged, first by train southeast to Harbin, then northeast in a Russian-built, single-engine biplane. No direct land route has yet pierced the wilderness that rules much of the terrain between Daqing and Yichun. On the flight I discovered the surprising resemblance of China's Northeast to our own New England. Rippling below us, mile after mile, was a carpet of autumn color that could have spread across the Green Mountains of Vermont. Daqing was a boomtown on the frontier; this, from above, seemed untouched land that awaited the cutting edge of the frontier.

The plane banked over the Tangwang River and dropped down to a broad tract of land raw from the felling of timber. Railroads zipped alongside the meandering river, and smoke drifted from the stacks of a few large buildings. We landed, bouncing along an airstrip and taxiing to a cache of fuel drums. Then I climbed into a van for another bouncing ride, over the rutted roads of Yichun, an enormous, sprawling village of mud and toil.

The road was crowded with horse-drawn carts full of red clay bricks, and wagons loaded with concrete forms, pulled by pairs of harnessed women. Crews were digging ditches and hauling off the dirt in baskets that swung from yokes. Other workers mixed dirt with water for mud bricks. All I could see rolling past the window of the van was a vast panorama of labor.

The workers are building what began in 1948 as a "forest city," hacked out of one of China's last great timber preserves. Now a thread of rail and road winds about 125 miles from the airstrip toward the Soviet border. A well populated frontier strengthens the Chinese presence in a tense area.

The Heilong Jiang, or Black Dragon River, forms the border here. The Russians call it the Amur. Some people have relatives on both sides, and I was told illegal visits are frequent, especially across the winter ice. When a cow, a boat, or a drunk strays across the river, a ritual begins. Upon discovering the stray, border guards raise their national flag. A flag on the other side answers. The two sides negotiate a meeting place and, after appropriate speeches, restore the stray to home ground. Sometimes, though, there are more than words. One night, on a radio in my room, I heard a Voice of America news report of an exchange of fire between border patrols. My Chinese hosts did not hear about the incident until the next day. The Chinese version had Soviet troops shooting an innocent Chinese farmer.

I ventured into Yichun's forest preserve. In the sharp air of fall, I felt at home with the pines, birches, maples, oaks—and chipmunks. There had been a light dusting of snow and a quick, sparkling fall of tiny hailstones. I saw a couple of birds that closely resembled American nuthatches, but that was all. Birdwatching seems to be unknown, and birds are scarce. Many habitats have been invaded and destroyed. People who have known famine have slaughtered birds as seed-eating pests—or for food. I had seen only one or two crows in acre after acre of cropland. There were few wild ducks in the marshes. And now, in this lovely wood, few birds and no birdsong.

The next day I was up to catch the 6 a.m. train to Jiamusi, a riverside city with a population of almost 500,000. I was on my way to the state-owned Friendship Farm, at the end of a narrow, bumpy road that begins in Jiamusi, 70 miles to the west. We made the trip in a huge, Japanese-built bus. Snow fell in big moist flakes. The radio played "The Stars and Stripes Forever" and the *New World* Symphony. Once the bus got stuck. At the end of a long day I was welcomed with smiles, handshakes, and tea.

To understand the setting and the breadth of the Friendship Farm, imagine the American prairie when it was a sea of grass beckoning the first homesteaders. That was China's Great Northern Wilderness as late as 1955, when the plow broke the prairie and turned up thick black soil. "I was there," one of the sodbusters proudly told me. "When we started to plow, the mice were jumping out of the grass around us, and the wolves came and had a feast. We did not kill the wolves then. It was good for them to eat the mice."

This farm built by Chinese pioneers bristles with numbers. A family is said to live on Farm No. 10 and work in Production Brigade No. 4. Statistics come from a rotund, moon-faced cadre who enumerates: 11 hospitals, 13 clinics, 132 schools . . . 840 tractors, 360 combines, 270 trucks . . . 52,850 pigs, 61,400 chickens, 2,778 horses, 379 cows, 4,493 beef cattle, 800 boxes of bees, "shipped south to keep them working in fall and winter."

I saw meadows once wild, now furrowed; marshes drained; the harvesting even of "weeds," wild papyrus-like plants used to make paper pulp. I listened to the farm's director, Lu Chunyu, a tall, slim man with a warm face and graceful hands that were always gesturing or holding a cigarette.

When Lu was sent here in 1958, China relied upon older, seasoned men and women for leadership. Today, he said, China looks to its youth. At the paper mill, Lu put his arm around the shoulders of a young man and introduced him as Ye, the manager of the mill. At 24, Ye was four years out of high school. He had learned to read and write before the decade-long educational blackout of the Cultural Revolution, unlike many workers only a few years younger. They try to recover their lost education by watching television courses, as I had seen many people doing in Daqing.

Like all Chinese state workers, Ye had been assigned to his job by the government. Married couples often are split up by needs of the state. A time card at Ye's mill, though it was blank and impersonal, gave me an understanding of life for a married worker. The card recorded work done each day. It authorized sick leave, "private business" leave, maternity leave, state holidays, and "time off to see family." This last type of absence, 12 to 14 days, is not for a laze-in-the-sun vacation. Unmarried workers go to their parents' homes; married workers visit their spouses. Thus, a man and wife separated by their jobs may well be together only 14 days a year. "That is a big problem in China," an official told me. "People dislike that more than anything else."

Farm No. 10 sustains 3,000 people, of whom 787 are agricultural workers growing wheat, soybeans, and sorghum. I saw blueprints for a community of the future that would have a 500-seat sports stadium, a cinema, an industrial area, and public baths.

Right now, many people live in two-story, cooperatively built houses that line a muddy lane swarming with chickens, pigs, an occasional dog, and ducks and geese that waddle in the puddles. This lane without a name is a friendly place, and the people seem happy. Each house has a small front yard, fenced and planted mostly in stooping sunflowers (the seeds are a popular snack). A brick shed (the summer kitchen) and a hand pump flank the packed-earth path that leads to the only door. Cabbages are piled on the thatched roof. Red peppers and bright yellow corn hang from roof posts and walls.

The wife of Shi, the farm's vice-director, showed me around her house. I entered a small kitchen with a waist-high clay pot of water, a cupboard, and a wood-burning clay stove connected to a little water boiler. The floors are brick, the walls whitewashed. To the left is the other first-story room, whitewashed, with a bed platform, a wooden wardrobe, a little table, and a mirror, its frame full of family snapshots. An ashtray and a tiny glass lamp with a long green cord and pink paper shade sit on the table. Up 13 concrete steps are two bedrooms. One bed has a mosquito-netting canopy. In each room a bare, unfrosted bulb hangs from a twisted electrical cord.

I knew I was being shown luxury. Certainly these houses were luxurious compared to the squat mud dwellings I saw everywhere else I traveled in the Northeast. But there was something disturbing here, a faith outside my experience, a faith in repetition, in sameness. In house after house, I saw the same few things arranged in the same way. It was as if a committee somewhere had decreed where people were to put their snapshots and what color they were to paint their mirror frames. The color was blue.

I walked across the lane from the Shi family's house to a row of new brick houses. In one of them I met a young couple, the Jiangs, and their yellow-eyed, tiger-striped cat. The wife, blushing and excited about discussing her future, explained that soon she would give up her job as an accountant to have her first and, under current strictures, only baby. She would enjoy her baby for 56 days of maternity leave, at full pay. On her return to work she would leave the baby in a nearby day-care center, and go to nurse it twice a day. She considered herself lucky. Many women, mainly in cities, must leave their babies in a nursery or with family members for the entire work week.

The houses in the Friendship Farm neighborhoods do not have indoor plumbing. The toilet for 18 families is a long brick outhouse with an L-shaped entrance at each end, one for men, one for women. The outhouse waste is periodically collected, hauled to the fields, and mixed with soil for fertilizer.

Often I saw lines of tank trucks and horse-drawn tank cars leaving cities in the morning, bound for the countryside to deliver this night soil. The Friendship Farm uses it extensively, except on one 4,115-acre experimental tract, where they demonstrate one of the four modernizations.

About 500 people would be needed to work this tract by hand. But here only 20 plow, plant, and harvest, using machines, commercial fertilizers, and pesticides. I watched huge green American-built combines chomp through a cornfield and spew ears into tractor-pulled wagons. The tense, well-trained combine drivers are called "mechanical workers," not farmers.

China has put most of its large farm machines and much of its hope for dependable harvests in the Northeast. Here, as nowhere else in China, you can sweep your eyes along the rich, flat lands and see the silhouettes of machines. But you can also turn your head and see, in a nearby field, workers pitching soybeans into an ox-drawn wooden wagon.

Allover China the commune is an idea from the past that is now being called into question. Today the commune is often an administrative facility, something like a county seat, rather than the original Maoist ideal with thousands or tens of thousands of people owning shops, factories, farms, and labor in common. Once, when I pointed to a cluster of houses and asked if that was part of a commune, an official said, "Please call it a village. Village is a softer word." It is also a word that characterizes the place people live—their *home*—rather than the system they work for.

Many villages flashed by the windows of trains, buses, and vans as I traveled the Northeast—clusters of yellow-mud houses; tilled fields; conical, thatched-roof silos. One day, south of Mudanjiang, my van rolled into the domain of the Bohai People's Commune. On a curve of the road stood a jumble of houses. I spotted a new wooden fence festooned with what turned out to be strips of pumpkin skin, a spectacle in a flat land of little color.

The pumpkin garlands, the fence, and the new brick house behind it all belonged to a friendly man named Yin. Once Yin worked only for work points from the commune, but now, he said, he earned regular wages at a cannery. I soon understood why the commune system no longer controlled Yin's life.

He had built his house with the help of neighbors, who worked for him on holidays and were paid with "a good meal and good wine." Money for lumber and bricks came from his cannery job and from what is officially more and more encouraged as "family sideline production"—known elsewhere as free enterprise. On a patch of land next to his house Yin grows vegetables and a cash crop of pumpkins for seeds. The skins that lured me to his house are dried, later to be steamed or used for soup. Some pumpkins are stored for winter, and bad ones are fed to his pigs. He sells about four pigs a year.

Yin owns a house bigger and more comfortable than any I had seen in China. He, his wife (a foundry worker), their three young sons, and his father (a retired cook) live in three large rooms with wooden floors and fresh flowers in big clay pots on the windowsills. He plans an addition to the house when he can get enough money together from his pig and pumpkin-seed profits.

The commune raises rice. In this region, rice-growing surprised me until I learned that about 25 percent of the commune members are of Korean descent, and that Koreans are renowned for being able to grow rice almost anywhere. I met some Koreans early one morning on the western edge of the commune. Four hunters on bicycles emerged from the mist. Rifles were slung on their shoulders, and a small deer was lashed to the back fender of one of the bikes. I went home with them to find a village much different from others I had seen. The mud houses were scattered along the slopes, not arranged in rows. It was a Korean-Chinese village, part of a commune production brigade.

While the hunters dressed and cut up the deer, a crowd gathered and a man stepped forward. Of the 500 villagers, he told me, five are pure Chinese, the rest Korean immigrants or descendants of Koreans who settled here 60 or 80 years ago. At the edge of the village, along a swift stream, is a small hydroelectric plant. A woman walked by, carrying on her head the clothes she had just washed in the stream.

We were in the neighborhood of ancient volcanic eruptions. Gray-green volcanic rocks flecked the mud and the tiny home gardens. Beyond, in the lifting mist, the fields resembled a lunar landscape somehow made a little fertile. In a far-off valley, richer fields were cabbage green or harvest gold. The hunters shouldered their rifles and pedaled off again. They and their fellow villagers struck me as vibrant, independent people. They seemed as detached from the Bohai People's Commune as Yin and his new house were.

I rode back over the rutted dirt road, to a crowded railway station in Mudanjiang, and through the long night to Harbin, railroad hub of the Northeast and capital of Heilongjiang Province. Harbin marks the edge of the frontier. From Harbin southward to the sea the rail network thickens and cities appear, strung along the tracks that spawned them.

Harbin was born as a railroad junction, a dot on the plain that Russian engineers selected in 1896 as the best place to begin laying track: northwest to their own railroad city of Chita, southeast to link Chita to their port of Vladivostok, and south to what the Russians would call Port Arthur. From Harbin, tsarist Russia would rule an empire whose land was Chinese but whose riches would be hauled to Russia on Russian rails laid down by coolie labor.

Russia lost its major hold on Manchuria in 1905 after a disastrous naval defeat that ended the Russo-Japanese War. By the 1930s the Japanese had become the new rulers. Russia's mark on Harbin was never erased, but now the city of two million belongs to the Chinese, their bicycles, and their sparking red-and-white electric trolley cars.

I wandered the broad streets of central Harbin. In a sea of people in blue and gray, a flash of color caught my eye: a black and orange dress, a maroon babushka. A Russian woman. I approached her, and she surprised me by speaking English. Her name was Nina Fetisova. Near her hovered a woman she called Galena, whom I took to be Chinese. We agreed to meet the next day.

In Galena's two-room, fifth-floor apartment, Nina told me her story. Born in Harbin in 1918, she went to a Russian Christian girls' school, where she learned English. Except for two trips to the country, she had never left Harbin. She made dresses for women of fashion in the Russian community. In a cloth bag she carried the only keepsake from her career, a packet of yellowed pages from the January 1958 issue of *Vogue*.

By 1965, most of Nina's Russian friends had died or emigrated, a few to the Soviet Union, most to Australia and Argentina. Now, she said, there are only about 60 left: "All old people. Many do not walk."

I asked about Christianity in Harbin. Nina said something in Russian to Galena, who is also Christian. From Galena, speaking through Nina, and from Nina herself, I got a picture of a religion gone underground.

After the Red Guards closed or destroyed the churches in the 1960s, the dwindling congregations celebrated Mass at the Christian graveyard. Candles burned on the tops of stone monuments. Communion was a piece of bread, not the traditional wafer. And then the graveyard became too public. The religion went into people's homes. Officially, Nina and Galena can now practice their religion. But I saw no church open for worship. There is no place to go except Galena's room, with the icon of the Virgin on the wall.

When the Russians made Harbin into a miniature Moscow, they built two-story apartment houses with tiny wrought-iron balconies. From one of those balconies, on a cool Sunday night, a smiling couple beckoned to me. I walked up a dark stairway to find a wedding celebration in a room seven feet wide by fifteen feet long. About twenty people had managed to crowd in. One couple danced to music from a tape recorder. The songs sounded Russian, and I guessed that they had been taped from Radio Moscow broadcasts.

The bride, Fang Sunhua, and the groom, Chen Jinchen, were both 25. They had been unceremoniously married a few hours before, simply by receiving at their office, Oil Company No. 6705, a stamp of approval on their marriage certificate. The room we stood in, sipping beer and munching on candy and pastry tidbits, was to be their new home. In the bedroom loft lay several quilts and blankets, traditional gifts. A new table and a new wardrobe held other gifts: a clock-radio, a pair of thermos bottles, assorted suitcases.

The couple will cook in the hallway, where the apartment house's other dozen or so second-floor families have set up gas hot plates on stacks of bricks. I can attest to the location of their communal lavatory. The groom and a helpful neighbor carrying a flashlight led me to it: down the unlighted stairs, out the front door, across the street, through a door in a tall wooden fence, down an alley to a large wooden outhouse.

The party spilled over to the next apartment, which was bigger. We danced, two couples at a time, as a small white cat with yellow eyes and a yellow tail stepped cautiously between the feet of the celebrators.

The train, its whistle long and sad in the night, rolls south from Harbin, out of the old Russian domain and toward Changchun, once the capital of Japan's empire in Manchuria. During the international city planning movement of the 1930s, the Japanese had laid out a grid of wide boulevards, circles, and parks. Upon this grid the Chinese have built a sprawling city that boasts of two very different industries. "Changchun," a local official proudly told me, "is the Hollywood of China and the Detroit of China."

The Hollywood part began in the final days of World War II, when the Soviet Union attacked Japanese forces in Manchuria. Soviet troops looted Changchun. When they withdrew in March 1946, Changchun was battered again, this time in civil war between Chiang Kai-shek's Nationalist troops and the Chinese Communists. Not until 1948 did the Communists finally gain control of Changchun.

Out of documentaries made during the civil war, a Communist film industry was born. Soon after victory, the Communists set up a film studio in the war-torn city. From the beginning, movies have immortalized the civil war and served the needs of the state.

On the set of *Red Phoenix Facing the Sun,* a melodrama about the embroidery industry, I watched the movie being made. I could talk and walk around out of camera range, for the sound was to be dubbed in later. The actors and actresses were speaking their parts only to provide lip movement.

"Prepare!" calls the assistant director. "Start!" The camera rolls forward.

Chen Ye, a beautiful young star playing a seamstress, sits on the edge of a hospital bed, despondent about her new blindness. "When shall I see again?" she asks the nurse who stands near the bed.

"Your eyes are seriously damaged," the nurse ventures. But her words end in a giggle that breaks up all the Chinese. She has blown her lines.

They shoot the scene again—and then again. The director speaks patiently to the nurse. The star looks bored and fusses with her hair and makeup. On the fourth try, the nurse manages her line. It turns out that she is an electrician pressed into service before the camera because the studio is making so many movies that there is a shortage of actors and actresses.

Later I chatted with two performers, Ye Linglong, who had just played an irate mother-in-law in a comedy, *Love, What Is Your Name?* and Ren Ye, who plays a Chinese Army general in *The Sparkling Sword.* I found that they knew little about Hollywood. Movie-making had fallen into disfavor during the Cultural Revolution, and so had American movies, previously very popular. The few films made during those vacant years were so bad, they told me, that people protested by withholding applause. One movie was so especially awful that patrons mailed their 20-fen (12-cent) tickets to the studio and asked for a 15-fen refund, saying that the movie was worth only 5 fen.

At the studio's property house, I was startled by enough U.S. Army equipment to outfit a platoon—canteens, knapsacks, uniforms. The prop man explained that they had been captured during the Korean War and used in war movies. He showed me an eagle-topped world globe with CHINA, UNITED STATES, and other places named in English. "In many movies," he recalled, "we had American Army officers gather around this globe and shout slogans against China." He paused. "But of course we have not made movies like that since the normalization of relations between our countries."

As China's Detroit, Changchun builds thousands of big blue or green Liberation trucks and a few big black Red Flag limousines. I was not allowed to see Red Flags being made, but I visited the huge Liberation plant, where 40,000 workers produce the nation's standard vehicle: a six-cylinder, 95-horsepower truck that can carry four tons. Nearly all of the truck chassis made here will be painted and bolted to blue or green, wooden-floored, wooden-staked bodies; some will be painted red and given fire-engine bodies; some will get oil-tank bodies. But all will be the same basic truck that the No. 1 Factory has been turning out since China and the Soviet Union built the plant in the 1950s.

Changchun, I was told, produces 60,000 trucks a year—more than any other city. But still China needs more trucks. A horse-drawn cart delivered oxygen cylinders to the factory. On the sidewalk nearby, stacks of parts stood next to piles of potatoes, cabbages, and other vegetables. Bicycling workers will haul the food home as best they can and store it for the winter.

Inside the factory large bulletin boards in every department showed photographs of "Advanced Production Workers," cited for such traits as enthusiasm, scientific ability, and intelligence. Other boards posted the percentage of parts that had passed final inspection; the lowest was 91 percent.

Engines, chassis, transmissions, wheels, bodies, and fenders weave overhead and along the assembly posts until, suddenly, trucks stand ready for the squirt of gas that will send them off the line on their own. With a quick test of lights and a first blare of horn, the truck comes to life, ready to travel, horn blasting continually, on the noisy streets and dusty roads of China.

Long before trucks and films and Communism, the Northeast produced what the Chinese call the "three precious products"—ginseng, deer antlers, and sable. All can be found in fields at the Institute of Special Products of Jilin, east of Changchun. As I was driven in, a small herd of does wandered along the edge of a reservoir. Deer drivers, cooing and snapping bamboo-handled whips, rounded them up. The males, their antlers already harvested, were confined elsewhere.

In a field, rows of ginseng plants grew under cotton strips, like American shade-grown tobacco. I saw sables snarling in rows of cages. I could understand why sable fur coats are a precious product. I was familiar with the stumpy, gnarled root of the ginseng plant. But ground-up deer antlers? Answers of a sort came in the Institute's specimen room, where the raw materials and their finished products were displayed. I copied the information from some of the labels:

Deer antlers in wafer-thin slices: to treat heart disease, heal wounds, restore bone marrow. Ginseng tonic: improves blood and kidneys; helps "women's problems." Tablets of ginseng and deer-antler powder: treat disorders of the spleen and bladder; ease aches in legs; prevent nightmares. Both ginseng and deer antlers were also recommended as aphrodisiacs.

Institute workers seemed to think I was merely being polite when I told them I recognized ginseng and some of their trees. Then I told them about "Gray's Puzzle," named after a 19th-century Harvard botanist who wondered why so many plants from northeastern North America resembled plants found in northeastern China. He solved his puzzle with a theory that I demonstrated by using my hands to signify mountain ridges. An audience gathered.

When the great glaciers began to grind southward, plants and animals retreated down valleys of mountain ranges that ran north-south (arms and hands pointed forward). But the glaciers' refugees were trapped and died if they lived on the flanks of mountain ranges that ran east-west (arms and hands flung sideways). China and northeastern North America had those life-saving ranges (arms and hands forward) and we shared many of the species that I saw here (hands sweeping outward). Everyone smiled, and I was convinced that they understood my performance.

South of Changchun lies Shenyang, the old Manchu capital of Mukden. The grid of parks and boulevards marks the city as another reminder of Japanese occupation. Farther south still is Anshan, an iron-and-steel city built by the Japanese upon the memory of a Ming walled town. East of Shenyang is Fushun, where the Japanese took away millions of tons of coal a year for the furnaces of Anshan. And at land's end is the great port of Dalian, long in Russian and Japanese hands under the names of Dalny and Dairen.

What the Japanese wrought exists today, but now the industrial complex

426

serves China, advancing the four modernizations and making China the world's fifth-largest producer of steel. At Anshan, factories, blast furnaces, rolling mills, chemical plants, and metallurgy labs cover more than six square miles. Just outside the town are five iron mines.

When I remarked on the steel mill's efficiency, Xia Yunzhi, the director of its ten blast furnaces, said, "This is my profession." I never heard that word used elsewhere in China. He also cited the workers' high wages. "The state interest and personal interest," he said, "are closely related."

In the steel mill, intense heat scorched my face as ladles, each carrying 20 tons of molten steel, moved to clusters of giant molds, each able to hold 5 tons. A worker stepped below the ladle, the size of a small house, and shoved it with a long pole to begin the flow. First in a trickle, then in a stream, steel poured into the molds, showering sparks on the workers and the floor. The air was heavy with metallic dust that glittered in the shafts of sunlight slanting through the high windows of the mill.

Outside I walked and coughed through black smoke, white smoke, red smoke. Red and gray dust covered the walls, roads, and walkways. Here and there flowers appeared, as if a few blossoms could somehow help Anshan's people bear the gritty air.

At a new oil harbor north of the port of Dalian, I found the end of a pipeline that begins at Daqing. From a long pier I saw a tanker, the *Daqing 252,* taking on the oil of China for distant ports. I was at the southern end of northeastern China, where that great mass of land and history ends in a ragged peninsula. My journey was nearly over.

But one day remained, and I went to an apple orchard—for this realm of factories is also an apple basket of China. Wan, the smiling leader of the orchard's apple-picking production brigade, handed me what tasted like a McIntosh. The apple trees, he told me, had been planted in the 1920s by Japanese who had transplanted themselves and their apples from California. "So you are eating apples from your own country," Wan said.

I nodded, remembering a day far to the north, when I had walked a country road with two Chinese farmers. Crows flapped up from the stubble of a cornfield. Reddening clouds streaked the fall sky, and the weight of distant snow hung in the air. We could see our breath as my companions questioned me about my American countryside, and I answered, pointing to a creek, to slender white birches, to feathery roadside weeds, to hills with trees already bare. All around me, I told them, was an autumn I had once thought only American. I had journeyed in a place of frontier and change, a place of birches and apples, oil and steel. On the land lived people I had never known, but it was a land that sometimes felt like home.

In the chill light of early morning, workers bear a length of pipe to one of the 8,000 wells that pierce the oil fields of Daqing. The abacus competes with the computer to measure production. Daqing accounts for almost half of China's crude oil. Fur hats and heavy clothes appear in early fall, prelude to a winter of relentless cold. Daqing sprawls across what once was a wilderness. When the first producing well was drilled in 1959, China began building "a city and a countryside"—the city that now houses some 135,000 oil workers and 12,000 petrochemical plant workers, the countryside to feed them. Much of the oil leaves here in a pipeline that ends at a tanker port near Dalian, sea gateway to the Northeast.

429

Under an airplane's rippling shadow, the forests of Yichun show their fall glory. The trees are related to North American oak, maple, birch, and pine. Few roads thread this timberland, a frontier of airstrips and isolated settlements.

Forest preserves protect trees from lumberjacks, but nimble climbers harvest another crop: pine nuts, an expensive delicacy. Some families earn a living by selling the nuts to the state or on the free market. Younger family members climb the pines and, with long bamboo poles, knock down cones to gatherers below. Older relatives, usually women, pound the cones with wooden clubs and extract nuts from the pulp.

431

Manpower, woman-power, and horsepower transform the trees of Yichun into the lumber of China. Women carry logs that will be hauled away by train. Other logs stay in a lumberyard, where workers take turns manning a two-story handsaw that strips timber of bark and rips away rough boards. Nearby, another two-man team shoes a trussed-up cart horse.

At the Friendship Timber Processing Plant in Yichun, a worker cleans the screens of a fiberboard press. Logs are ground into chips, which are made into pulp, pressed, and dried. Of the plant's 2,700 workers, 500 are women. All work a 48-hour week.

Centuries of clearcutting and slash-and-burn farming depleted much of China's forestland, and contributed to disastrous floods. Only about 12.7 percent of China is forested today (compared to 33 percent of the United States). Aiming toward a land with a 20 percent cover, China is planting and sloganeering: "Spare the saplings today. They will be beams for Communism tomorrow."

433

The colors of harvest brighten the state-owned Friendship Farm, a showcase of modern agriculture. Soybeans pour from a Chinese-built combine, part of a fleet that includes machines from the United States, Canada, East Germany, and the Soviet Union. Corn hangs high to dry near new brick housing, which replaces mud houses built by pioneers who came here in the 1950s. Children's play reflects a principle of the farm: organized activity. People are put in production brigades of about 270 agricultural workers (half of them women) plus 730 other workers and family members. The farm, which covers 722 square miles, supports about 100,000 people and produces enough surplus to operate without government subsidies in good years. Most of China's mechanized farming is concentrated in the Northeast, where flatlands make large-scale agriculture practical.

Food on the hoof and on the wing supplements silo-stored grain—and dramatizes changes in China's agricultural policies. Wolf fur warms a farm boy, whose home-raised goose belongs to him, not the state. The biking hunters will share their deer among themselves, not with their production brigade. But the silo's grain, collectively produced, will earn more for the state than for the farmers who grew it. After years of running a society based on collectives called communes, Chinese leaders are experimenting with a "responsibility system," in which households must meet communal obligations, but may keep more of their harvest than in the past. They can sell their surplus in a free market. Under the new system, says People's Daily, there is "less scolding and beating of commune members . . . less wandering about without taking part in physical labor."

437

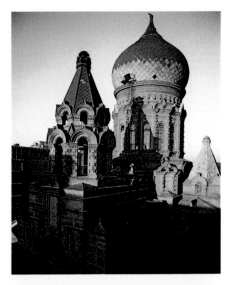

R*ush hour in Harbin pits cyclist against trolley and truck. Women being trucked to work wear veils against the wind. In the "metropolis of the north," wintry cold may last six months and temperatures drop to 25 below. Chilly streets sometimes serve as temporary open-air refrigerators for slabs of meat and piles of produce.*

Oldtimers can remember when Harbin was more Russian than Chinese, when the onion-shaped domes of Orthodox churches loomed over the largest Russian city outside the Soviet Union. Founded as a center for Russian railways, Harbin later came under Japanese control. But the city never lost its Russian look. Several churches still stand, their sanctuaries now warehouses, offices, schools, or apartments. In the late 1960s, during the Cultural Revolution, many other churches were damaged or razed by rampaging Red Guards.

OVERLEAF. *A nurse in Harbin's No. 1 Hospital tends the newborn. A baby boy is in an incubator against the wall. A red mark on a baby's forehead shows that the child has been given a test for tuberculosis. All births, except cesarean, are without anesthetic.*

State policy encourages a couple to have only one child. An only child earns parents a bonus and gets privileges, such as better schooling, that are denied a second child. In some areas, a couple refusing abortion of a third pregnancy are fined 10 percent of their income until the child is 14 years old.

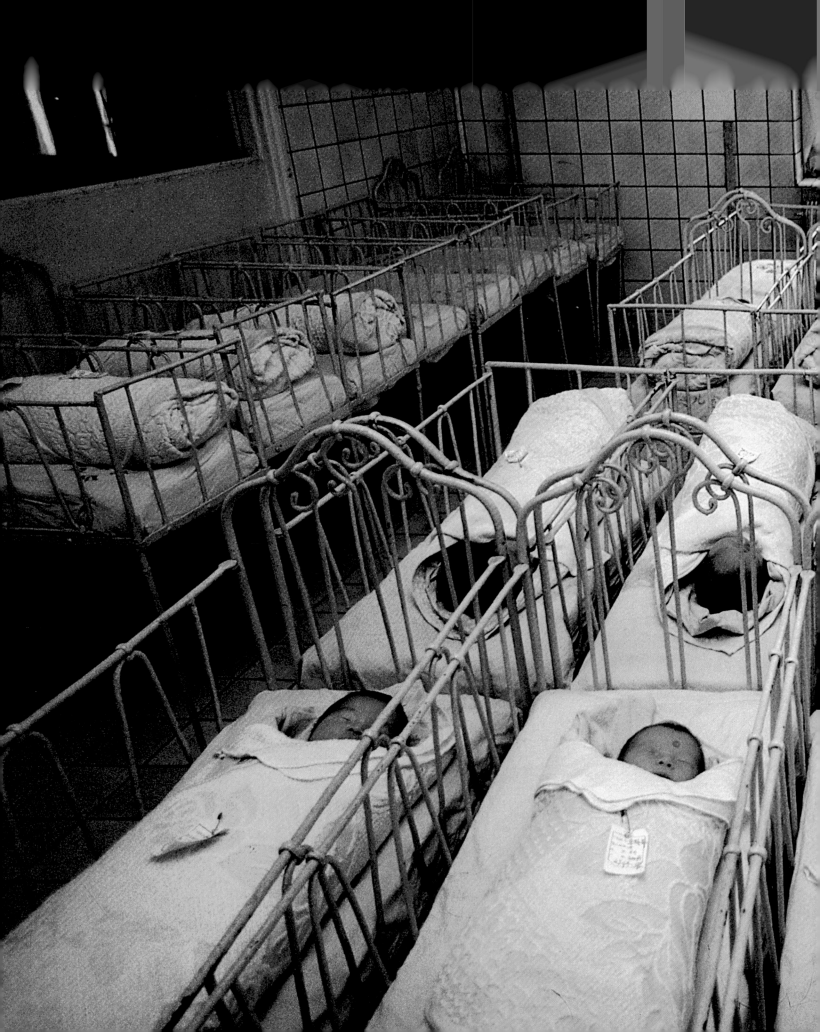

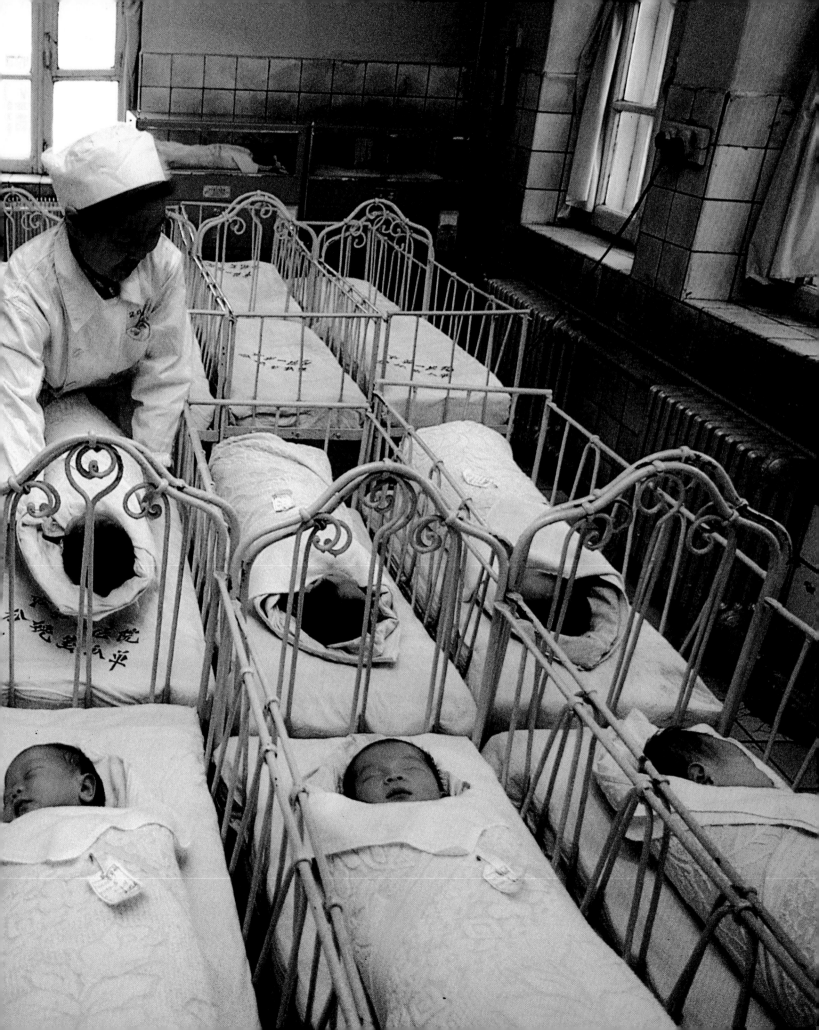

Tooting or studying, pupils at Harbin's Garden Primary School wear the red kerchiefs of Young Pioneers. Potentially good citizens 7 to 14 are eligible—and that means about 95 percent of China's children. Good Pioneers may pass on to the Communist Youth League, milestone on the path to coveted party membership. "Diligently study. Climb the peak," says the slogan on the blackboard at a Pioneer meeting. The school has 1,000 students and 70 teachers. Here, as in many schools, English is first taught in the third grade.

443

Beneath the city built by tsarist Russia hums the Underground City, shelter built by the people of Harbin because the government fears modern Russia's missiles and bombs. In one of the Underground City's factories an experienced lathe operator teaches an apprentice. The red flag on her machine states that it is "in good condition." She and the other workers file in and out through domed tunnels 46 feet below the surface. In wartime, they would live in the complex of dormitories, dining halls, warehouses, hospitals, and factories—an area large enough to hold 3,000 average American homes.

Civil defense philosophy calls for protecting people and maintaining an industrial base. Shelters in many Chinese cities follow a Chinese saying—"Make one thing serve two purposes"—by doubling as a hotel, a restaurant, a cinema, or even as a roller-skating rink. These peaceful places were designed to be converted quickly into bastions of war.

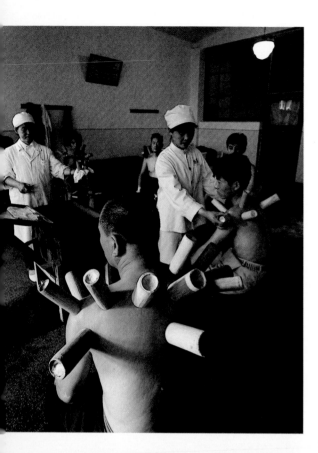

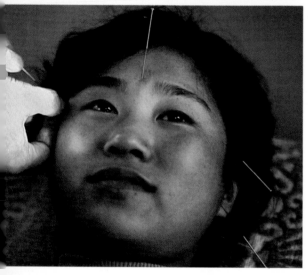

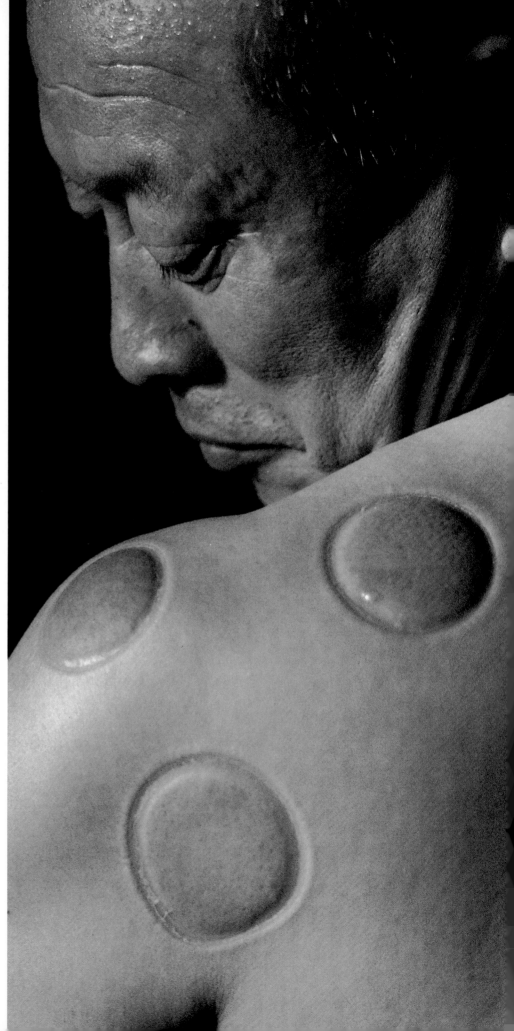

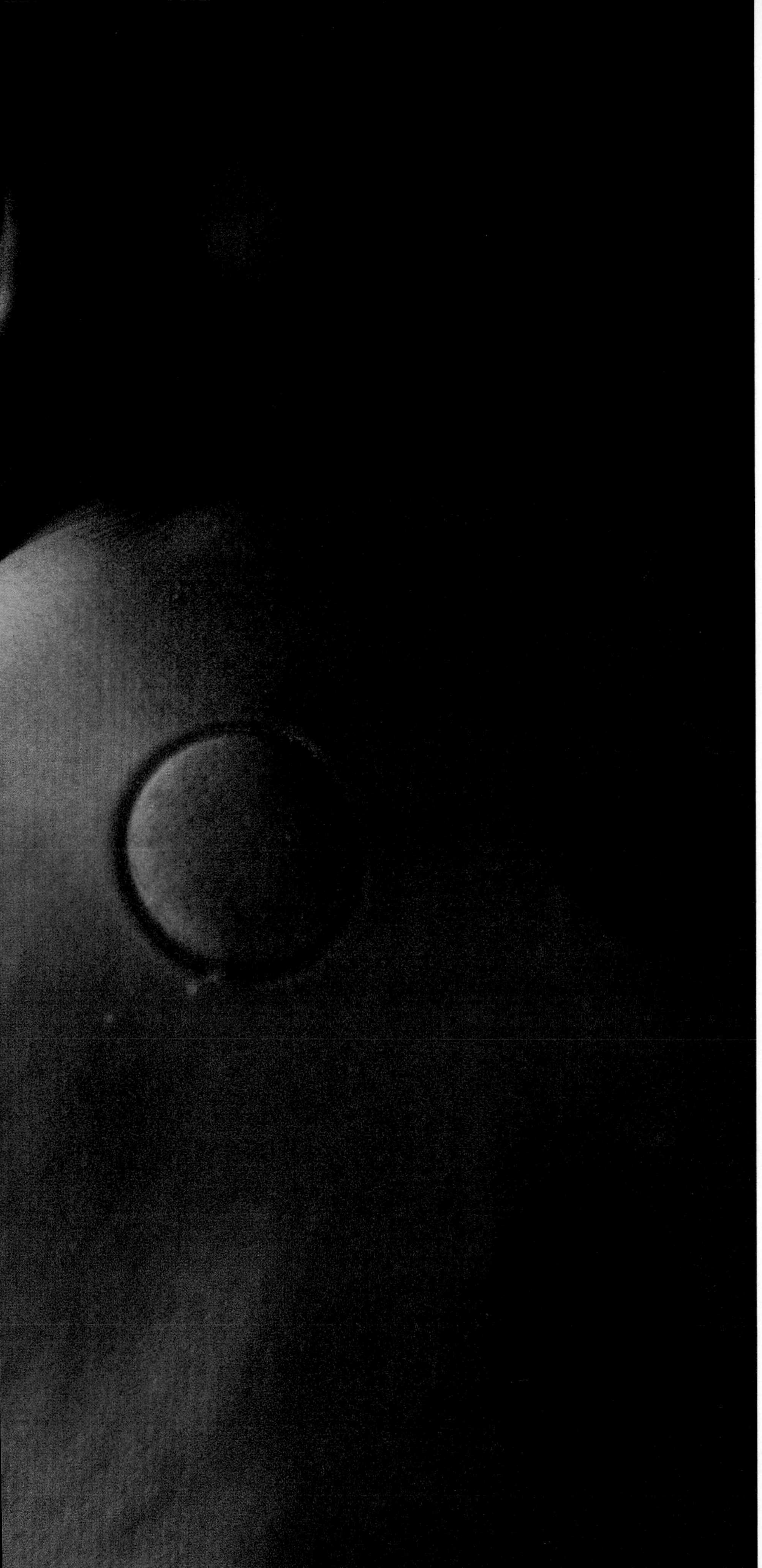

A man suffering from rheumatoid arthritis bears the marks of his cupping treatment—like acupuncture, an old folk cure. He is a patient at the Tanggangzi Sanatorium near the steel city of Anshan. Nurses, treating several patients at once, dip bamboo tubes into water piped from a hot spring. When a tube is applied to the skin, the hot air in the tube cools and contracts, producing suction. The tubes may be stuck at the same places where, in acupuncture, needles would be inserted.

Needles stud the places for headache cure in the head of a tranquil young woman at the sanatorium. Relief from pain is one of acupuncture's oldest claims—and the one most accepted by skeptical Western physicians. Many doctors who have studied the 2,500-year-old treatment believe that the needles may block nerve impulses in other parts of the body by closing "gates" in the spinal cord.

The traditional Chinese theory held that health depended upon a balance of a mysterious life fluid. Disease came from an imbalance. The fluid circulated through a network of channels that could be reached at hundreds of specific points on the body. A needle inserted at one of those points could drain bad fluid or allow fresh fluid to flow in.

Modern Chinese medicine points to cures, not theories. At the sanatorium, for example, success is claimed in the treatment of arthritis, migraine headaches, and what Western practitioners would call psychological disorders.

OVERLEAF. Ice adorns trees along a riverside street in Jilin. An icy fog rises from the Songhua River, unfrozen because of heat from a power plant. Borne on cold night winds, the vapor enamels the trees and freezes into white jade. Behind the cross-pierced wall thrusts the spire of a church devastated by Red Guards. Repaired with state funds, it serves Jilin's diminished Catholic community.

Overleaf: Chinese photograph

447

While their mothers work at the No. 1 Auto-Truck Factory in Changchun, children three to six years old play, exercise, and sleep at a nursery on the plant grounds. Boys and girls strip down to pants and socks for an "air bath," cold-weather version of the cold-water bath they take in the summer. The bath is calisthenics with a folded towel.

Sleep and play are collectivized. Before naptime, costumed six-year-olds danced and acted out ideology. An eagle (a boy) swooped down upon a swan (a girl). Six other girl swans drove off the eagle, and the rescued swan sang, "Collectivism is good." The six swans, after saving her again, proclaimed in tiny voices, "Unity is power." Then they took their nap.

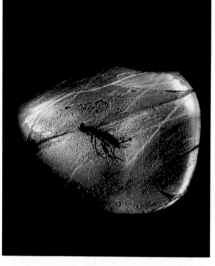

Walls of China's biggest opencut coal mine, the great pit at Fushun, rise more than 900 feet from the shovels ever digging deeper. Work trains follow a spiraling route that spans a mine 11 miles long and more than a mile across. Russians began the dig in 1905. Teams of hunters search the mine for amber. A piece imprisoning an insect—this one, a mosquito—can be worth a miner's wages for 10 months.

452

Hands, feet, and head work for the state in the training hall of the Shenyang Acrobatic Troupe. The girl balancing bowls on head and foot, the boy timing his headstand with an alarm clock, the teenager losing his duel with gravity—all work in a special kind of show business. The acrobats are often sent to other countries as ambassadors of art. The troupe triumphantly toured the United States even before China and the U. S. agreed on diplomatic relations.

Young recruits practice twice a day six days a week, but still go to school in the troupe's headquarters. After three years of training, successful graduates join one of the troupe's four 60-person teams. Following a year of apprenticeship, the youngster—perhaps only 13—becomes a full-fledged performer.

R ed-crowned Cranes, trained to come when called, flock to their keeper at the Zalong Nature Refuge near Qiqihar. Researchers tamed wild cranes in order to learn about their habits—and to learn how to save them. Revered as a symbol of good luck and immortality, the long-lived crane seemed destined for extinction, primarily because its wetland habitats were being drained for farming.

Of the 15 species in the world, 6 have been found at the refuge. Among the most endangered are the Redcrowns. To preserve them and the other species dying out here, the Chinese government set up the refuge in 1979. The Redcrowns then numbered about 100. The count has risen to 160. The Red-crowned Cranes breed here in spring and fly southward to winter. Both Korea and southern China claim to be the winter resort of these good-luck birds from Zalong. Refuge scientists are banding the birds to solve the mystery.

Olympic skier Wang Guizhen speeds down a snowy trail in the Changbai—Ever White—Mountains, which dominate one of China's largest forest reserves. A lone jeep travels a road in the 494,000-acre reserve. The forest is divided into two parts: a semiprotected area, where limited hunting and lumbering are allowed, and an area off limits to both guns and axes. Manchurian tigers and black bears prowl this borderland with North Korea. More than 300 species of medicinal herbs grow in habitats that range from alpine to heath.

459

Chinese photograph (also lower and opposite)

Feasting begins a Korean wedding and dancing ends it—hours later. Though the party takes place in Jilin Province, the fun came from over the border. China officially endorses austere weddings, but tradition flourishes when members of the Northeast's largest minority group get married. The bride and her aunt watch over the wedding feast at the groom's home. The bride's parents do not accompany her. The table, burdened with food, is spread before a backdrop of pine trees and cranes, symbols of longevity in China, Korea, and Japan. The rooster and the rooster-shaped cookies signify fidelity. At the celebrations, the bride and groom perform—a dance to an accordion, a game, eating an apple together—and recite the history of their courtship.

460

461

Oroqen women, who long have lived off a frigid land, embroider wolf skins with symmetrical designs that reflect motifs from nature and, through repeated patterns, symbolize wifely loyalty. Silk has replaced grass as thread, but women still use the antler of a roe deer to carve designs on birchbark sewing boxes. Nomads until recent years, some 3,000 Oroqen have settled in villages along the northern rim of Heilongjiang Province, where a year may bring only 100 frost-free days. Men still ride off to hunt, leaving chores to women, who are forbidden to touch tools used by men.

OVERLEAF. Oroqen men sipping tea around a campfire evoke a time when their society was built upon hunting parties, and families lived in huts of birchbark and hides.

462

Dalian, safe harbor for fisherman and merchantman, ranks behind Shanghai as China's second largest port. The colonnaded passenger terminal and forest of cranes (above) attest to the port's versatility. Dalian offers 48 berths. Nearby is a deep-water oil port, where a pipeline from Daqing ends. Boats sail to fishing grounds off Dalian, sometimes spending a month at sea. They bring home a catch of prawn, plaice, bluefish, and skate, a delicacy. Salted and hung to dry, the skates seem to be grimacing, but the false face has nostrils, not eyes, above the mouth; eyes are topside. Flattened relatives of sharks, skates usually feed along coastal sea floors.

SAMPAN PORTS AND THE TIDES OF CHANGE

By David D. Pearce
Photographs by James P. Blair

It was a cold, gray January dawn. The Toyota minibus picked its way down the busy two-lane road that threads Fujian Province's narrow coastal plain. Even at this early hour, the highway was clogged with bicyclists, commune trucks, and field workers toting shoulder poles. We veered east toward Chongwu, a walled fishing village on the Formosa Strait. With one hand on the wheel, the driver leaned over, flicked on the radio, and tuned in pop music from Taiwan, which lies just over 100 miles across the water.

Like so many other towns along this coast, Chongwu is a cluster of one- and two-story granite houses. The wall girding the town was built in the Ming era, when Japanese pirates were ravaging the coast of Fujian. We pulled up near the sheltered harbor. A large junk had been heaved ashore for repairs, and I watched as workmen handcrafted new timbers, hammered them fast with long iron nails, and caulked their seams with a silver paste of tung oil, lime, cement, and bamboo shavings. I strolled through town to the shore, past a charcoal factory where the road was black with dust from piles of round, honeycombed briquets.

Green-clad limestone hills loom over lush rice fields near Guilin. By Thomas Nebbia.

A fleet of 180 junks serves this town of 24,000 and that day, with the sky wind-driven and menacing, most of them bobbed at anchor in leaden chop offshore. The 30- to 50-foot vessels, each crewed by about 20 men, range the coast of Fujian and neighboring Zhejiang Province for ten days or more at a time, fishing with net, hook, and line for hairtail, mackerel, sturgeon, shark, eel, grouper, and squid. The fishermen sell about 30 percent of their catch to the Chongwu fishing commune; the rest they divide among themselves according to rank and seniority.

The fishermen's bad luck was my good fortune: In better weather, the boats would have been out. I asked to meet one of the fishermen, and commune official Wu Xinjin obligingly led me through the narrow, twisting alleys of the town to the granite-block home of Zhang Jiahong. Zhang's house gave onto a central courtyard shared by other members of his family.

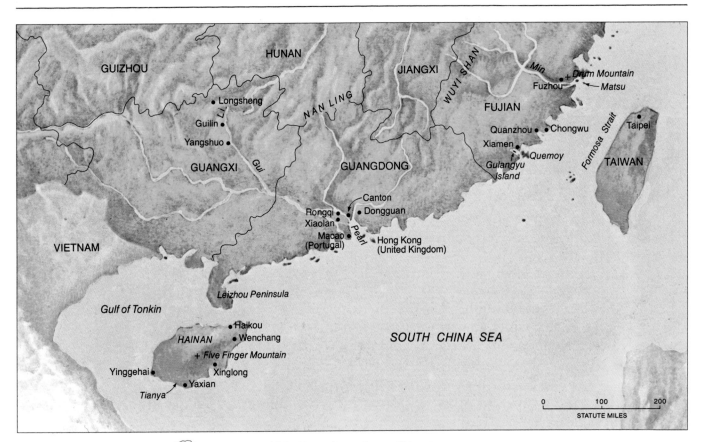

David D. Pearce's southeast China journey took him from the Formosa Strait coast to the Guangxi region bordering Vietnam. He saw pine-covered mountains in Fujian Province and sprawling rubber plantations on Hainan, a Holland-size island in the South China Sea. He explored Canton, focal point of a region that still produces more emigrants than the rest of China combined.

The wiry, weatherbeaten fisherman welcomed me into a cramped room dominated by a large, shellacked four-poster bed that he had bought for the marriage of his eldest son. Zhang sat crosslegged on the bed, wearing a brown jersey and faded gray cotton trousers. Despite the chill weather, he was barefoot. I asked him if he had any relatives on Taiwan. After his wife had served tea, he lit a cigarette and, pulling on it steadily, acknowledged that his younger brother had been there for the past 28 years.

"He was captured in 1953 while fishing in the strait. We don't see each other now, but pass news through fishermen who meet on the sea." In 1973 the brother managed to sneak across, but by that time he had married a Taiwanese girl and had five children, so he returned to the island. Zhang said that authorities there found out about the trip and threw his brother in jail for two months. "Since then, he's been afraid to come."

One feels the presence of the rival Chinese regime all along the coast of the southeast, but especially in Fujian. Although the actual war between the mainland and the Taiwan-held islands of Quemoy and Matsu tapered off in the 1960s, the battle for hearts and minds continues unabated. It is waged on the radio waves and by means of balloons and bottles stuffed with propaganda and committed to winds and tides. One coastal dweller I met said he and his friends sometimes find bottles from Taiwan when there is an east wind. The messages describe how good life is and urge mainlanders to come and "join the prosperity." Were they tempted to go? "We'd love to, but we can't," he replied. If the government found out, they'd be locked up, he went on to say, just as the authorities on Taiwan had imprisoned Zhang's brother.

Contacts on the high seas between Taiwanese and mainland fishermen, officially sanctioned by Peking since 1979, have led to smuggling. The medicinal herbs from the mainland that Chinese on Taiwan prize are swapped for articles like radios and wristwatches. Figures are not available on the extent of the smuggling, but one official said that the government has mounted a crackdown, putting spies in the markets and vastly increasing sea patrols. "We let Fujianese fishermen have contacts with Taiwanese fishermen, and some opportunists take advantage of the situation," the official said.

Beginning in Fujian, I traveled for more than six weeks in southeast China—a region that geography destined to be China's window on the world. For centuries, wave after wave of foreign goods, customs, and ideas buffeted the southeast coast, while rugged inland mountains served as a barrier to the rest of China. Thus, with their backs to a wall of rock and the ocean spread wide open before them, southeasterners tended to go overseas, not inland, during times of famine and political upheaval. Of the estimated 20 to 25 million Chinese scattered from Singapore to

London to San Francisco, more than 90 percent trace their roots to the southeast. Among those who remain, geographic isolation fosters a spirit of independence. Succeeding rulers have often found the fractious, worldly-wise southeasterners quick to revolt and difficult to pacify.

I walked around Chongwu after my talk with Zhang. I saw World War II wounds: holes in the town wall from Japanese shells. Just inside a town gate, I found a small folk temple dedicated to a third-century warrior hero, Guan Yu. About a dozen women prayed as joss sticks exhaled delicate, scented ribbons of smoke. "The women pray for the safety of their men," explained the attendant. "When the men go out, it's for their safety and that they may return with a boat full of fish. When they come back, it's to give thanks for a safe return."

In recent years, Fujian's economy has lagged behind that of other provinces. Barely 5 percent of its land is arable, and until 1979 when relations with Taiwan began to improve, state planners were reluctant to invest heavily in the region because of the chance of hostilities. But Fujian was not always economically backward. During the 13th century, Marco Polo described a trip down this same coast as "a constant succession of flourishing cities, towns, and villages, rich in every product." This Mississippi-size province was marked by a period of settlement and growth, then by decline and emigration. Since the Tang Dynasty, settlers had been pouring into Fujian from the north. They came first to escape the ravages of nomadic invasions, then to partake in the prosperity of burgeoning trading cities such as Quanzhou (which Arab traders named Zaytun after an indigenous thorn tree, the *citong*). But population growth began to outstrip the province's agricultural capacity, and by the late 1300s, world trade patterns had shifted away, Zaytun's harbor had silted up, and Japanese pirates were plundering the coast. The region's sons and daughters started to emigrate, especially to Taiwan and Southeast Asia. Although China's Ming rulers attempted to enforce a ban on emigration, the flow continued through Qing rule to modern times.

Quanzhou is only 22 miles from Chongwu. Looking at the drab little market town, I found it hard to believe that this city was once one of the world's greatest ports. And yet, in Zaytun's heyday during the Yuan Dynasty, it drew merchants from India, Arabia, Persia, and Southeast Asia with spices and jewelry. Relics of those days include a ruined mosque, a Song-era ship dredged out of the old harbor, and a graveyard for foreigners outside town. Later eclipsed by other cities, Zaytun for many years was the main maritime gateway to the Middle Kingdom.

The most conspicuous survivor of old Zaytun in modern Quanzhou is the Buddhist Kaiyuan Temple. Built in A.D. 686 and restored in the Ming period, the temple's twin pagodas are often pictured as the trademark for local products. Kaiyuan abbot Shi Miaolian escorted me around the temple and showed me some of the treasures in the old monastery's Hall of Scriptures. Among them was a 13th-century copy of the Buddhist Lotus Sutra, a slender, folding volume filled with large, rust-colored Chinese characters. The abbot said the scripture had been copied in blood by a monk named Shi Ruzhao as a mark of devotion to the Buddha. The monk fasted from salt to retard clotting, pricked the tip of his tongue with a needle, and dripped the blood into a container from which he wrote a few characters a day. It took him three years to write seven volumes this way.

But the treasure of modern Quanzhou is a puppet troupe. On the night I was there, the Quanzhou troupe performed the *Flaming Mountain,* an action-packed story about a monkey with magic powers who is protecting a Buddhist monk on a trip to India to fetch sacred scriptures. The impish protagonist clashes with the beautiful but dastardly Princess Iron Fan. In the end, the monkey succeeds in wresting from her a magic fan, which allows the monk to pass safely by the Flaming Mountain to India.

As the lights went out in the packed meeting hall, children shrieked with delight. Young and old who couldn't get inside pressed against the windows. The sets and costumes were rich and exquisite in detail. A speaker system boomed out the lines and slides flashed color and scenery in the background. Remarkably realistic birds and butterflies flitted over the stage, and the tiniest flickers of the puppet-characters' hands, limbs, trunks, heads, and eyes were painstakingly articulated. There were clouds of smoke, schools of fish swimming in midair, flames (paper strips blown by a fan from underneath), storm winds, twirling batons, and fighting with swords, staves, and hoes. In one great magical melee, puppets appeared and disappeared in puffs of smoke, changing form as they did so. Manipulation of this lively, colorful cast was by string, rod, and glove.

"Give us 11 pieces of bamboo and 3 blankets and we will give you a stage," promised master puppeteer Huang Yique, reciting one of the maxims of his craft. "Give us 36 puppets and 4 puppeteers and we will give you a million generals and soldiers." It is a prestigious thing to be admitted to the Quanzhou troupe. Fujian's puppeteers are acknowledged to be the best in China and among the best in the world. When entrance examinations were last held in 1978, some 800 people applied for the 30 available places. It takes five years of hard training to become a Quanzhou puppeteer.

From Quanzhou, whose glory lies in its past, I continued on down the coast to Xiamen, the port that promises to be Fujian's commercial heart in the future. Linked to the mainland by three miles of causeways, this island city, with its fine natural harbor, wide arcaded streets, and colorful back alleys, is a centerpiece of government efforts to promote foreign trade in long-neglected Fujian. Plans call for increasing the current port capacity by more than a million tons. In addition, the city contains a special economic zone, one of half a dozen such zones planned in the southeast. With low duties and inexpensive labor as inducements, the Chinese hope to entice foreign companies to the zones for joint ventures with local firms. At the Amoy Cigarette Factory in Xiamen (Xiamen is called Amoy in local dialect), I ran into a team of technicians from a North Carolina tobacco company that was already teaching Chinese workers how to operate about $500,000 worth of complicated cigarette-making machinery.

Chinese authorities also seek to tap the resources of the Overseas Chinese communities. Capitalizing on the powerful bonds of culture and affection that tie millions of Overseas Chinese to their ancestral homeland, the government has spared no effort to lure them—and their money—back. Overseas Chinese are encouraged to buy bonds, reclaim family homes, and invest in joint ventures. Special hotels offer them far better accommodations than the guest houses most Chinese stay in while traveling. And at well-stocked Overseas Chinese stores, the visitors and their relatives use special exchange coupons issued by the central bank to buy consumer goods not readily available to the vast majority of Chinese.

Along the Fujian coastal highway I saw many large, ornate houses owned by Overseas Chinese. One house I stopped at belonged to a Kuala Lumpur businessman and sheltered no fewer than 20 of his relatives. The graceful structure had carved beams, grilled windows, murals, and wall panels—all gaily painted in red, white, green, and blue. The relatives told me the owner plans to retire there one day.

Not all Overseas Chinese return to tour or to retire, however. Some come back to escape persecution in other Asian countries, where Chinese sometimes are resented for their wealth and clannishness or, more often, suspected of being agents of Peking. In a quiet, tree-shaded neighborhood of two-story houses set aside for returning Overseas Chinese in Xiamen, I met one such woman. Zeng Shuwan told me she was forced to flee Indonesia in 1960.

"They were chasing the Chinese out of Indonesia," the 75-year-old retired schoolteacher said. "When we left, they put our fingerprints to a statement and made us swear on it never to go back again."

Ironically, Zeng Shuwan's troubles did not end with her return to China. A few years later, the Cultural Revolution struck Fujian. Rival factions battled in the streets. With their special privileges, different life-styles, and contacts abroad, Overseas Chinese were suspect. Some were held up to the ridicule of frenzied mobs at mass "struggle" sessions. Some were beaten. Some were killed. Zeng Shuwan told me what life in the city was like then:

"The two [Red Guard] factions fought each other with guns here. I was afraid to go out. We moved to the back of the house and slept on the floor. Kids were shooting wildly all over the place."

Until the Sino-Japanese War and the subsequent transformation of Fujian into the front line between the mainland and Taiwan, Xiamen had been a busy port with many foreign consulates. The foreign community lived on Gulangyu, a 405-acre island only minutes from Xiamen Island. Leaning over the rail of a crowded ferry, I spotted navy gunboats amid the small craft—reminders that the island of Quemoy is just offshore. At Gulangyu I stepped off the boat to tranquil tree-shaded streets lined with old, European-style villas.

Near the landing, I found the old United States Consulate: a two-story brick structure behind four stout white columns. On the pediment above the portico a large red star was outlined with white light bulbs. The sign by the door said Fujian Ocean Research Institute. I wandered around the side of the building and peered in the windows. A large office facing the water with a fine marble fireplace and elegant pilasters must have been the consul's. A picture of Chairman Mao hung over the hearth where Franklin D. Roosevelt's image may once have held pride of place.

The old caretaker, Zhao Wenjin, lives in a nearby building with his wife, son, daughter-in-law, and three grandchildren. When the American staff was evacuated during World War II, Zhao stayed behind to watch the consulate buildings. The United States has been paying him since 1926, through the Swedes and the British during our absence from China, and now through our embassy in Peking. In 1981, after 55 years of service, Zhao received from Washington a lump-sum payment of $6,000 and a pension of $122 a month— double the salary he had been making.

One day, perhaps, diplomats will again work at the consulate on Gulangyu. At Canton (Guangzhou), my next destination, the United States already operates its largest consulate in the country. This city near the apex of the fertile Pearl River Delta is the most important trading center in south China. It exports textiles, sugar, fruit, silk, timber, tea, and medicinal herbs, and imports industrial equipment and manufactured goods. Canton is also a growing center of light industry, churning out articles such as bicycles, watches, and radios. At the Canton Radio Factory, I discovered that the Cantonese are even trading with Taiwan. Factory manager Liu Zhilian, a genial, middle-aged man who took charge of the radio-assembly plant in 1980, produced for me a radio-cassette player that he said had come from Taiwan via Hong Kong. It was a large, smart-looking machine that would be the pride of any household. I turned it over. Nothing on the cassette player indicated where it was made. All the Canton factory had added was the Pearl River (Zhu Jiang) brand label.

In early 1979 the Peking authorities eliminated all customs duties to and from Taiwan. Today great quantities of goods flow through Hong Kong both ways. From the mainland go medicinal herbs and from Taiwan come items such as television sets, radios, umbrellas, and clothing.

"There are no politics in business," quipped Liu. "The Hong Kong-based representatives from Taiwan have been here many times since last year. After 32 years this is the first step toward establishing contacts again."

Large numbers of foreigners are also seeking to do business in Canton. But with its many parks, broad streets, squares, and arcades, Canton today is very different from the city it was in the last century, when many foreigners lived there. There are still narrow alleys and cul-de-sacs, but they are a far cry from the filthy byways that led turn-of-the-century American writer Eliza R. Scidmore to describe Canton as "this unspeakable city of dreadful dirt." Bubonic plague, dysentery, malaria, and cholera ravaged its crowded streets and sunless alleys. Fetid canals crisscrossed the urban land. Hundreds of thousands of people lived on boats along the waterfront, and pirates infested the waterways. Beggars were legion. In 1902 Miss Scidmore detailed a trip through the city in a sedan chair: "Street children jeer; larger enemies make faces and the cutthroat sign, and hurl epithets and invectives after one. . . . The foreigner is best hated in Canton of all Chinese cities." Today, disease and starvation have been mostly eliminated, although housing is very overcrowded and I occasionally saw beggars in the streets.

In the late 19th century, foreigners took refuge from Canton's disease-plagued masses on Shamian Island, once a Pearl River sand bar. Protected by guards and barbed wire, they built hotels, parks, and tennis courts. Crossing over a narrow bridge to Shamian, I found that the island still manages to preserve its aloofness from the hurly-burly of the city. The old banyan trees stand in rows and the crumbling mansions retain a certain dowager dignity. On South Street, there are two ancient, but still playable, red-clay tennis courts. As I stood by them, an old Cantonese with cap and cane walked up and introduced himself in English. He said he was a 1926 graduate of Cornell—and a lifelong tennis player.

I asked him what the city was like before 1949.

"There were thousands of boats with almost half a million people living on them all along the waterfront," he said. "Prostitution was permitted, and anybody who wanted to smoke opium could find a place to go. Gambling of every sort went on. On Shamian, both bridges were guarded by Chinese police, and Indians were employed as guards by the foreigners here. Sure, I was happy to see things change."

I asked him how he felt about the return of foreigners to Canton. "I think it is good for both of us that the foreigners are coming back," he said. "We are looking for a better life."

From Canton, I traveled deep into the Pearl Delta through flooded rice paddies being readied for transplanting, past thick stands of sugarcane and innumerable fish farms. Houseboats, with laundry flying like colored flags, clogged the waterways. In the center of the delta—about 30 miles and many ferry crossings from Canton—I came to Xiaolan Commune, an agglomeration of 107,000 people that includes the town of Xiaolan and a number of outlying villages, all incorporated as brigades of the commune. Xiaolan's roofline, like those of other delta towns, bears a lacy crown of television antennas, a badge of wealth and overseas connections. The antennas are canted toward Hong Kong and its Western-style programming. Xiaolan officials told me that about 30 percent of the people in the delta town own television sets and that Overseas Chinese visitors from Singapore, Hong Kong, Macao, and Thailand bring about two million dollars to Xiaolan each year.

Money from relatives overseas is important, but I could also see that some peasants in the area were becoming rich from their own enterprise. One such man was Zhang Yutang, a member of Xiaolan's Luxiyi Production Brigade. In a country where most people make less than 50 yuan ($30) a month, this chunky 48-year-old had made, last year, over 3,300 yuan ($1,980) a month by running a flower-growing business in the hours after his fieldwork for the brigade was done. He was, by Chinese standards, a millionaire.

Zhang's home had two stories, painted wall panels, and a tile roof. A large Japanese console color television, an AM-FM shortwave radio, a pendulum clock, and a case stocked with candy and liquor crowded the living room. He offered me tea, pastries, and Million-brand cigarettes.

What were the reasons for his success? Simple, he said. "I put in a great many hours and a great deal of hard work, and I raise a greater variety of flowers than anybody else."

I couldn't help wondering why everybody there didn't raise flowers, if it was so profitable. "Growing sugarcane is a lot easier," Zhang explained.

Rich peasants like Zhang have sparked considerable debate in China over the future course of the country's modernization effort. Pragmatists in the Communist Party argue that initiative and innovation must be encouraged and rewarded, while doctrinaire party members insist that such policies encourage capitalist behavior.

Over the villages of the south loom old watchtowers, relics of bitter feuding between towns over such matters as land and water rights. Clan ties have long had great importance, and many single-surname towns line the maze of canals and channels that crisscross the delta. At the Longrui Brigade, a village of 3,300 that is part of Xiaolan Commune, everybody bears the surname Liu. At the neighboring village-brigade of about 2,000, everybody is named Gao. The Liu and Gao clans had been feuding for over half a century—until 1949, that is, when the Communist authorities stepped in and settled the problem by executing ten of the ringleaders on both sides.

"In the old days, when the Gaos caught a Liu, they would take him and grind his head on a grindstone until he was dead," says Liu Guoyuan, the 40-year-old Longrui Brigade vice-director. "If the Lius caught a Gao, they would steam him to death in a pottery jug, like a dumpling. These were the traditional ways of murder during the feuds." Now, the old vendettas have been replaced by healthier rivalries, such as Ping-Pong and basketball. Even intermarriages are not unheard of.

477

I wanted to fly to my next destination, Guilin (Kueilin). Set in the rugged mountains of the Guangxi Zhuang Autonomous Region about 250 miles northwest of Canton, Guilin is famous as a wartime base of Gen. Claire L. Chennault's American Volunteer Group, the Flying Tigers. From the Guilin base, Chennault's pilots tracked Japanese forces in south China and gave valuable support to the Chinese resistance effort. In 1944, at the orders of Gen. Joseph W. "Vinegar Joe" Stilwell, Chennault blew up the buildings and supplies at the Guilin airfield to keep them from the Japanese. Theodore H. White, then a war correspondent in the China theater, described the evening as "a wild and wonderful thunder-popping, flame-streaked, explosion-rocked orgy of destruction that is the most scarlet-and-brilliant night of my memory."

Unfortunately, I could not fly into Guilin because the airport was closed for repairs. So after about 450 miles of roundabout routing, I pulled in by train to a rather ordinary-looking town of block buildings in a most extraordinary setting of limestone hills, called tower karst. From my hotel window overlooking the Li River, it was easy to see why this landscape has inspired so much art and poetry. The hills, formed by the erosion of an ancient uplifted seabed, cast a spell on Chinese and foreigners alike. The green peaks lie like jagged chunks of jade, links in a giant necklace draped over the mist-shrouded landscape. Through this enchanted region winds the silver ribbon of the Li, plied by cargo sampans and chuffing tourist boats. With ballet-like grace and dexterity, cormorant fishermen pole the long, narrow rafts that skim back and forth across the river. The cormorant handlers curse the black, long-necked birds (prevented by choke collars from swallowing their catch) and splash them, spanking the water with poles to make the reluctant fowl dive.

For two days I drifted down the river. Our cargo sampan followed its course between the clefts of the hills 20 miles to Yangshuo. Capt. Huang Jifa guided the craft, which he had built himself. The crew included his brother, wife, daughter, and five-year-old son.

Sitting in a rattan chair, I slid between the lofty karst, the silence engendering a sense of serenity. A light drizzle disturbed the Li's placid surface with a million silver winks. The water was low, but Huang stuck to the side, because the center could be six or seven meters deep, too deep to pole comfortably. In April, when the rains come, the river could rise to 40 meters, the captain said.

Captain Huang's brother set off in a bamboo raft for one of the family's fishing nets about 50 yards away. He returned with a 14-inch carp, which he secured to a line under the raft, and then tied the raft to the sampan. The carp stayed fresh in the running river until lunchtime, when it lost its head on the chopping block together with a chicken that had been hauled squawking from the hold. Huang's wife simmered the chicken and fish together with spring onions and ginger in a wok mounted on a brazier. We washed this delicious concoction down with Tsingtao beer.

Sitting on the edge of the sampan after lunch, I watched the Huang brothers dig the poles in at the front of the boat, then lean into shoulder crutches and walk the bamboo shafts back along the catwalks on both sides of

478

the sampan. With my feet in the cool river, I savored the fresh, sweet air blowing over the water. On both banks grew stands of bamboo, clumpy sentinels with green plumes nodding in the breeze. The only sounds were the lap and slap of water against the hull and the crash of steel points as the poles found purchase between the rounded stones of the river bottom.

Other sampans passed us at intervals, making the more difficult passage upstream. Crude, square sails set on collapsible masts helped them somewhat, but most of their progress was through brute strength, a combination of poling by those on board while other crew members, often women, trudged laboriously along the shore straining to pull the sampan against the current. The crew members grunted and heaved against their poles. As they did, they uttered an eerie, almost mournful, whining cry, "O-yo-yo."

We spent the night at Xingping Commune, and left soon after dawn the next day for the last leg of our trip. Pink and ocher clouds glowed behind the village; the hills were veiled in haze. We sculled through the water, Huang's wife and daughter pumping furiously on the rear sweep. Rounding a bend, we found the morning mist hanging over the karst, slicing off the tops of the tooth-shaped hills. Several white-collared magpies, crow-size, flew through the middle air. The light was silver. A lone hawk wheeled with ragged-tip wings just below the mist-cloud, about 500 feet up. Another joined him, a *pas de deux*. The sun appeared as a bright, silver-yellow disk behind the mist, then burst forth, throwing a spotlight glare of light on the river, full in our faces as we came about out of a rapids. Now the mist dropped like a robe about the waist and feet of the karst, and only the crests were visible in the pale yellow light. A stiff breeze gave a rough texture to the surface of the water. All too soon, we slipped through this magic scene and arrived at Yangshuo.

From mountainous Guangxi, I returned to Canton for a flight to Hainan Island at the southern tip of China. Because of its strategic location opposite Vietnam, Hainan was long off limits to foreigners. I would be one of the first Westerners to visit it in many years.

Over the South China Sea the clouds parted. The sun was setting into the Gulf of Tonkin as the plane banked south toward Hainan's capital, Haikou. To starboard lay the Leizhou Peninsula; the sinking sun cast the sea around it in metallic orange. A junk scudded far below under full sail, the bamboo rib battens of its mainsail clearly visible as it raced the dying day.

It was hazy and warm as I stepped onto the tarmac at Haikou airport. Fronds of coconut palms waved in the tropical zephyr. When I had left Canton two hours earlier, it had been about 45°F—cold, gray, and windy. Here, it was 77 degrees and balmy. Haikou had the crowds of people and bicycles I was used to seeing by now, but its lush vegetation made it different.

I was given a room in the Communist Party guest house, set in a lovely green compound with palm trees rising tall over spongy grass. The room was large, pleasantly furnished—and full of mosquitoes. Since the weather on my trip had been fairly cold so far, I welcomed the warmth and sunshine, even if it meant a few bugs. What I really looked forward to was coffee. Hainan is one of China's major coffee-producing regions, and I was grateful for a cup after a month of nothing but tea.

H ainan had long been a place of banishment, the Chinese equivalent of Devil's Island. To northern Chinese, it symbolized the very edge of the earth, a place of evil spirits, bugs, snakes, and wild tribesmen. Government officials who displeased the emperor would find themselves making the dread passage across the strait to Hainan and exile. Now this very isolation and the island's tropical beauty make it a popular resting spot for high-level government officials. The island's remoteness tempered the effects of the Cultural Revolution on Hainan. One official, who lives at Yaxian on the south coast, said, "The Cultural Revolution was like the cold wind from Mongolia. By the time it got here, it didn't have much strength."

The road from Wenchang, in the northeast, inland to the Overseas Chinese State Farm at Xinglong is red, rutted, dusty, and lined with Australian pine. Great rubber groves and distant mountains began to appear in the west. The state farm, a resettlement camp for returning Overseas Chinese, grows many of Hainan's crops: rubber, rice, cocoa, coffee, hemp, coconut, and oil palm. Refugees from Vietnam account for more than a quarter of the nearly 20,000 Overseas Chinese on the farm. "In the 1950s, they [the refugees] came mostly from Malaysia. In the 1960s from Indonesia. In the 1970s from Vietnam," said farm director Li Buhai, a gruff ex-army officer who took part in the fight to expel Chiang Kai-shek's forces from the island in 1950.

Down the east coast toward the island's southern tip, the landscape grows more severe. The dusty road stretches through scrub pine and sandy soil, relieved occasionally by palm trees and rice paddies. The South China Sea was on my left. Somewhere out there to the east, beyond the coral reef where the distant breakers traced a thin white line against the blue horizon, were the Philippines. To the west, Vietnam, and to the northeast, Taiwan.

With only 5.5 million people, Hainan is one of the most sparsely settled areas of south China, capable of absorbing the overflow from other regions. It is heavily garrisoned, an ocean-walled fortress staring west across the water at Haiphong and south to Da Nang. But Hainan could have great appeal for tourists. Splendid sand beaches stretch along the coast, fringed with pine and palm trees. Mottled, luminescent cowrie shells wash up on the strand. Tiny hermit crabs peek out like timid pirates from plundered murex shells.

On one such beach at Yaxian, I met an American doctor who had been living and working in China for 48 years. Dr. George Hatem was vacationing with Rewi Alley, an expatriate New Zealander, and Manny Granich and his wife. Granich, former editor of an English-language newspaper in Shanghai, now lives on Cape Cod. One evening at Rewi Alley's bungalow under the pines, I asked Hatem what made him forsake his native Buffalo, N.Y., in 1933 for a lifetime of working to improve health care in China.

"I came to China and saw the poverty and the misery," he said. "You either walked away, went nuts, or became a revolutionary. Some did walk away. I didn't. I went northwest and joined the Red Army."

Today at 71 Hatem is a Chinese citizen, a Communist Party member, and an adviser to the Ministry of Public Health. His Chinese wife is a movie director and his son a photographer for the magazine *China Reconstructs*.

I thought of Hatem the next day as we drove into the mountainous interior of Hainan, where one peak rises to 6,000 feet and thick rain forest covers the ground. "About 20 years ago," he had told me, "I walked barefoot up these mountains with a bamboo pole carrying stick—a sleeping mat, towel, and soap in the front basket; my stethoscope and medical kit in the back."

After a final night in Haikou, I flew back to Canton. Soon I was boarding a Hovercraft for the two-and-a-half-hour ride down the Pearl River to Hong Kong. Down this same waterway, thousands of Chinese laborers had sailed en route to work in distant countries. Up the river had flowed the currents of foreign influence since the third century. Past these shores, with bulging holds and billowing sails, had come the vessels of Indian, Persian, and Arab traders, followed by the ships—and gunships—of the Portuguese, British, Dutch, French, Americans, and Japanese.

As the Hovercraft edged away from the dock and slowly gathered speed, the old city of Canton slipped past to port. To starboard, the industrial suburbs gradually receded. The Pearl spread itself luxuriantly at Canton's feet, a humming flow of sampans, passenger ferries, barges, and small craft. Tall buildings gave way to smaller structures and finally to flat delta punctuated by rocky outcroppings. The sleek, black-hulled Hong Kong Hovercraft hurtled at full speed over the widening, ruffled waters. About twelve miles downriver, we passed the clustered freighters and loading cranes of the Huangpu (Whampoa) docks. The delta was slipping away faster now, as the estuary grew broad and choppy. The Hovercraft bounced lightly over the cresting chop, throwing up plumes of foam. It sped by Zhongshan County, where Sun Yat-sen was born nearly 120 years ago.

Soon Hong Kong lay before us, with its gleaming buildings and mighty harbor. On the road that winds along the shore I could see cars instead of bicycles. Suddenly I experienced a common traveler's sensation: momentary doubt that the trip I had just completed had ever taken place. I had just spent six weeks in a land of water buffalo, rice paddies, and sampans, and now, as though I had stepped into another dimension, I was in a machine of steel, plastic, and chrome, whizzing effortlessly over the water to a different world.

Seagoing junks rub elbows with skiffs and sampans in Fuzhou's broad Min River estuary. The Min is the master stream of a river system that furnishes mountainous Fujian with hydroelectric power and transport for upland-grown timber and tea. The system rises in western Fujian's Wuyi Shan mountain range and flows southeast to the Formosa Strait.

Forest products of heavily wooded, subtropical Fujian are put to many uses, such as rain gear for a young mountain dweller (above). His winglike cape is woven of palm-bark fiber.

Fuzhou, Fujian's capital, was once China's chief tea port. The province still exports fine teas as well as other products like porcelain and lacquerware.

482

Buddhist nuns file through a temple on Drum Mountain outside Fuzhou (opposite). They invoke Amituofo, the Buddha who promised rebirth for all who repeat his name.

In Fujian, local granite goes into buildings, walls, utility poles—and even the fence around a pig pit (above) at Quanzhou. The pigs signify good times. Relaxation of curbs on private enterprise spurred peasants to raise so many animals that a "pig glut" developed.

The Japanese watches in a Fuzhou window (left) attract stares. Imported watches can cost up to $170, six months' wages for many workers.

The orange-tile roofs of Gulangyu, Xiamen's old foreign quarter, spread out below Sunburst Cliff (far left). The island enclave is now a popular resting spot for high-level officials. A ban on cars and bicycles invests it with a dozy tranquillity that contrasts sharply with Xiamen's busy waterfront across the channel. Island shoppers (above) can choose from a variety of eggs sold on the street.

Formerly a treaty port in which foreigners could do business, Xiamen today refines a major share of Fujian's sugar, a product vital to the province's economy. A worker at a sugarcane processing plant (left) bundles cane for the crusher.

487

A veil of mist spills over the rippling hills and terraces of a remote Guangxi river valley (opposite). Isolated upland villages, like this one in Longsheng County, are the traditional abode of the Zhuang, China's largest minority. Now assimilated except in such remote areas, the Zhuang comprise more than a third of Guangxi's population of 34 million. Another million Zhuang live in the adjoining provinces of Yunnan, Guangdong, and Guizhou.

Recent excavations have shown that 2,000 years ago the Zhuang were already settled in the area. Hundreds of finely crafted bronze drums attest to their ancient skill as artisans.

Two Zhuang women wash clothes at a communal pipe at Jinzhu, a village in Longsheng County (right). Behind them, a Zhuang house rises on wooden stilts. Livestock, a latrine, and stored fuel and tools fill the open area under the house. Only vehicles with four-wheel drive can negotiate the rough road to Jinzhu.

Cooking smoke from a wok in Liao Cuirong's Jinzhu home (opposite) cures strips of pork hanging overhead—and also combats termites, villagers say.

At a Jinzhu bridal banquet (left), Zhuang men lift bowls of warm rice wine in a toast. After the meal at the bride's home, friends of the groom (above) lead the way to Baishi village, 12 miles away, where the groom and his family await them. The men bear gifts of cake, wine, and cloth shoes made by the bride for her in-laws. A sheaf of rice symbolizes hope that the bride will bring her new family abundance. Behind the men walk the bride and nine friends, the "ten sisters." Their open umbrellas provide symbolic shelter from misfortune.

George F. Mobley (also left). Overleaf: Thomas Nebbia

A coxswain shouts the strokes to his straining crew (left) during the dragon-boat race on the Miluo River in Hunan Province. Excited spectators spill over the river banks (above). The ancient summer festival honors the virtuous third-century-B.C. poet-reformer Qu Yuan. Despairing at the futility of his efforts, Qu jumped into the Miluo River. Fishermen paddled furiously but vainly to save him. Today's racers recreate the heroic attempt.

OVERLEAF. Peaks like dragon's teeth throw shadows across a sunset reflection on the Li River; a lone fisherman barely ruffles the glassy calm. The Li winds through Guilin, a region famous for its eroded limestone hills.

Thomas Nebbia (also left)

At mealtime on a floating house (left), a harried woman supervises four youngsters, a dog, and 18 ducklings. Such scenes abound along the Li, where families often live on their sampans. In the scenic, rugged mountains of northern Guangxi, the river serves as both home and highway. A traveler (above) shades himself and a child from the south China sun. At water's edge, curling plumes of bamboo nod below tower karst robed in leafy emerald. The karst, or limestone landscape, formed when an ancient uplifted seabed eroded.

OVERLEAF. Canton stretches along the banks of the Pearl River. With nearly three million people, it is the south's largest city. The European-style Customs House, with its domed clock tower, stands in silent testimony to Canton's enduring position as south China's center of foreign trade.

497

At the Dongguan Fireworks Factory near Canton (far left), workers roll paper tubes for firecrackers. Two other employees (above) attach the required classification labels to Flying Colors Butterfly Rockets destined for the American market. Wearing protective boots and gloves, a worker (left) uses a block of wood and a copper dowel to compact gunpowder in the tubes. Fascination with fireworks endures among the people who invented gunpowder more than a thousand years ago. The Chinese once set off firecrackers to frighten evil spirits. Today they use them to mark auspicious occasions, such as weddings, births, holidays, and the arrival of guests.

501

lasted scraps of firecracker paper *(left)* litter the ground at Rongqi in the Pearl River Delta during a Lion Dance marking the lunar New Year. In the dance, which dates back to the seventh century, a masked performer *(opposite, below)* teases a gaudily-painted papier-mâché lion with a palm fan. The creature responds by rearing and bowing, shaking its head, rolling its eyes, snapping its hinged jaws, and charging in rage. All this occurs amid a din of drumbeats *(opposite, above)*, crashing cymbals, and exploding firecrackers. The raucous pantomime was originally a demon-expelling ceremony. Lions, nonexistent in south China, were thought to be especially effective. Now called Spring Festival in China, the holiday no longer centers on exorcism. But it remains a time for cleaning house, settling obligations, and generally putting one's affairs in order.

503

Thomas Nebbia

Bruce Dale

Stretched out on a bed of nails (opposite), a young street performer in Canton holds her breath as her father tries to smash a slab of stone balanced on her stomach. Behind them, a gong-wielding sister attempts to drum up donations. The large red poster proclaims, "Great Fervor for the Four Modernizations!"

Canton offers unusual cuisine, as well as unusual sights. At the window of a snake restaurant (right), passersby peer at cobras destined for the dinner table.

In Canton, south China's most modern city (above), most people get around on foot or bicycle. Canton has long been the main point of contact for foreigners seeking to do business with China. In the late 17th century, European traders began to make regular calls. To limit unwanted foreign influence, the Chinese confined the merchants, or "factors," to trading posts called "factories" and ordered them off Chinese soil at the end of a prescribed trading season. For similar reasons, imperial China refused to establish diplomatic relations with England, and also tried to suppress the illicit British opium trade. The result was China's defeat in the 1839-1842 Opium War and the opening of several treaty ports, including Canton, to foreign trade. Cantonese chafed at the power of foreigners, but they also chafed under corrupt Qing rule. From Canton, Sun Yat-sen spearheaded the revolution that toppled the monarchy in 1911. During the 1920s, Mao Zedong, Chiang Kai-shek, and Zhou Enlai all launched their careers in Canton under Sun's leadership.

Palm trees sway beside a bright checkerboard of freshly transplanted rice on tropical Hainan Island (left), as a peasant carries shoots from seedbed to paddy. China's second largest island after Taiwan, Hainan has a hot climate that yields three crops of rice annually, compared to two crops elsewhere in southeast China. An agile Hainan climber (above) reaches for a coconut, a product for which the island is famous throughout China.

M id-February marks the start of spring rice planting in parts of the south. Baskets of seed (right) await as workers prepare a muddy field for sowing. Roughly 25 days after sowing, when the rice shoots are about seven inches high, workers will dig them out of the crowded seedbed and transplant them to a paddy. Men and buffalo (above) ready a flooded paddy to receive the young plants. Women transplant the spiky green seedlings in neat rows (opposite). The crop will be harvested about three months after transplanting.

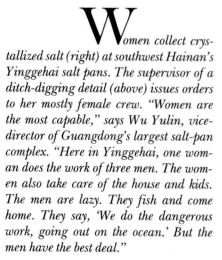
Women collect crystallized salt (right) at southwest Hainan's Yinggehai salt pans. The supervisor of a ditch-digging detail (above) issues orders to her mostly female crew. "Women are the most capable," says Wu Yulin, vice-director of Guangdong's largest salt-pan complex. "Here in Yinggehai, one woman does the work of three men. The women also take care of the house and kids. The men are lazy. They fish and come home. They say, 'We do the dangerous work, going out on the ocean.' But the men have the best deal."

OVERLEAF. On Hainan's hilly southernmost shore, the South China Sea laps shelving sand and stony headland. Tradition says that in 1097 the poet Su Dongpo named this desolate stretch Tianya, or the Edge of Heaven.

Thomas B. Allen, former National Geographic book editor and co-author of the biography *Rickover,* now works as a freelance writer in Bethesda, Maryland.

Mike Edwards, senior writer on the staff of NATIONAL GEOGRAPHIC, has published articles on India, Pakistan, Tunisia, Mexico, Canada, Shanghai, and the Danube.

William Graves, NATIONAL GEOGRAPHIC Senior Assistant Editor of Expeditions, has published articles on Tokyo, Iran, Portugal, Bangkok, Denmark, Finland, and the Rhine.

Donald R. Katz, a New York City freelance writer, won the Overseas Press Club's award for the best magazine interpretation of foreign affairs in 1978, and has worked in Ethiopia, Egypt, Israel, the Canadian Arctic, France, and Northern Ireland.

Jay and Linda Mathews covered China for *The Washington Post* and *The Los Angeles Times,* respectively, until the end of 1980, when their newspapers transferred them to Los Angeles. They published *One Billion: A Chinese Chronicle* in 1983.

David D. Pearce covered the revolution in Portugal (1975-76) and conflict in the Middle East (1976-79) for United Press International. He was a National Geographic book editor before joining the U. S. Foreign Service in January 1982.

Robert M. Poole covered national politics for *The Winston-Salem Journal* and *The Richmond Times-Dispatch* before joining the National Geographic as a book editor in 1980.

Roy Reed covered the 1960s civil rights movement, national politics, and the British Isles for *The New York Times* before moving to the Ozarks to farm, write, and teach journalism at the University of Arkansas.

Griffin Smith, Jr., a freelance writer from Little Rock, Arkansas, has written articles on Sarawak and Thailand and speeches for President Jimmy Carter. NATIONAL GEOGRAPHIC published his article on Mexican Americans in June 1980.

Jonathan D. Spence, a native Englishman who now teaches Chinese history at Yale University, has published *The Death of Woman Wang, To Change China,* and *The Gate of Heavenly Peace.*

Shirley Sun, a Shanghai-born American citizen, is a filmmaker and scholar as well as a writer. She is a fellow of the Aspen Institute of Humanistic Studies.

ACKNOWLEDGMENTS & BIBLIOGRAPHY

In addition to our chief consultants, listed in the front of the book, we wish to thank many individuals and government agencies for their help with *Journey Into China.* In particular, we are indebted to Senator Howard H. Baker, Jr., and Senator David H. Pryor; Charles Freeman, Department of State; and Norris P. Smith, International Communication Agency. We are also grateful for the advice of Jonathan Chaves, George Washington University; Victor Falkenheim, University of Toronto; David Finkelstein; Harry Harding, Stanford University; David N. Keightley and Jeffery Riegel, University of California; Edward I. M. Lipman, Canadian Department of External Affairs; William L. Parish, University of Chicago; and Constant C. Shih. And our warm thanks go to Virginia A. Bachant, Mary B. Hunsiker, Ann Campana Judge, and Karen Enroth Lischick of the National Geographic Travel Office for their efforts on behalf of all our travelers.

We have made extensive use of government and private research centers, and of the resources and staff of the Library of Congress, as well as our own National Geographic Society Library and staff. Our special appreciation goes to George Archibald, International Crane Foundation; Judith Banister, Bureau of the Census; Teresa Chao; the staff of the Committee on Scholarly Communication with the People's Republic of China; and Edward W. Doherty, U. S. Catholic Conference. Also to Theodore R. Dudley, National Arboretum; John Seidensticker, Smithsonian Institution; Marianna Graham, National Council for U. S.-China Trade; Charles Liu, Department of Agriculture; Leo Orleans and Chu Mi Wiens, Library of Congress.

In a book of this scope, we have relied heavily on the firsthand knowledge of many scholars and others who know China and its history well. These include James E. Bosson, University of California; Albert Dien, Stanford University; June T. Dreyer, University of Miami; John Grobowski; Earl and Nazima Kowall; David M. Lampton, Ohio State University. Also Steven Levine, American University; Jonathan Lipman, Mt. Holyoke College; Lobsang Lhalungpa; John McCoy, Cornell University; Susan Meinheit; Roberta H. Stalberg; and Frances Thargay, The Office of Tibet.

And, of course, we could never have produced *Journey Into China* without the kindness and help of the Chinese Embassy in Washington, D. C., and of the many Chinese individuals and organizations who escorted us on our trips and handled the complicated local logistics of such an undertaking. We are also grateful to Chinese photographers for the pictures on pages 170-172, 173 right, 174, 176-177, 323, 366-367, 448-449, and 458 through 465.

Since our book is chiefly about modern China, much of our reference material came from current newspapers, magazines, and journals published in China and the West. Many books of a general nature aided us too. These included the following: *The Chinese* by David Bonavia; *Food in Chinese Culture* edited by K. C. Chang; *The United States and China* by John King Fairbank; *China: Tradition and Transformation* by John K. Fairbank and Edwin O. Reischauer; *The Chinese* by John Fraser; *China's Imperial Past* by Charles O. Hucker; *Encyclopedia of China Today* by Fredric M. Kaplan and others; *Chinese Shadows* by Simon Leys; *Nagel's China;* the series *Science and Civilisation in China* by Joseph Needham; *China: Its History and Culture* by W. Scott Morton; *The Arts of China* by Michael Sullivan; *China: A Geographical Survey* by T. R. Tregear; *Chinese Civilization* by Yong Yap and Arthur Cotterell; and Marco Polo's travel accounts translated by Sir Henry Yule and others.

More specialized books included: *Mao's China* by Maurice Meisner. *Peking* by Felix Greene; *The Forbidden City* by Roderick MacFarquhar; and *The Imperial Ming Tombs* by Ann Paludan. *The Great Wall of China* by Jonathan Fryer; *The Great Wall of China* by William E. Geil; *Inner Asian Frontiers of China* by Owen Lattimore; *The Great Wall* by Luo Zewen and others; and *The Great Wall of China* by Robert Silverberg. *The Archaeology of Ancient China* and *Shang Civilization* by Kwang-chih Chang; *Water Management in the Yellow River Basin of China* by Charles Greer; *The Great Bronze Age of China,* Metropolitan Museum of Art; and *Mandarins, Jews, and Missionaries* by Michael Pollak.

Also helpful were *The Silk Road* by Luce Boulnois; *My Life as an Explorer* by Sven A. Hedin; *Foreign Devils on the Silk Road* by Peter Hopkirk; and *Ruins of Desert Cathay* by Mark Aurel Stein. *Daily Life in China* by Jacques Gernet; and *The Chinese Garden* by Maggie Keswick. *Junks and Sampans of the Yangtze* by G.R.G. Worcester. *Seven Years in Tibet* by Heinrich Harrer; *The Changing Face of Tibet* by Pradyumna P. Karan; *Tibet: A Lost World* by Valrae Reynolds; *A Cultural History of Tibet* by David Snellgrove and Hugh Richardson; and *The Splendors of Tibet* by Audrey Topping.

The editors gratefully acknowledge permission to reprint the excerpt on page 93 from a poem in *The Jade Mountain* by Kiang Kang-hu, translated by Witter Bynner, © 1957 Alfred A. Knopf, Inc.

INDEX

Type composition by National Geographic's Photographic Services. Color separations by Beck Engraving Co., Inc., Philadelphia, Pa.; Beck Offset Color Co., Pennsauken, N.J.; Chanticleer Co., Inc., New York, N.Y.; Lehigh Press Inc., Alexandria, Va.; The Lanman-Progressive Companies, Washington, D. C.; Offset Separations Corp., New York, N.Y. Printed and bound by R. R. Donnelley & Sons Co., Chicago, Ill. Paper by Mead Paper Co., New York, N.Y.

Library of Congress CIP Data
Main entry under title:

Journey into China.

Bibliography: p.
Includes index.
1. China—Description and travel—1976-
I. National Geographic Society (U.S.).
DS712.J68 1982 915.1′0457 82-14132
ISBN 0-87044-437-9
ISBN 0-87044-449-2 (deluxe)